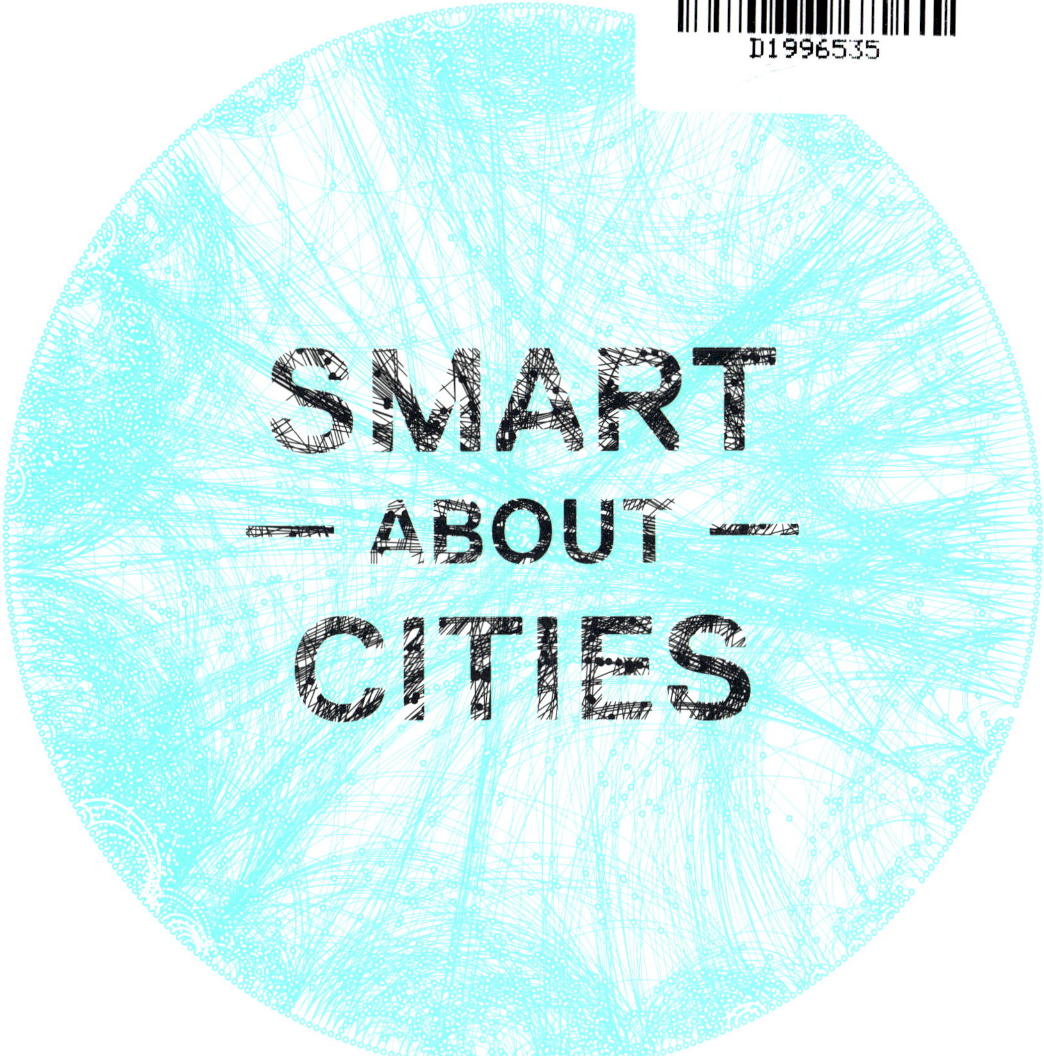

SMART — ABOUT — CITIES

'We need a globally networked urbanism'

VISUALISING THE CHALLENGE FOR 21ST CENTURY URBANISM

Maarten Hajer
& Ton Dassen

nai010 publishers /
pbl publishers

Smart about Cities – Visualising the Challenge for 21st Century Urbanism shows the metabolism of an urbanised country such as the Netherlands. A country that functions as an organism with its own metabolism – that processes and needs the inflow and outflow of a variety of foods, resources and materials. These flows, often, span the entire globe. Flows that not only consist of construction materials and fuels, food, water, air and waste, but also of people who work to achieve the healthiest and most efficient metabolism, using their transport and other technologies. With this book, PBL Netherlands Environmental Assessment Agency fits in with the theme of the sixth edition of the International Architecture Biennale Rotterdam: the IABR 2014 –Urban by Nature-. This motto definitely applies to the small country of the Netherlands with its high level of urbanisation, but also to the world of the 21st century. Urban metabolism, therefore, is receiving a great deal of international attention. This has become apparent from leading organisations, such as the World Bank and the United Nations, calling on cities to map their metabolism to subsequently base their strategic planning on. Only then will they be able to make the crucial connection between spatial and environmental policy.

Scientists long ago already showed there to be 'limits to growth'. To date, this has not resulted in any actual change, but society's transition has now become a necessity. What is needed is a science that is embedded within society. In addition, creative reform is needed, with the vital input of designers.

The book opens with the essay 'On Being Smart about Cities; Seven Considerations for a New Urban Planning and Design' that further elaborates on this science that is closely connected to society. We are going to need 'smart' technology, but also – and more importantly – we must connect with a continuing, open and social form of innovation. The essay draws some of its inspiration from the past and builds on a new self-confidence for cities. This then leads to seven considerations for urban planning and design.

Maarten Hajer
Director-General at PBL Netherlands Environmental Assessment Agency
Professor of Public Policy at the University of Amsterdam

Dirk Sijmons
Curator IABR–2014–URBAN BY NATURE–

George Brugmans
General Manager International Architecture Biennale Rotterdam

CONTENT

Seven Considerations for a New
Urban Planning & Design

SMART CITIES OR SMART URBANISM

Every once in a while, cities are confronted with a period of transition. Over the last 200 years, we experienced at least two of those transitions. In the 19th century, Western cities adjusted from having medieval city structures to becoming industrial cities. In Europe, city walls were torn down and made way for a new infrastructure of factories, railways for transport, and housing for the flocks of newly arrived workers. To fight the diseases that came with the rapidly growing cities, we subsequently installed an elaborate sanitary infrastructure. A second transition occurred in the 20th century, when the arrival of the car called for large-scale readjustments. It was the era of ring roads, high rise tower blocks, Central Business Districts and the invention of the 'suburb'. Now, we are on the verge of a new transition. We must find a way to make cities eco-efficient, with renewable energy, recycling of waste and environmentally friendly traffic management, and fewer CO_2 emissions. Eco-efficiency is no longer merely 'nice to have'; it has become a necessity. Cities that do not respond run great risks, both financially and in terms of operational liability (UNEP 2013a).

Interestingly, a solution is argued to be in sight, in the form of smart cities. Everywhere we go we hear snippets of the discourse. 'The driverless car is on its way'; 'Big data will make public transport much more efficient'; 'Smart meters and smart grids will reduce CO_2 emissions'.

The discourse on the smart city promises an era of innovative urban planning, driven by smart urban technologies that will make cities safer, cleaner and, above all, more efficient. Behind it all is the application of ICT technologies. Smart cities will 'sense' behaviour via big data and use this feedback to manage urban dynamics and fine-tune services. City planning will become a continuous experiment, with cities serving as 'living labs' for new products and services. The optimism is captivating.

This book is written from the awareness that this sustainability transition is now indispensable. It aims to show how far off we are from a sustainable and resilient urban system. But it also calls for reflection. An urban transition is not a matter of simply matching problems to solutions; it is a complex and multi-faceted endeavour. Reflecting on the past may show us what it takes to get moving and what we are likely to encounter on the way; transitions are never going to be easy. People will push back, vested interests will resist, and some solutions will not work out. But cities will always continue to develop. The argument here is that urbanisation, ultimately, is the outcome of a process of 'discourse formation' in which coalitions are shaped that will effectively push a particular agenda. In that sense, studying 'smart cities' is of paramount importance. What exactly is this 'discursive take' on cities about? Could it work? Where would it contribute, what pitfalls may we anticipate? Can it deliver?

For the first time, we will need to think about urbanisation as a global phenomenon. Demographic calculations that suggest we are moving towards a world in which, by 2050, up to 70% of people will live in cities, with much of the new urbanisation taking place in Asia and Sub-Saharan Africa (UN 2012). The most significant figures suggest that we are looking at mind-boggling investments in urban infrastructure. Reports by global consultancies, such as Booz Allen Hamilton and the Boston Consultancy Group, are the

> **The World Bank suggests a USD 30 to 50 trillion investment in urban infrastructure**

basis for the World Bank's estimates. The World Bank suggests a USD 30 to 50 trillion investment in urban infrastructure over the next 20 to 30 years – very big money indeed (Doshi et al. 2007; Airoldi et al. 2010; Hoornweg and Freire 2013). This equals the value of all companies listed worldwide on the stock exchange (World Bank 2014). Part of this money will be needed to extend the infrastructure of the developing world; part of it will be needed to retrofit the urban infrastructure in the developed world, where some essential infrastructure systems date back to the 19th century.

In this spectrum, the 'smart city' agenda proposes a digital 'upgrade' that will make cities more efficient. Efficiency is not future-proof, however. Of course, it makes sense to explore how we can use the possibilities raised by new digital technology and the big data that this may generate. But it seems as if we have collectively forgotten that this promise of a great efficiency dividend was made before. Twentieth-century century planning was dominated by the discourse on the modern, 'functional' city. It promised a healthy urban life for all, with free flowing traffic and, using the future technology of nuclear energy, electricity that would be 'too cheap to meter'. Considering smart cities we are excited about the possibilities for the future, but we tend to forget about the failures of the past.

The debate on the future of our cities is of paramount importance. Yet, it deserves to be grounded in an understanding of the history of urbanism. This can help us frame a resilient and broadly shared programme for what we want our cities to achieve. If we fail to formulate this orienting vision, there is a good chance that investments will flow towards short-term agendas. Money will be spent

> **The debate on the future of our cities cannot be held without an understanding of the history of urbanism**

on 'default' options and will simply extend the way we thought about urban planning over the last century, making an outdated model more efficient. A 20th century agenda is now deeply problematic. Our 'urban metabolism', as this book illustrates, is completely out of sync. Getting this right could provide inspiration for designers and planners worldwide.

So, if it is something smart that we need, it is a 'smart urbanism' – a powerful integrative and action-oriented body of thought on cities that emphasises their particular histories, the social composition of cities, analyses the resources it takes to 'run' a city, provides insights into the intricate ways in which design, politics and business interrelate, and helps to think of the institutional formats and practices that can help deliver on the transition needed. The future calls for smart urbanism rather than smart cities. Here, we examine if we can infuse the discourse on smart cities with an understanding of what cities are, what they are capable of, how governance can function, and how we can organise learning, both in and among cities.

THE SMART CITY AS DISCOURSE

Urbanisation rates as one of the crucial challenges for the 21st century. The World Bank recently reminded us that we are going to experience as much urbanisation in the next 40 to 50 years, as we have been over the last 200 years (Hoornweg and Freire 2013). This implies that in '...just 40 years, cities will need to build the infrastructure for an additional 2.7 billion people.' (ibid. p.125). China wants to rehouse 250 million people from rural areas to cities, by 2030 (OECD 2013). In 2009, UNDESA expected African cities to house an additional 800 million people by 2050 (ibid. p.33).

The World Bank reflects that, on a global level, 'As their populations increase and people become more affluent, the cities are faced with daunting challenges in managing transportation, water and wastewater, solid waste, and energy, with demand far outstripping supply. In addition, uncoordinated growth of cities over the past few years has dispersed their populations, with more people living in the urban peripheries and thereby increasing the cost of infrastructure and service provision.' (Hoornweg and Freire 2013, p.34)

At this point, smart cities are sometimes introduced as the logical way forward. The World Bank publication states that the application of smart city technology could realise a 7.8 Gt CO_2 emission reduction by 2020 (ibid. p.9). This is a sizeable figure, compared to the national emissions in the United States (5.2 Gt) and China (9.9 Gt) in 2012 (Olivier et al. 2013). Perhaps it is indicative of how the 'smart city' discourse frames urban realities; we could calculate the effects of the full application of smart technology, but implementing such tech solutions in an existing urban fabric is of course incredibly complicated, both politically and physically.

> **Here, the debate risks getting caught in a dichotomy where a priori value preferences predict contributions and responses**

In policy and politics, we see how 'smart cities' are often taken to be a set of devices, proposals and instruments that could be adopted, installed, and operated. Policymakers see it as a programme, opening up space for big corporations, such as IBM, Cisco Systems or Siemens, to sell tech solutions that address real and urgent problems, such as those related to health and aging, traffic congestion and environmental quality. Typically, this proposition is then criticised from a 'bottom up' perspective, focusing on 'smart citizens' and open platforms (Townsend 2013; Greenfield 2013). Here, the debate risks getting caught in a dichotomy where a priori value preferences ('small is beautiful' or 'big problems require integrated solutions') predict contributions and responses.

This is not how real change comes about. What we typically see is the emergence of coalitions of forces that, between them, create the persuasive power to bring about change. The actors operating in this coalition do not necessarily agree on all the details, but they agree on a strategic orientation and share a language to discuss cities. I regard smart cities for the moment as such a discourse, a way of seeing and talking that highlights some aspects of our urban reality, but, out of necessity, pays less attention to other aspects. Elsewhere, I have defined a discourse as: 'an ensemble of notions, ideas, concepts and categorisations through which meaning is allocated to social and physical phenomena, and which is produced and reproduced in an identifiable set of practices.' (Hajer 2009, p.59–60). In this sense, 'Keynesianism' or neo-liberalism could be considered a discourse. Both are ways of seeing, which, over time, became deeply influential as discourse institutionalised into new rules and routines (Hall 1986). What started as language and ideas, in the end, had consequences for tax regimes, anti-cyclical spending (or the opposite), or indeed the preferred role of the state in infrastructural projects. This is why discourse analysis postulates that language really matters. Through language 'some issues are organised into politics while others are organised out', (cf. Schattschneider 1960).

If we look at smart cities as a form of discourse, we see, first of all, a dominance of concepts such as 'smart grids', '(big) data', 'efficiency', 'infrastructure', 'system', 'energy', 'monitoring' and 'information'. This highlights a managerial take on cities, with new possibilities coming from the application of ICT tools. This is then applied to urban problems, such as those related to environmental quality and health, security, and the efficiency of service delivery. The dominance of ICT technology leads urbanist Mark Swilling to see smart city as a form of 'algorithmic urbanism' (Swilling 2014a).

Second, discourses do their political work as the 'glue' of coalitions. Such 'discourse coalitions' (Hajer 1995) reproduce a particular way of seeing throughout society. Smart cities are typically discussed in new, cross-over fora in which business, government and knowledge institutes find each other. Cisco Systems organised a string of meetings on various continents under the heading 'Meeting of the Minds'; BMW launched a 'Guggenheim lab' travelling from New York to Berlin and Mumbai; and Siemens built a complete pavilion, the Crystal, in London, to showcase the future of the smart city. Interestingly, their enthusiasm has not spilled over into academic debate.

Third, smart cities are oriented to a particular organisational idea. New opportunities are linked to public–private partnerships in which business helps public service delivery. As part of this shift from public infra to public–private partnerships, the way in which consumers pay for their urban services is likely to change. 'Public works' will be replaced by a 'pay per' approach (Graham and Marvin 2001). These are potentially big changes. They may provide an excellent private business proposition, but what gets less attention is how particular understandings of the smart city relate to the existing system of governance, or indeed, the civil society of cities.

Fourth, smart city discourse approaches innovation as primarily a technological matter. Here, it often touches on the technological sublime, glorifying new possibilities. The trouble with the quick move from problem to solution is that the very conditions under which a future of liveable, stimulating cities has to be achieved, are

> **The trouble with an overly fast move from problem to solution is the rather short amount of time in which to hold the debate**

not really discussed. This is an omission, as the complex urban world does not allow for a quick application or transplantation of solutions. Knowing how difficult successful implementations of ICT projects have proven to be, even in much more mundane environments such as government bureaucracies, it seems important to pay more attention to the conditionalities of successful applications. This is, incidentally, also what comes out of one of the very first comprehensive studies of a 'smart cities' partnership, the T-City in the German city of Friedrichshafen (Hatzelhoffer et al. 2012).

Fifth, smart city discourse is notoriously weak on historical awareness. Why are things the way they are? What appear to be 'inefficiencies' in smart city discourse may be the result of the political battles of the past. For instance, in the heart of Amsterdam stands a bridge wide enough to fit a four-lane motorway. It carries only a one-way street and a bicycle lane. In New York, Fifth Avenue ends at a T-crossing where Washington Square Park starts. Undoubtedly inefficient, but the situation with the Amsterdam bridge was the result of Nieuwmarkt community protests against a car-oriented city development in the 1970s, while the Manhattan example was the outcome of Jane Jacobs and others protesting against the infringement of new car-oriented technologies on their own community spaces. In cases such as these, citizens can actually be proud of the inefficiencies of their cities. And we would now probably agree that this were the better urban planning solutions.

When it comes to cities, there are no 'set' solutions. Urban politics will always remain a matter of making difficult choices, and, to the extent that cities are run in a democratic way, urban politics is about making these choices, following an open deliberation between citizens and policymakers, constantly taking into consideration the interests of all those affected by the decisions (Barber 1984; Hajer 2009).

In all, the challenge may be to avoid the dichotomy between 'big' tech solutions and a world of 'bottom up' planning. First of all, because we are guided by a strong conviction that we have to make it work. Continuing to build cities in the 'default' way is leading to cities that are nasty to live in, costly to get around in, and that are hardly based on the employment of the imagination of either our citizens or our best designers. At the same time, we see how governments often have become more vulnerable and lack the authority, legitimacy and funding to really 'bend the trend'. We need to find a way to align the agents of change that can make this ideal of the 21st century as the age of a planet with liveable cities becomes a reality. What we need is a collaborative smart urbanism. And that very much still needs to be invented and defined. The best way to do this may actually be to be open and seek the debate.

THE TRANSITIONS OF THE 19TH AND 20TH CENTURY IN RETROSPECT

THE SANITARY REFORM MOVEMENT

The problems contemporary cities are facing may seem daunting. But they are not without precedent. It is particularly instructive to reflect on the period from the middle of the 19th century onwards, when the industrial city got its first public infrastructure. From 1840 to 1920, the US urban population grew from about 1.8 million to more than 54 million (Angel 2013). Between 1880 and 1920, over 20 million immigrants entered the United States. People escaped poverty and moved away to work in the newly industrialising cities, such as Chicago, Detroit and New York.

Housing quality was extremely poor and diseases spread rapidly. Public health became a prime concern. The first sanitary survey of New York City was organised in 1864, a crucial moment in the history of American public health.

> **The problems contemporary cities are facing may seem daunting. But they are not without precedent**

'The inspectors wrote about overflowing privies, slime-covered streets filled with horse manure, and slaughterhouses and fat-boiling establishments dispersed among overcrowded tenements. One inspector reported that blood and liquid animal remains flowed for two blocks down 39th Street from a slaughterhouse to the river.' (Pizzi 2014)

In Europe, cities such as London, Paris and Berlin were similarly facing the consequences of slum life. In response to the urban problems of the second half of the 19th century and early 20th century, the construction of the sanitation infrastructure to fight the 'city of the dreadful night' as Peter Hall called it (1988) began in earnest. The slum clearance and installation of proper sewage systems and provisions for good drinking water ultimately put an end to the horrors of urban disease in the cities of the West.

In hindsight, the installation of the urban sanitary infrastructure seems a coherent exercise. In actual fact, it was beset by political conflict, resistance by vested interests and coalition building. The issue was put on the agenda by reformers, such as Edwin Chadwick (1800–1890) who studied the sanitary situation of the poor, and journalists who found the right tone to get the message across to a wider audience. This then led to the appointment of a Royal Commission, such as the one on the Housing of the Working Classes in 1884 (Hall 1988, p.16). Major infrastructural works were the product of a discourse coalition, the 'sanitary movement', which combined the social cause of ending urban blight with the push to install particular new infrastructure in the cities. British reformers Edwin Chadwick and Charles Booth (1840–1916) organised surveys and first produced the statistics that helped

| In what type of city would we like to live?

create a broader awareness needed to really push this retrofit of sanitary infrastructure onto the cities. Vested interests were only persuaded once stubborn statistical work illuminated the need to install proper water provision infra. In Paris, the construction of sewers was combined with the broader (politically driven) project of slum eradication and the development of the boulevards (Graham and Marvin 2001, p.55 ff.). In the United States a similar development took place. Here, Frederick Law Olmsted embarked on a project on city parks to help create another attitude and value-set for the working poor. 'The remedies then were different. But the problem, and the perception of it, was similar on both sides of the Atlantic' (Hall 1988, p.44). And, in all cases, it was not simply a technical debate about infrastructure, but rather was led by a notion of what type of city we wanted to live in, and what sort of morals and values should find their expression. In what type of city would we like to live?

This new discourse on sanitation subsequently inspired a generation of planners and designers to come up with visions on the future of the city. Frederick Law Olmsted, Ebenhezer Howard and

Patrick Geddes all responded to the call for more liveable cities, and they, each in their own particular way, invented forms of city planning that were meant to cope with the interaction between nature and the urban. Whether by interlacing the urban areas with green spaces, by the creation of 'garden cities' or via the idea of a more regional approach to planning, thus focusing on the interaction of 'the country' and 'the city', all three sought to reconnect the city to its natural environment. What is more, by doing so, they all worked with their own ideas of what constitutes a 'good society', hoping that the new organisation of the urban space would bring out the best in people. Often, this was a moral politics aimed at 'educating' or even disciplining the urban poor, but in all cases the designs were inspired by the sense of a possibility of a more harmonious world.

The influence of planners and designers was never direct. Planners were taken up in discourse coalitions where their ideas became an element in a concrete political practice that always moulded the original ideas, often because of the emergence of new technological inventions, because of political ideology or choices for a particular organisational form. Howard's garden city paved the way for the suburb, but was stripped of his anti-urban community-oriented societal idealism, along the way.

The history of the sanitary movement of the 19th century illustrates the important role of the broader socio-political debate on the public problems of that day. Public health was a widely shared concern. The successful strategies that were adopted derived their effectiveness from this broader societal legitimation.

THE MODERN CITY

A second instructive period of transition was the era of modernist planning. Starting in the 1920s, urban planning came to be dominated by the 'modern' movement. The movement was epitomised by the Swiss/French architect Le Corbusier (1887–1965), but with many other deeply influential thinkers, such as Siegfried Giedion, Walter Gropius, Bruno Taut and J.J.P. Oud, who gathered in the Congrès International d'Architecture Moderne (CIAM). Its modernism was reflected in its commitment to explore and use the possibilities of new materials and methods of construction. Steel, concrete and prefab materials allowed for a new way of organising construction. Buildings could be higher and cheaper, thus allowing the deployment of these techniques for social purposes. The modern movement broke away from the traditional styles in architecture, but initially continued the morphological search for garden cities, such as in Siemensstadt and the 'Onkel Toms Hütte Siedlung' near Berlin.

The movement was socially utopian; the purpose of using the new materials was to help overcome the public health problems and often even outright nastiness of the 19th century housing stock and architecture. Linking architecture to urban planning also showed ways of improving the living conditions of many by separating dirty work from living. The 'functional' city sought solutions to issues of urban planning by spatially differentiating work, transport, living and leisure, and by opening up the urban fabric. The 19th century city proximity was the basis, and the new modern technological inventions allowed for a separation between functions. People were able to enjoy fresh air, light and green space. With plan Voisin and La Ville Radieuse, Corbusier introduced the idea of the high-rise in the park.

Nature was not absent in modernist planning, but was rigidly conceptualised in terms of access to good air quality and, in particular, the positioning of buildings, to allow for direct sun light to enter homes. Here, the modern movement again took city slums as its starting point, with their notoriously bad air quality and where hardly any sun entered into dwellings.

The modern movement was based on a firm belief in the possibilities of science. It proclaimed the functional city as solution to the urban problems of its time, and this functional city was to be based on good statistical analysis. Using survey analysis, the movement aimed to find the most efficient solutions for planning cities; zoning rather than detailed design was key. This modernist planning gave us the pioneering Amsterdams Uitbreidingsplan by Cornelis van Eesteren and Theo K. van Lohuizen (1934) and the Abercrombie plan for London (1944). Most of the time, however, the ideas of planning were not to be realised according to the intellectual ambitions of the founding fathers. The modernists were strongly positivist and had a belief in general laws and generic optimal solutions. Corbusier developed with a 'modular man' and claimed he had found a yardstick to measure good urban form, from doorknobs to a full city layout (the Arts Council of Great Britain 1987). But, apart from a few exceptions, such as the designs for the new cities of Brasilia and Chandigarh (India), the modern movement was never able to fully impose its own design logic on cities.

In the end, modernist design was outpaced by technological development and eroded by social critique. After the Second World War, the prospects of the urban world had changed. The combustion-engined car had become available as a mass product. Pioneered by Henry Ford in the 1910s, this was a typical product of the modern age. Based on the full exploitation of the benefits of modern mass production, car mobility created new possibilities to handle the issue of transport and distance in cities. What is more, it called for major breakthroughs in the existing urban fabric to guarantee the flow of traffic on the existing streets of the inner city (cf. Berman 1983). Urban planners such as Robert Moses acted in a complicated discourse coalition that also included real estate interests, mobility management concerns and bureaucratic strive between different agencies. In all, the modern movement relied on its strong ties to city governments. It had a persuasive story line on how the application of the latest insights and technologies could help realise politicians' dreams. Rationality and efficiency were key. Just as the sanitation movement of the 19th century was propelled by the dystopia of the urban blithe, the 20th century modern movement captured the imagination via an utopian vision of an automobile city – clean and smooth, laid out in space. It suggested that cities were defunct and in need of an upgrade. And that upgrade was thought to be readily available.

This vision captured the imagination of policy elites who, at the time, had not enough eye for the vulnerabilities of the particular urban communities that were to be rehoused to the modernist tower blocks. Neither were they aware that the imposition of this modernist format on existing cities would hurt the cities in their very essence; as places of exchange, inspiration and openness. This was precisely what led to the social critique of the discourse of modern planning in the late 1960s. It was stopped by 'a shout in the street', as Marshall Berman famously put it (Berman 1983).

THE GREAT ACCELERATION

The lead up to the third transition that we face today started in the 1950s. After the Second World War, planners realised that the car was the technology of the future. The inner city of Rotterdam, bombed by the Nazis early on in the Second World War, was reconstructed in a new, more open layout, to accommodate the many cars that were expected to dominate city life. Indeed, it is hard to overestimate the influence of the automobile, not only in the inner cities, but also in the region. The emergence of the car

> **After the Second World War, planners realised that the car was the technology of the future**

as a means of mass transport extended the socio-spatial scope of the modern planning projects. As the car allowed for a higher 'time-space compression', the suburbs came within reach for those that earned enough in city jobs to consider commuting to work on a daily basis. All of this took off in the 1950s and 1960s. It was the time of the National Highway Defence Act (1956) that laid the basis for the US interstate highway system (cf. Chakrabarti 2013, p.104 ff.) and similar schemes elsewhere.

The car extended the dream of the functionalist city and set work and living apart in ways that had been unimaginable before. Not only did it allow for the invention and materialisation of the 'suburb' as a new way of living, it also allowed for a new expression of spatial differentiation in urban societies. The suburb allowed the new middle classes to escape the vicinity and directly felt presence of the urban poor.

> **The car extended the dream of the functionalist city and set work and living apart in ways that had been unimaginable before**

The suburb became a corner stone of the 'American Dream'. A new 'way of life' for the new middle classes, who now could use a refrigerator to store perishable goods and, thus, avoid more frequent trips to the corner shop. Suburban living was a lifestyle, well expressed in advertisements, film and television (cf. Chakrabarti 2013). People were able to reach the city but no longer needed to be living in it.

In European countries, the 'suburbanisation' was seen as 'urban sprawl'. Attempts were made to guide the overflow in to 'new towns'. These purpose-built new cities, such as Milton Keynes in the United Kingdom, Vällingby in Sweden, and Purmerend and Lelystad in the Netherlands, were constructed at longer distances from the main urban centres and often had priority public transport connectivity. The regional scope of the city found its new expression.

> **Post-war cities have set up the centralised, fossil-fuel-based energy systems**

Notice that the story of the modern city is mostly told in terms of the way in which it organised housing and transport. Less realised perhaps, but not less meaningful; modern post-war cities mostly set-up centralised fossil-based energy systems that generated electricity and delivered it to our homes via a grid. Coal and oil, over time, were replaced by gas and electricity to generate heat.

In all, the transition towards the modern city illustrates how 20th century urban development was the product of a discourse coalition in which planners and designers only played a certain part. The idealism of the modernist planner must be seen in the context of the industry's push for the car as a consumer good, the continued economic growth and the emergence of a broadly shared sense of the good life being related to a suburban way of living. Socio-politically this model was supported by the possibility to constantly use new economic growth to create the preconditions for better lives. Ecologically, it ran on the seemingly unproblematic intake of natural resources, most notably fossil fuels for electricity and cars. High productivity agriculture guaranteed rich diets, often based on a high input of fertilisers and pesticides. Waste and water were managed beyond the city perimeter or were not managed at all. Urban metabolism played no role in strategic planning.

The second half of the 20th century was a period of unprecedented improvements in quality of life. The Western world experienced a rise in the standard of living that made its style of living into an aspirational model for the world at large. In the last decade, the newly developing countries started to follow in the tracks of the West. Yet, this progress came at a cost. The rise of modern city living coincided with what Will Steffen called 'the great acceleration'. Looking back we see how, around the 1950s, our extractions from nature and our emissions to nature rose at an unprecedented speed:

'One feature stands out as remarkable. The second half of the 20th century is unique in the entire history of human existence on Earth. Many human activities reached take-off points sometime in the 20th century and have accelerated sharply towards the end of the century. The last 50 years have without doubt seen the most rapid transformation of the human relationship with the natural world in the history of humankind.' (Steffen et al. 2004, p.18)

This great acceleration did deliver prosperity, but now we are being confronted by its unintended consequences.

CITIES IN THE ANTROPOCENE

Until recently, nature performed benignly. It functioned as a wonderful 'hinterland' for cities that could be drawn upon for all those things needed to make urban society excel. It provided the input of building materials, fuels, water and food. On the 'output' side, nature seemed to function as a sink, which cleared away whatever we produced in terms of waste or emissions. For some decades, we were able to live in the illusion that nature was resilient. Nature supplied the cities with what they needed, in the way of food, a-biotic resources and energy. And the rivers, soils and air cleared away the urban muck.

These days, we are well aware of the seriously disrupted cohesion between nature and society. The 20th century cities run on fossil energy that cause global warming, they extract too much drinking water, do not recoup waste water and nutrients and pile up waste in landfills. Our modern system is one in which non-renewable resources, such as phosphorous, flow into our rivers and seas where they cause environmental havoc. Many countries have hidden their waste in landfills, little aware that, in the generic waste heaps, we also throw away precious metals. The IRP calculated that for only 18 of 69 metals and metalloids the recycling rate is above 50%. For some crucial metals, such as lithium and arsenic, the recycling rate is below 1% (Graedel et al. 2011).

> **Now we have the knowledge that shows how seriously the nature-society nexus is out of sync**

In the early 1990s, it was Nobel Prize Laureate Paul Crutzen who first suggested that our industrial way of living had *geological* consequences. He coined the term 'the Antropocene' to express this (Crutzen 2002). Subsequent work by Rockström, Steffen and others has only reinforced this call. We are crossing planetary boundaries (Rockström et al. 2009; Steffen et al. 2004), in terms of climate change, biodiversity loss and the nitrogen cycle, and we risk crossing the boundaries in many other domains. Cities, occupying less than 2% of the land of the planet, are the areas for which most of these resources are used. Based on this awareness of the Antropocene, cities now have to rethink how they function and accept that there are natural limits beyond which their continued and safe existence becomes impossible.

The failure to conceptualise the relation between the city and the natural environment, in metabolic terms, is one of the tragedies of 20th century planning. In the early 1920s, planner Patrick Geddes had been very firm in his insistence on an integrated approach to the city and its 'hinterland'. But after that, modernist thinking was growth-oriented and driven by a belief in engineering and science for finding solutions. The concept of the 'tabula rasa', a 'clean slate' to start thinking about best urban form illustrates the extent to which the notion of good city life had become decontextualised. For city planning, this has become a major obstacle to making our cities resilient. Most 20th century cities now show a massive 'lock in' with infrastructure that is based on a fossil-fuel-based economy that we need to get away from. Yet, lock ins such as in the energy domain are institutionally embedded and make it difficult to organise the transition towards an ecologically acceptable metabolism.

The tragedy of our time is that we are currently seeing how the rapid urbanisation of the new cities of the global South, by and large, follows the default trajectory that was pioneered in the cities of the Western world in the 20th century. There is currently no place on Earth where we can see this more vividly than in the cities of China. The 'airpocalypse' in Beijing and other cities not only creates serious health hazards, but now starts to affect agricultural production, as the growing season is hampered by lower photosynthesis rates. What is more, air pollution has started to have a measurable negative effect on economic performance (The Guardian, 27 February 2014).

> **Nature and society, today, are so much out of sync that, as scientists, we can no longer address singular problems in a meaningful way**

Nature and society, today, are so much out of sync that, as scientists, we can no longer address singular problems in a meaningful way. Today, we speak of 'nexus' problems in which issues around climate change, energy consumption, land use and biodiversity loss are seen as fundamentally intertwined.

Take, for instance, the land-related consequences of urbanisation. The current pattern of urbanisation also consumes arable land at a high cost. Without policy interventions, settlements and infrastructures are expected to expand by around 260 to 420 million hectares by 2050 (Kemp-Benedict et al. 2002). Angel (2012) calculated that around half of all urban expansion occurs on what was previously agricultural land. This often concerns fertile land in river valleys and deltas, and causes agricultural activities to shift towards soil that delivers a lower yield. This, in turn, means that more land is required to feed the growing and wealthier world population, despite agricultural developments and improvements. The agricultural land expansion is projected to amount to at least 400 million hectares, in the period up to 2050 (PBL 2012). The point of closely coupled challenges is made by the FAO statement that 'If we fail to meet our goal and a food shortage occurs, there will be a high risk of social and political unrest, civil wars and terrorism, and world security as a whole might be affected' (FAO 2013).

In the West, we saw a first wave of environmental measures to act on those urban flows that hit people most directly some 40 years ago. In the 1970s, we introduced wastewater treatment, air quality control, soil pollution protection and noise level control. But we failed to allow the cities of the global South to 'leapfrog'. As a result, they are now, four decades later, experiencing exactly the same type of problem but on a grander scale.

Most daunting, perhaps, is the water situation in the cities of the South. While New Delhi homes may have toilets, their wastewater spills untreated into the Yamuna river, which supplies the drinking water to cities downstream. Biswas and Brabeck-Letmathe cite a 2011 survey by the Central Pollution Control Board of India indicating that only 160 of 8,000 towns had both a sewerage system and a sewage-treatment plant (CPCB 2013). In 2011, the water in more than half of China's and India's rivers and lakes was found to be unfit for consumption. In 2013, 72% of Pakistan's samples from the water delivery system were found to be unfit for consumption (Biswas and Brabeck 2014).

Child mortality from diarrhoea – caused by unsafe drinking water and poor sanitation – is projected to decrease from 1.8 million today, to an estimated 0.5 million by 2050. Fortunately, worldwide access to improved water sources and sanitation is getting better (WHO and Unicef 2013). However, the failure to address the interaction with nature will result in continuing, tremendous health risks. Here, the improvements in the lack of access to basic sanitation can hardly compensate for the deteriorating urban air quality situation. By 2050, outdoor air pollution (particulate matter and ground-level ozone) is projected to become the top cause of environment-related deaths worldwide, according to the OECD Environmental Outlook Baseline scenario (OECD 2012). Air pollution concentrations in some cities, particularly in Asia, are already far above acceptable health standards (World Health Organization's Air Quality Guideline).

We need to put the new wave of urbanisation on another footing to avoid human hardship and ecological waste. There is only one way to get this done: we must think of another planning strategy and the cities of the South must find ways of 'leapfrogging', using all available know-how to reconfigure the urban metabolism of cities in developed and developing countries.

SMART URBANISM: AN AGENDA FOR PLANNING AND DESIGN

We are currently experiencing a discursive shift in urban planning and design. We are inventing new terms and concepts that will create the new practices of 21st century planning. Discourse analysis differentiates between 'discourse structuration' and 'discourse institutionalisation' (Hajer 1995, pp.60–61). Discourse structuration describes the process in which a particular way of conceiving reality settles, to become a generally accepted way of talking. With it, a particular sense of problems and solutions compete over centre stage. Over time, such a discourse may become the new 'normal', accepted way of seeing. It then starts to institutionalise in new rules and routines, in laws, new business models, new roles for state agencies and market, citizens and experts, and even newly shared values.

Moments of discursive shift are moments of opportunity

Moments of discursive shift are moments of opportunity. The old institutionalised power relationships offer a chance for debate. At such moments, new actors characteristically discuss new issues in the established fora. This is exactly what we see happening around the notion of the 'smart city'. Here, we are discussing the future of planning and design. It is important to make sure that this reordering is informed by a good sense of the challenge that cities face. That is why this book presents the important statistics on our urban metabolism in a visualised way (see part two of the book). First, we provide seven considerations for the agenda for planning and design.

1 / 'DECOUPLING' AS THE STRATEGIC ORIENTATION

In the following decades, we will need to strongly 'decouple' the prosperity of the city from the use of resources. By and large, we need to find ways to create the same sort of wealth and welfare with only a tenth of global greenhouse gas emissions. The *City-Level Decoupling Report* published by UNEP's International Resource Panel (IRP) brought this perspective on to the wider urban agenda (UNEP 2013a and UNEP 2013b).

Decoupling wealth from resource use is a major break away from the current urbanisation by default that stems from the replication of 20th century urban development strategies. Continuing on this path is going to result in pollution, rising emission levels, congestion and rising input costs as prices absorb the downstream effects of resource depletion.

> **The default urbanisation that is still being applied today, is based on the duplication of 20th century development strategies**

Achieving decoupling alone will not be enough. Those most concerned with the decoupling regimes are well aware that this should be realised in a broader social perspective. We should not only stay in the 'safe operating space' within 'planetary boundaries'; this space should also be socially just (Rockström et al. 2009; Raworth 2012; Swilling and Annecke 2012). Fusing socially just and safe operating spaces lies at the heart of the current debate on 'Sustainable Development Goals' (SDGs). Creating a separate urban SDG would be a way to link urban development to this broader normative debate.

2 / A PERSUASIVE STORY LINE ABOUT THE FUTURE

The American planning theorist James Throgmorton once described planning as 'persuasive story-telling about the future'. His argument was that the essence of planning was not about ends and means, ordering, organisation and reorganisation; instead he found that underlying effective planning was a vision, a persuasive story. That persuasive story had a generative capacity: it informed the daily activities of all those working on plan making, restructuring, organising and logistics (Throgmorton 1996).

We need new, persuasive ideas for the city of the 21st century. Ideas that mobilise actors throughout society; ideas that are able to mobilise resources and give city officials the confidence that they can use it as the persuasive story line to make their mark on their respective urban futures.

The concept of 'smart cities' currently mobilise much positive energy among the elite, and its discourse is truly of the 21st century, yet it lacks connection to a broader social reform agenda. This is something that must still be established if it is to become a generating story line. People come to cities to improve their lives. We need to rethink the city so as to make it an environment, a configuration that is sustainable, socially just and resilient to future shocks.

What do we want these smart technologies to help achieve? Currently, we see lots of excitement about new possibilities that I would classify as 'nice to have', whereas decoupling is a pressing 'need to have' agenda that could do with some smart support. Smart cities should be judged in terms of their capacity to really add to the transition towards a healthy, safe and ultimately liveable urban future that is embedded in ecological sustainability and regional bio-economies.

Smart cities are related to concrete aspects of urban planning and policymaking. Ideally, such innovations allow for an enhanced efficiency, making cities cheaper and easier to navigate, explore and exploit them for citizens and business, and cheaper and easier to manage for public policy officials. Smart urbanism calls for a language that expresses more than efficiency and technology. After the initial excitement over all the new gadgets and technological possibilities, we should now explore what the new technologies achieve for those spheres that make up a good city. A team from the Technical University of Vienna came up with six themes to assess the contribution of a smart city approach (discussed in Hatzelhoffer et al. 2012, p.22):

→ SMART ECONOMY / dealing with innovation and entrepreneurship

→ SMART PEOPLE / the contributions to social and human capital, 'including educational attainment, lifelong learning, openness to what is "new", and integration into public life'

→ SMART GOVERNANCE / public participation, an accessible local administration and good service delivery

→ **SMART MOBILITY** / applications that help local and international accessibility and innovations towards sustainable mobility

→ **SMART ENVIRONMENT** / everything related to environmental protection, resource management and the preservation of green space, water aquifers, among other things

→ **SMART LIVING** / relating to quality of life; for example, the effects on services in the domain of health care, cultural institutions, security and social cohesion

3 / USE URBAN METABOLISMS AS FRAMEWORKS FOR STRATEGIC DECISION-MAKING

Metabolism takes place 'off stage' of the urban spectacle; it is barely visible. Yet, for its performance, a city is dependent on a constant flow of input and output, but improvements to sewage systems do not win elections. However, sometimes, sustainable metabolism is very obvious. Think of interventions in public space, such as the recent pedestrianisation of Times Square in Manhattan. It is an illustrative symbol of a governance that strives for a responsible handling of the flows within the city. These metabolic flows were basically 'assumed' in the modern city, but now need our full attention. These metabolic flows are a profoundly useful way of conceptualising the challenge of urban sustainability. So, think of cities in terms of their metabolic flows: water, energy and food (UNEP 2013a; Swilling et al. 2012; Ferrao and Fernandez 2013). Cities need vast quantities of materials, such as steel, sand and cement. And they produce heaps of waste and emissions of various sorts. This 'metabolism' is a prerequisite for what we love about cities as places of human improvement, creativity and exchange. Nevertheless, as the smog in Chinese cities shows, if we do not put urban metabolisms at the heart of our strategic planning, we run the risk of triggering a negative feedback loop that will undermine urban liveability. What is more, cities that do not improve the efficiency of their metabolic system will be vulnerable to the inevitable price effects from the resource scarcities predicted by the assessments of organisations such as the UNEP IRP.

The strange fact is that we do not have a good sense of the modern city's metabolisms. Even rich cities in the global North often lack the statistics on input and output. We are running our cities in a way similar to driving a car without a fuel gauge on the dashboard. We know our speed, but we have no idea about how long we could keep on going. Tracking the metabolism of society will shed light on the flip side of our progress and is something we now urgently have to come to grips with. Initiatives such as the Large Urban Areas Compendium initiated by the World Bank (Hoornweg and Freire 2013) and the Global City Indicators Facility (http://www.cityindicators.org/Default.aspx) are therefore more than timely.

Understanding our urban metabolism is not only a matter of being able to stay within limits. It also calls for a focus on potentials, transformations and the transition. Here, designers and planners can really contribute. It also calls for a monitoring of achievements and an analysis of the reasons for success. This would be a task for scientists and policy scholars.

4 / FOCUS ON THE DEFAULT IN INFRASTRUCTURE

Connecting smart city discourse to a sustainable urban metabolism would give it a better sense of purpose. This is a challenging agenda. The IRP identified the crucial role of urban infrastructure in all of this. 'The design, construction and operation of infrastructures also shape the "way of life" of citizens and how they procure, use and dispose of the resources they require. City-level infrastructures are therefore key to increased efforts to promote resource efficiency and decoupling at the city level, as well as well-being and access to services of their citizens.' (UNEP 2013b, p.7)

> **Infrastructure is static and mostly embedded in all types of systems**

In their path-breaking Splintering Urbanism, Stephen Graham and Simon Marvin included a quote from the report Cities and their Vital Systems: 'Cities', write Herman and Ausubel (1988), 'are the summation and densest expressions of infrastructure, or more accurately a set of infrastructures, working sometimes in harmony, sometimes with frustrating discord, to provide us with shelter, contact, energy, water and means to meet other human needs. The infrastructure is a reflection of our social and historical evolution. It is a symbol of what we are collectively, and its forms and functions sharpen our understanding of the similarities and differences among regions, groups and cultures. The physical infrastructure consists of various structures, buildings, pipes, roads, rail, bridges, tunnels and wires. Equally important and subject to change is the 'software' for the physical infrastructure, all the formal and informal rules for the operation of the systems' (Ausubel and Herman (1988), cited in Graham and Marvin, 2001, p.1).

From a governance point of view, infrastructure is a deeply problematic field. Infrastructure is static and mostly embedded in all types of systems. Infrastructures of cities are the result of decades or indeed centuries of cumulative investment. Infrastructures are notoriously difficult to disentangle and change. And infrastructures are essential to daily life within cities; hence, maintaining them is very complex, let alone changing their configuration.

Infrastructure development is crucially important if we want to decouple urban economic growth rates from those of resource consumption. But infrastructure is deeply political as well, be it that this is not always recognised. Infrastructure sets the defaults. First of all, via the hardware of urban infrastructure networks. It is safer, for instance, to get around in London with a car than with a bike although vehicle speed is notoriously slow. And in the second place, via the rules that determines how we use those networks. For instance, a rule that gives renewable energy priority access to the grid, creates the business case for small holders. In the domain of infrastructure smart technology could really make a contribution. It would enable us to change the way we use our roads (for cars, bicycles or pedestrians) even at different moments of the day, much more easily; likewise, smart grids, if regulated with rules that facilitate renewables, would allow for a powerful push from citizens and firms to become active electricity producers. Here, governments can facilitate a shift, making capital productive for a more sustainable infrastructure (cf. Swilling 2013).

The challenge for smart cities is not simply that of adopting a given technology. Rules and ownership are the crucial 'soft' dimensions of infrastructure. Infrastructure always comes with a default, and privileges certain uses over others. These rules can become problematic if values are changing, think of the implicit priorities in traffic, and the way these are now becoming politicised in London, Paris and New York, where bicyclists claim a right to use the streets safely. Policymakers need to reflect carefully on the social consequences of the rules they adopt. In the 20th century, they fully supported the company structures of utility companies that were completely focused on centralised energy supply and large-scale economic thinking. Today, such company structures increasingly more often are under pressure. Small-scale, renewable energy technologies and smart grids offer opportunities for alternative approaches (Richter 2013). Smart energy grids and meters today present possibilities for realising long-term ambitions for energy generation with a low CO_2 emission level. Although some of the new rules are to the advantage of citizens, the majority appear to benefit the business community. Particularly energy suppliers benefit from the optimisation of energy supply and energy prices using smart grids and smart meters. New issues of dependency are emerging. The guarantee of broad access always stimulates innovation, whereas closed systems of provision and ownership stifle it.

In the days of modern city planning, we may have aimed to develop a strategic framework for a desired infrastructure configuration in advance of the dynamics of urban development (Angel 2013, p.57). Nowadays, this no longer speaks to our realities. In the West, we think in terms of open planning and a large part of the urbanisation will take place in countries with a weak governance system and low regulatory capacity anyway. The days of blueprints are over, and rightly so. Weak capabilities for strategic forward planning may now be compensated by the potential of peer-to-peer learning. Hence decoupling may be more about experience, learning and duplication than about elaborate bureaucratic planning. Such seemingly spontaneous leapfrogging already took place in Sub-Saharan Africa with mobile telephony. There is no reason why such leapfrogging could not be achieved with other socio-technical systems.

5 / BEYOND THE SMART CITY 'FROM A BOX'

With the World Bank arguing that 'smart cities' could 'reduce greenhouse gas emissions by as much as 7.8 Gt in 2020', we seem to have an example of the 'we've got the technology' fallacy. They calculated what the effect would be of a full application of a given technology on the urban world.

> **The idea of 'smart cities from a box' – generic concepts that are imposed on cities – will not work**

The idea of 'smart cities from a box' – generic concepts that are imposed on cities – will not work. Experimental green cities, such as Songdo in South Korea, Masdar in the United Arab Emirates and Dongtan in China, stand witness to what happens if we opt for sustainability but continue following the planning concepts of the 20th century. These are, in the end, smart cities on a modernist footing; the 21st century equivalents of Brasilia and Chandigarh. And, even though they were created in a 'politically easy' *tabula rasa* situation, they have not lived up to their promises (Kuecker 2013; Townsend 2013; Ferrao and Fernandez 2013; p.131 ff.; Premalatha et al. 2013).

Cities illustrate how the technological and social aspects are interlinked in complicated ways. Engineers cannot decouple cities by themselves. A car is not just a technical artefact that can be meaningfully analysed in isolation. Instead, the impact of the car is related to the way in which it became an element of a much broader 'socio-technical system' that has been perfected to include multilane motorways with giant petrol stations, parking facilities in inner cities, out-of-town shopping centres, as well as much of our urban fabric and form, from the tangible cul-de-sac to the idea of suburban life style being a blend between city and country living. This large socio-technical system also comprises a powerful 'car industrial complex' that is a crucial component of the economy, creates jobs, generates know-how and drives the direction of innovation.

Hence, when we now think of smart cities as solutions to urban problems, we need to think about the technologies within context. We need to consider smart cities as being more than the effects that their singular artefacts may have on city life, and we need to also think beyond those artefacts; often, social innovations are needed as much as technological ones, in order to achieve sustainable urban metabolism. Here, technological innovation may help. Great examples of this include the various websites that organise a shared usage of tools and services in neighbourhoods. In the end,

> **Social innovations are needed as much as technological ones, in order to achieve sustainable urban metabolism**

it is most likely that a new blend of social innovations, new technologies, and new business models will provide the 'disruptive' force needed to change the dominant modern system. One may think of the combined effects of a shift to the *driverless car* (developed by outsider technology firms), a business model that moves from car ownership to mobility as a service, and the value shift from the car being the life structuring status symbol towards a life structured by the smart phone.

6 / A NEW OPEN AND COLLABORATIVE POLITICS

The established political system has become vulnerable. It is based on the assumption of a primacy of political decision-making by an elected council, supported by a monopoly of knowledge. However, the idea that the 21st century will still be about 'decisive acts' by a City Council is misguided. Innovation, both in terms of technology and of new social forms of organisation, outpace the capacities of classical-modernist forms of government (cf. Hajer 2009, Chapter One).

In 'Seeing like a State' (1998), the anthropologist James Scott studies how schemes that were 'meant to improve the Human Condition have failed'. He analysed not only the fate of high modernist urban planning but also that of intellectually similar efforts to improve agricultural productivity in Tanzania. He saw a 'high-modernist' ideology at play that was overconfident about the possibilities of solving problems by applying scientific insights and the latest technology. When a state is overconfident and a civil society is too weak to raise questions or resist particular schemes, this leads to the implementation of plans that do not connect and put an undue burden on the state to execute schemes that often lead to the adoption of authoritarian methods; thus, weakening the possibilities of joint implementation and learning.

We need a new mindset for the smart, liveable city to become a reality. In some cases, it requires more ongoing creative response to developments that take place, than to focus on the 'decisive act' of adopting, let alone on buying a 'turn key' technological scheme. Smart urbanism is about continuous learning, inspiration, measurements, analyses and readjustments.

> **We need a new mindset for the smart, liveable city to become a reality**

This requires a rethink on how public administrations operate. Policy can no longer be imposed. Everyday we can see examples of how the new civil society full of well-educated citizens raises so many astute questions and produces so many new demands that a classical bureaucracy becomes a defence industry. The classical 'decide, announce, defend' model is vulnerable in a world of continuous learning and shared and open information. Weberian bureaucracies worked much better in an era where government held the monopoly on good knowledge. Those days are over. ICT technology brings 'proto professionalisation' within reach of many. Governments now face an 'energetic society' (Hajer 2011) of citizens, who you either relate to by making them part of the (search for) solution(s), or who you will find opposing you. Twenty-first century cities increasingly have an opinionated and often well-informed citizenry who will resist, quarrel, raise questions, call for amendments, and oppose. And often for good reason. In planning, the trick is to use the intelligence of energetic citizens.

Interestingly, the 21st century seems an era in which a pragmatist philosophy of 'learning by doing' carries much better prospects than does the analytical idea of first stabilising knowledge and then allowing elected politicians to make big choices for us. The ideas of John Dewey, and later on the writings of Don Schön, on learning or the rethink on public policy by authors such as Majone, Pressman and Wildavsky (who saw implementation as a phase of continuous learning), (cf. Pressman and Wildavsky 1984), fit very well with an energetic society of people who think along (whether you ask them or not) and a technological environment that enhances their power to do so.

This being said, it is by no means obvious that cities will follow these suggestions. Intellectually we may see the limits of classical-modernist government, but in reality it is still a possibility that governments would follow the established classical-modernist model and aim for a big contract with a single party or a consortium of parties. In that case, this government would embark on an upgrade of the city infrastructure that is easier to control, in terms of contract and performance measurement, but, most likely, far less able to learn and readjust.

Elsewhere, I argued for a *radical incrementalism*, in a plea to use the enhanced collective intelligence of cities, to move towards a future in which learning really performs like a continued 'leapfrogging' movement (Hajer 2011). Radical incrementalism requires an open format that allows, indeed stimulates, the entrepreneurial spirit to outperform the public goals set to make cities sustainable and smart. It assumes that city governments strategically conceive of infrastructures as being the backbone of a new city life and guarantee the possibilities for continuous learning with respect to that backbone. For instance, the fibre-optic cable network is an infrastructure for which an openness should be guaranteed to make sure a variety of entrepreneurs will be able to use it, to provide new, often as yet unthought-of services. A city may impose a congestion charge, but rather than prescribing a technological meter to collect it, this would better be left to the market to invent the most efficient way to make people pay. A city could opt for a new rapid transit bus system, but it would be better advised to describe the desired performance and then leave it to entrepreneurs to find ways to achieve that performance.

In all, we should think carefully about the governance of a transition in infrastructure. On the one hand, we need a strong coalition to make such a transition by decoupling, a strategic possibility. On the other, the organisations currently promoting smart cities are so powerful that citizens are easily being left out. In this respect, Amsterdam's 'smart city' agenda is an interesting blend of both high end, high tech interventions, and a scattered set of experiments with citizen involvement or collaborative projects of shopkeepers to essentially implement 'decoupling' at street level (cf. http://amsterdamsmartcity.com).

Collaborative governance always implies a certain openness as to what exactly should be achieved. Collaboration is never effective if it is merely regarded as a tool to facilitate the implementation of a fixed set of pre-determined goals. Rather, it should be about true coalition building, with people adding concerns and wishes within an open-source environment. This then leads to the creativity of combination and implementation. For many, this may be counter-intuitive because it is about *adding* complexity that allows collaborative governance to find the best solutions (cf. Swilling 2014b). This, in turn, results in a reinvigorated idea of local democracy.

7 / CREATE A GLOBALLY NETWORKED URBANISM

Today, we need to think about urbanism from a global perspective. However, this time, it is not the globalism of a grand and all-encompassing vision. We can expect more from a networked one that links grounded concrete experiences together to plumb them and share insights and doubts. Such a globally networked urbanism should help avoid a repetition of the 20th century mistakes made in the West. Put differently, the 'task of the century' may be to succeed in this new global approach to urbanisation, bringing back the ideal of cities as a place of exchange, inspiration, social mobility, enhanced quality of life, inclusion and reconnectedness to nature.

The modernist city was the city of the blueprint: survey, analysis, plan. The cities of the 21st century cannot work with this model. What is more, I think that we are now too smart for thinking in terms of blueprints and linearity. We can now use complex networks of learning to radically speed up sharing solutions. We see a great variety of these horizontal networks emerging. C40 Cities, ICLEI, UN Global Compact, Global Initiative for Resource Efficient Cities, and the IHDP Sustainable Urbanisation initiative are just a few examples of the many initiatives. Horizontal exchange can lead to showcasing solutions and sharing enthusiasm among mayors and policymakers. Yet, there is much room for improvement if we would be able to add the analysis of *why* and *to what extent* particular examples contributed to learning and effective decoupling.

Given the challenges cities face, we now need cities that can adapt, correct, adopt, and add on to existing practices and knowledge. Modernist thinking relied on coordination and had a linear division between thinking (science), deciding (politics) and execution (implementation). If we want the 21st century to use its newly gained capabilities, urbanism is not going to be a coordinated effort – and that is a good thing. It is much more likely that we will achieve city-level decoupling if we manage to stage (creative) 'co-opetition'. A creative *co-opetition* requires citizens to stage and share successes and invites cities to excel.

> **Given the challenges cities face, we now need cities that can adapt, correct, adopt, and add on to existing practices and knowledge**

We now also look towards a new way of connecting science and analysis to policymaking by using and extending the important work on global databases, such as the Global City Indicators Facility (GCIF) or the IRP Cities Working Group. If cities do not know their metabolisms they cannot act on them. Yet, this time around, we should also be open to develop a much more grounded type of policy practice. It still is surprising to see how little use is being made by policymakers of the knowledge among street-level bureaucrats (cf. Lipsky 1980). In the 21st century, we should allow everyday life into policy-making, in order to avoid repeating the mistakes of the 20th century.

Learning requires more than statistics. City governments need good policy analysis, as well. We could use complexity science to analyse big data that is now available, and spot patterns and opportunities for intervention that may enhance the effectiveness of policies. We are looking towards a new reality in which policy analysis gives a much faster feedback, thus, allowing cities to readjust policy measures and regulatory regimes, accordingly.

A globally networked urbanism requires us to develop the science of 'transplantation' which allows us to determine under what conditions particular schemes or solutions have worked. Such science may help to assess whether a success could be copied. A 'Guggenheim' may have worked for Bilbao but was not a solution for many of the cities that tried to copy the success of the capital of the Basque country. Similar conditionalities apply to smart grids, rapid bus transit systems, green buildings, sewage treatment plants and solid waste management systems, or to the ways to involve citizens in the management of their own neighbourhoods and services. This new learning will be much more about inspiration and collaboration than about 'analyse and instruct'.

To connect the new possibilities of big data statistics to the everyday life of street-level bureaucrats and citizens is one of the critical challenges of today. When hearing the debates about the possibilities of big data, one is often struck by the echoes of the modernist past. Added is the sentiment that 'this time we can get it right'. That seems to deny the importance of political debate, urban conflict and the various interests. A deliberative policy-making (cf. Hajer and Wagenaar 2003) would aim to connect those without ending up in a new variation of technocracy.

The modernist planning of the 20th century has been written up in terms of big characters: Le Corbusier, Robert Moses and Jane Jacobs standing up to Robert Moses (Flint 2009). Most likely, 21st century planning will not have a figurehead. It will all be about networks. Smart city urbanism is most likely to be successful if its configuration is able to change and adjust, continuously. In terms of achieving a decoupling, we would do better to approach smart city urbanism as a 'project of projects', which leads to leapfrogging, because we put much emphasis on the evaluation of individual projects, as well as on sharing the results. Twenty-first century urbanism should become the 'feedback of all feedbacks' project, connecting cities, in order for us to learn faster than ever before.

The future of our cities is the 'project of all projects'. Smart urbanism would create the conditions for continuous learning, reflection and adjustment, in order to improve the urban condition for its inhabitants. And the only way to do that is to be open and share experiences and solutions.

CONCLUSION

Cities stand in the front line of sustainable development. Often built in the deltas of major rivers and bordering on seas and oceans, they are most threatened by climate change; they contribute most to CO_2 emissions and other resource use; but they are also most capable of innovation and change.

City-level decoupling is a daunting yet necessary ambition. Considering what is at stake, it would not be far fetched to say it is *the* task of the century. A brief look at the urban past shows that we have been ambitious and successful before. It also suggests that we need a broader engagement than we have seen so far. The sanitary reform movement of the 19th century gives us a sense of what is required to bring such major shifts about. In his discussion of smart cities, Anthony Townsend argues 'Like Patrick Geddes, I believe that it will take a social movement that enlists science, the humanities, and us all to address the challenges we face building a planet of cities that can survive.' (Townsend 2013, p.320).

Cities are social organisms. You cannot just 'pop the hood' and fix them. Thus far, smart city discourse is a-historic and has shown little appreciation of the societal contexts in which our cities will have to be built, rebuilt and retrofitted. Yet, if we really want to get this right, we must act now and quickly correct the technological orientation in smart city discourses. The fate of 20th century modernism shows the pitfalls of a technocratic approach.

We need to reconnect the bio-physical to the social domain. A first task is to broaden the awareness of what it would take to make a city run. Our urban metabolism is literally hidden. Visualising the urban metabolism shows what current city life entails and gives us a sense of what decoupling would require.

END NOTE

I would like to take this opportunity to thank Mark Swilling, Zef Hemel, Ries van der Wouden, David Hamers, Hiddo Huitzing, Ton Dassen and particularly David Laws for their review of earlier versions on this essay.

Maarten Hajer

People make a city; they travel around it, build and consume. Without people there would be no traffic, no construction pits, no waste, and no water or gas pipes.

A proper understanding of the city requires knowledge on the continuous flow of people that bring it to life. The people arriving or leaving and those living and working in the city, together, cause it to eat, absorb, digest, and discharge.

When we look at cities as organisms with their own metabolisms it becomes clear that they are not separate entities. All over the world, cities use nature as their supplier of fuel, food, resource materials and water, and, subsequently, nature also absorbs the waste generated by those cities. Adding all cities together, these flows are enormous.

The world population is growing at a considerable rate. How long nature will be able to keep up with this is debatable. Climate change, water scarcity and rising resource prices show at an increasing rate that nature's abilities are not inexhaustible. A future-oriented city, therefore, must have insight into its own metabolism. This starts with a clear understanding of its own population, but there is more. Flows of people 'elsewhere' have an ever-increasing influence on what nature is able to deliver. In order to set up an effective and action-oriented urban agenda, insight into these global flows of people is crucial.

This first chapter of part 2 of this book, therefore, begins by showing how the Dutch population and cities have developed in the past and how they are likely to develop in the future. This is followed by an image of the development of the world population and the related role of world cities.

1.1 / EVER MORE AND EVER OLDER

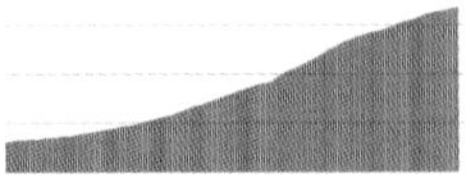

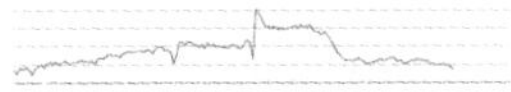

Over the centuries, as has been happening all over the world, the population of the Netherlands also has increased considerably. Up to the mid 19th century, this increase was slow but steady. Then, between 1850 and 1950, the size of the Dutch population began to grow dramatically, from 3 to 10 million people. Immigration in those days was hardly heard of; population growth was caused by the large numbers of newborn children in combination with a decrease in the number of deaths. A well-known example is the wave of births known as the Baby Boom, following the Second World War. It was not until many 'guest workers' arrived in the 1960s that the Netherlands became an immigration country.

The Netherlands, currently, has close to 17 million inhabitants. The strong population growth has decreased since the 1980s, and projections for the future even indicate that fewer children will be born than the number of elderly people expected to die. This will cause the aging of the population to increase. According to the population projections of Statistics Netherlands, the Dutch population will reach its peak in 2060, with close to 18 million inhabitants.

The Dutch have reached an increasingly older age, over the past centuries. Currently, men have a life expectancy of 79 and for women this is 83. This is twice as high as the life expectancy of men and women one hundred years ago. A combination of hygienic measures (e.g. the construction of water mains and sewage systems), better housing, abolishment of child labour, better medical knowledge and health care (vaccinations) have all lead to a steady decrease in the mortality rate. Epidemics, such as the small pocks and cholera epidemics of the 19th century, became increasingly rare. The most recent large epidemic to hit the Netherlands was the Spanish flu, in the 1918 – 1919 period, following the end of the First World War.

During the Second World War, many people died prematurely due to violence and malnutrition. After the 1950s, life expectancy for women increased rather strongly, while it remained more or less stable for men; many men were smokers in those days and women hardly smoked, which meant that men, in particular, were dying of smoking-related illnesses.

POPULATION SIZE (IN MILLIONS, THE NETHERLANDS)

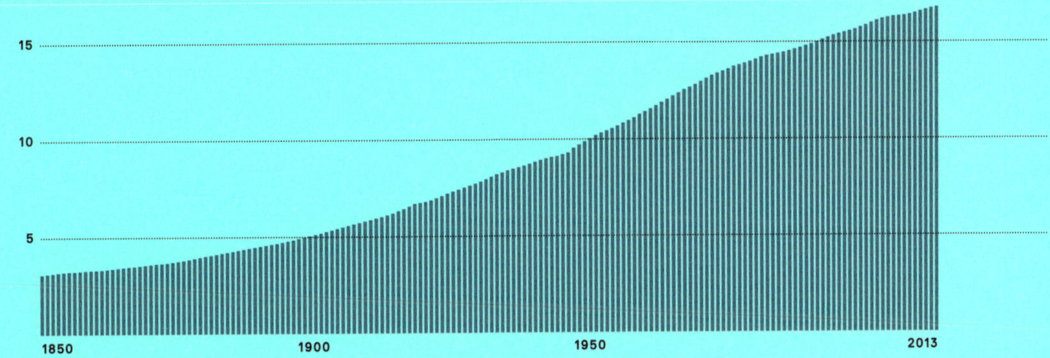

BIRTH-DEATH BALANCE AND IMMIGRATION-EMIGRATION BALANCE (THE NETHERLANDS)

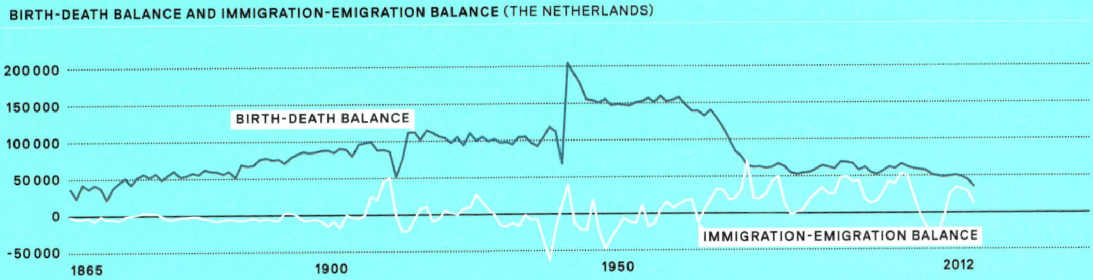

LIFE EXPECTANCY AT BIRTH (THE NETHERLANDS)

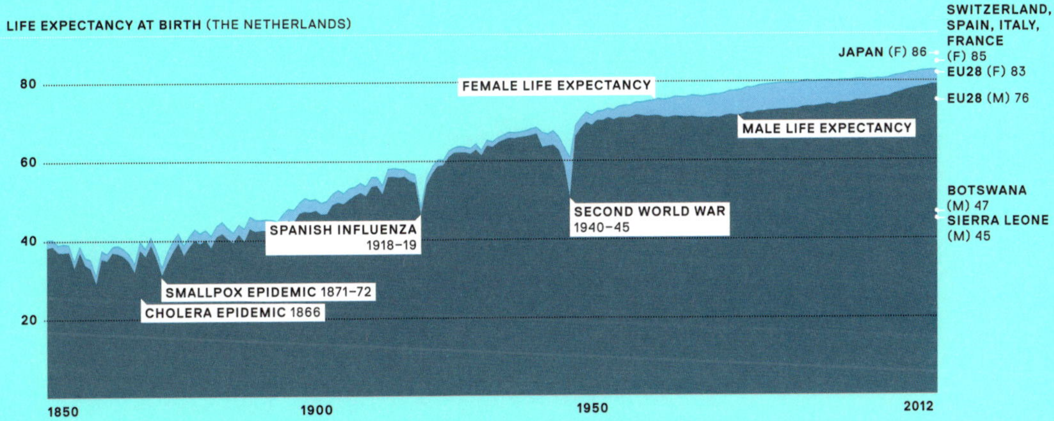

1.1 / EVER MORE AND EVER OLDER

The population of the Netherlands has grown from 3 million in 1850 to almost 17 million today. Population growth accelerated after 1950, when birth rates became much higher than death rates, and the Netherlands also became an immigration country. For decades, life expectancy has been increasing: the Dutch keep on growing older.

Sources: CBS, NIDI

Over the last decades, the longevity of men has increased again, partly due to a rapid decline in the percentage of smokers among men, and this made the difference in longevity between the sexes smaller. The Dutch are projected to continue to live longer, also in the future. Life expectancy is expected to increase to 87 for men and to 90 for women, by 2060. However, not everyone has the same chance of reaching such an old age. Higher educated people will live more than 6 years longer than those who are lower educated; and they will even feel healthier for 14 more years. There are no indications of this difference becoming smaller in the future.

1.2 A / FLOWS OF PEOPLE

Births, deaths, and people settling and leaving, together, determine the size and composition of the population. Changes are continuous and vary per country, region and municipality. In the Netherlands, the numbers of births and deaths mostly determine population development. Over 85% of the population growth over the past 10 years can be attributed to the birth surplus; more people were born than the number that died. Just under 15% of population growth was due to the fact that more people moved to the Netherlands than the number of people that left the country – the migration surplus. During this period, close to 1.9 million children were born and nearly 1.4 people died. The average number of children per woman was between 1.7 and 1.8, over the past years. This is higher than the European average of between 1.5 and 1.6 children per woman.

Fertility rates are higher for non-western immigrants in the Netherlands. For Moroccan and Turkish women, the respective average number of children per woman is just over 3 and 2. Around 25% of newborn children are of non-native origin. With respect to deaths, only around 10% is non-native. This share is low because most non-native inhabitants are relatively young; they entered the Netherlands in the last decades as young adults, or were born here.

The number of migrants, thus, has less of an impact on population growth than the numbers of births and deaths. Over the past decade, there were nearly 1.3 million immigrants and over 1.2 million emigrants.

There is a considerable flow of returning emigrants; native Dutch people who come back to the Netherlands after having lived abroad for a number of years. On balance, as this obviously does not apply to every emigrant, there is a considerable outflow of native Dutch people, with a total of 250,000 over the past decade.

1.2 B / FROM ALL OVER THE WORLD

Currently, the Netherlands has 3.5 million non-native inhabitants – people who themselves were born abroad or at least one parent of whom was born abroad. Around 1.5 million of them originate from western countries and 2 million from non-western countries.

Over the past 50 years, the Netherlands clearly became an immigration country, with more immigrants than emigrants in nearly every year. In the 1960s and 1970s, the guest workers arrived; first from southern Europe, then mostly from Turkey and Morocco. Around the time of the independency of the Dutch colony Surinam in 1975, and shortly after, many Surinamese people moved to the Netherlands. In the 1980s, family unification was started, with many wives of guest workers joining their husbands. In later years, their children often found a partner in the country of origin and these partners then also immigrated to the Netherlands. In the 1990s, refugees from war-torn countries or disaster areas came to the Netherlands, such as from former Yugoslavia, Iraq and Ethiopia. Following the expansion of the European Union in 2004, many migrants arrived from central and eastern Europe. In addition, there is a group of highly educated expats temporarily living in the Netherlands. Nearly all immigrants prefer the larger cities, because of the networks of fellow countrymen, employment opportunities, shops and cultural or religious facilities.

MIGRATION FLOWS, BIRTHS AND DEATHS IN THE NETHERLANDS BETWEEN 2003 AND 2012, IN THOUSANDS

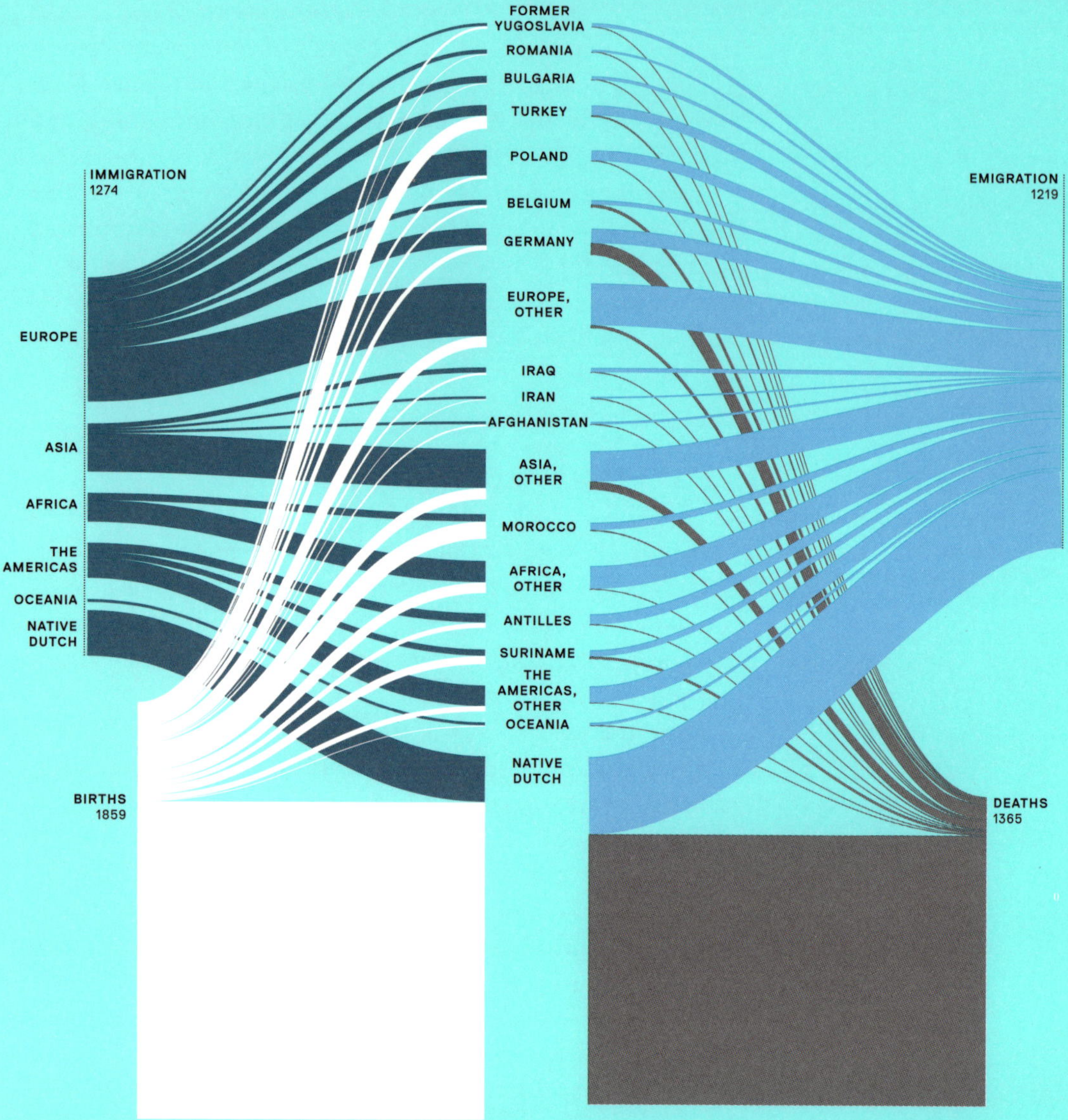

1.2 A / FLOWS OF PEOPLE

In the Netherlands, over the last decade, almost 2 million children were born and close to 1.5 million people died. Furthermore, over 1 million immigrants arrived in the country, while over 1 million emigrants left. Presently, the Dutch population includes 3.5 million people who are either foreign-born or have at least one foreign-born parent.

Source: CBS

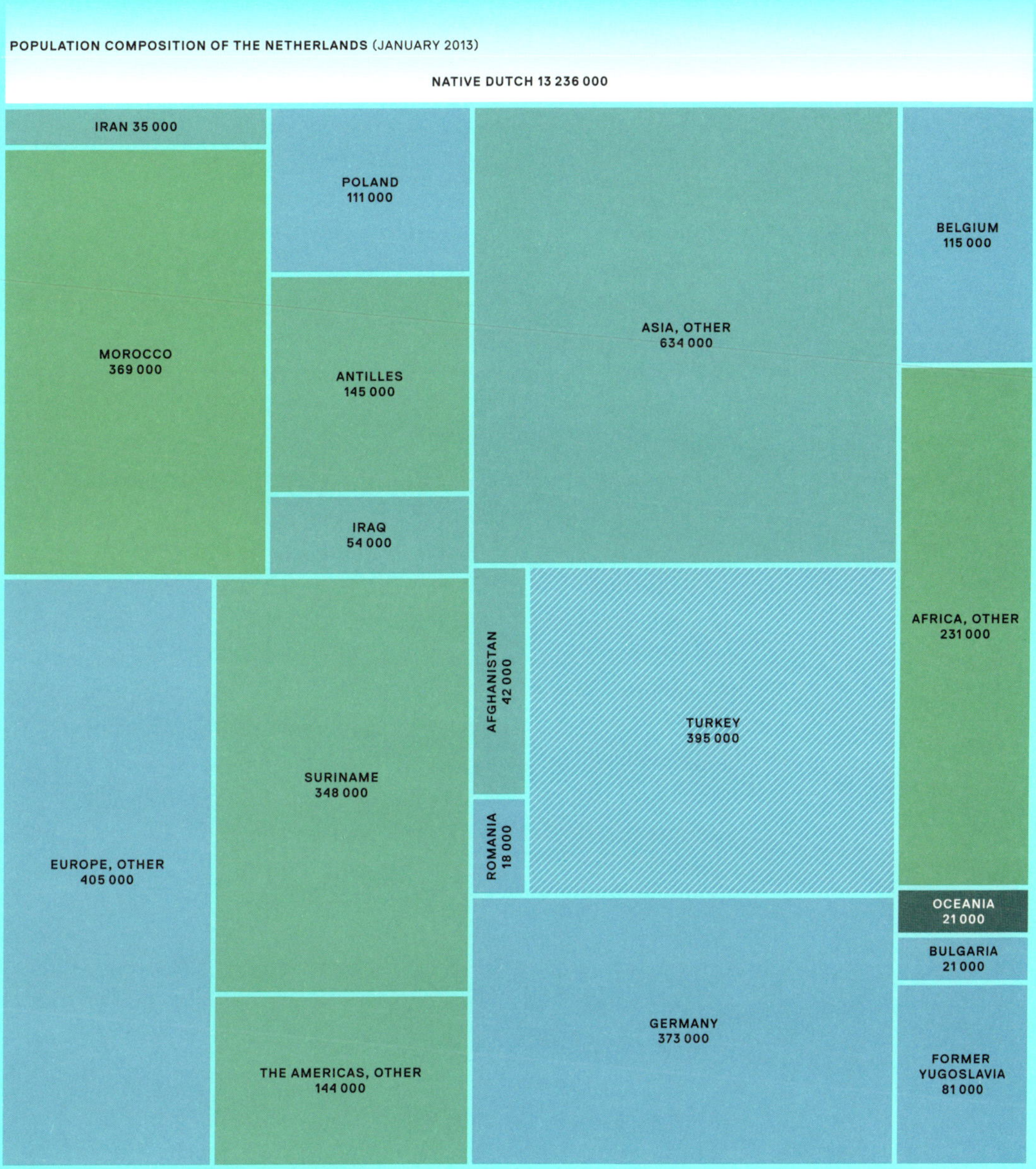

1.2 B / FROM ALL OVER THE WORLD

Close to 80% of the Dutch population is endigenous. The other 20% is either non-native or has at least one non-native parent. Around one third of them originate from European countries and nearly one quarter from Asia. The remaining 30% is formed by three groups consisting of Moroccans, Turks and Surinamese; each group forms around 10% of the non-native population.

Source: CBS

1.3 A / THE MOVE TO THE RANDSTAD

Each year, around 1.5 million people (nearly 10% of the population) move to another place of residence, within the Netherlands. Young people often move as they become independent or set up a household with their partner, or because they start a university study or their first job. The main reasons why middle-aged adults move house are that of a better house or living environment, a new job or, for example, the ending of a personal relationship. For the elderly, their state of health is an important reason to move. Of all people who move house, around 40% moves to another municipality. Relatively many of them move to the western part of the country. This is where the Randstad is located, which has been attracting many people for decades now. The Randstad has a relatively large number of jobs, educational institutes and other facilities.

People move to the Randstad from all corners of the country, but mostly from the south. Although the Randstad only makes up a quarter of the land surface of the Netherlands, nearly half of all inhabitants live there. Between 2005 and 2010, the Randstad population increased by over 200,000 people, 15% of whom came from abroad and 10% from the rest of the Netherlands. The largest part of the population growth, however, was caused by a birth surplus (70%).

1.3 B / SHRINKAGE VERSUS GROWTH

In the overall majority of Dutch municipalities, population numbers increased over the last years. Nearly everywhere, more children were born compared to the number of deaths, and more people moved to, rather than away from, the larger towns and cities.

However, this does not apply to all municipalities. Some rural areas have been experiencing shrinkage over the last two decades. These areas are mostly located around the edges of the country, such as in eastern Groningen, southern Limburg and Zeeland. Here, relatively few children were born and relatively many people died. Furthermore, young people move away from these areas towards the big cities, for employment

CHANGES IN POPULATION FOR 4 REGIONS (2006–2010)

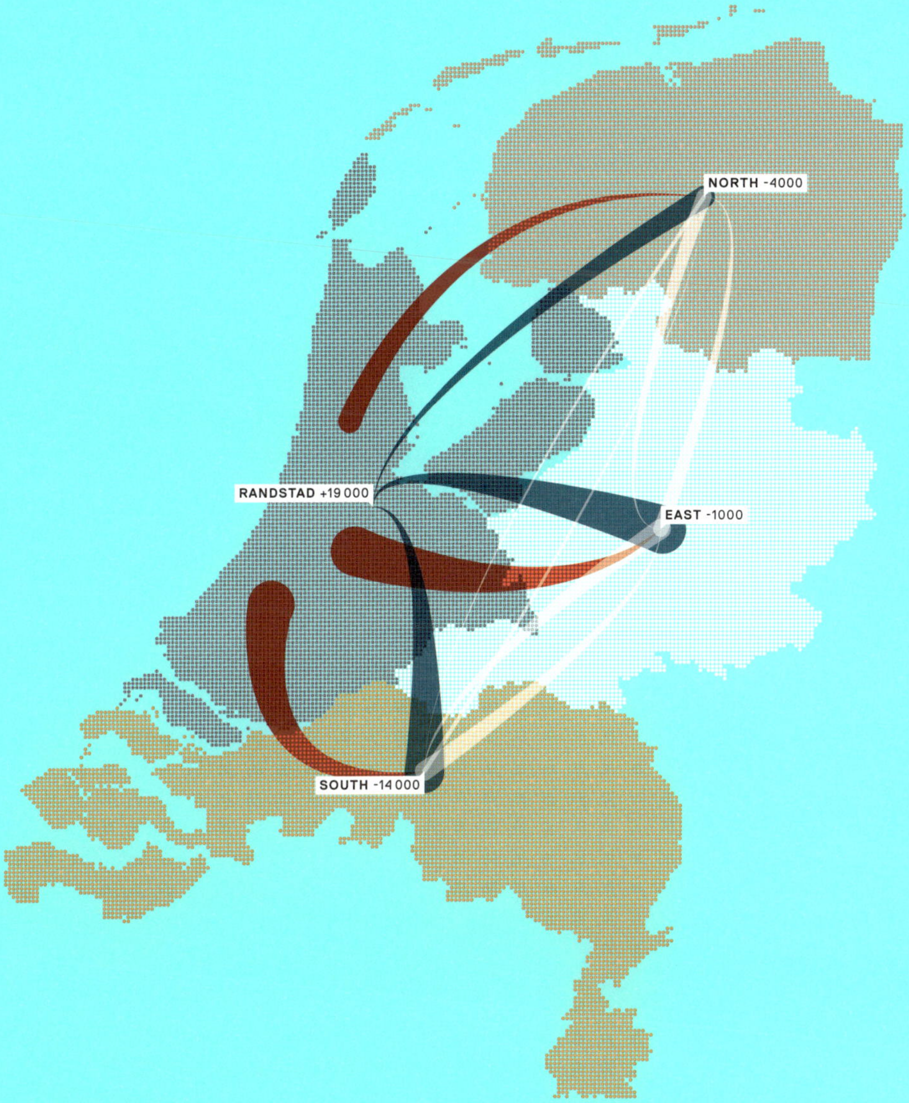

NUMBER OF PERSONS MOVING BETWEEN REGIONS/ MIGRATION SURPLUS

- 2000
- 20 000
- FROM / TO
- TO RANDSTAD
- FROM RANDSTAD
- OTHER
- +19 000 BALANCE BETWEEN PEOPLE SETTLING AND LEAVING

1.3 A / THE MOVE TO THE RANDSTAD

Internal migration flows are not equally distributed between regions. The Randstad conurbation, which is the economic heart of the country including Amsterdam, Rotterdam, The Hague and Utrecht, has an immigration surplus; particularly young people move here for work or education. The other regions show a (small) negative migration balance. Half of the Dutch population currently lives in the Randstad.

Source: CBS

or educational purposes. Further inland, shrinkage remains limited, as in many rural communities young families take the place of young people; in particular, because of the opportunities for cheap, spacious and green living.

Over the last years, large cities have grown rather strongly, with Utrecht and Amsterdam as frontrunners. This has meant that the Netherlands is becoming increasingly more urbanised. The current popularity of the large cities was not always a fact. Between 1965 and 1985, cities lost many of their inhabitants to the so-called growth centres. The government was looking to manage the population increases of the large municipalities by constructing many new housing projects in a number of surrounding areas to meet the increasing housing demand. Well-known growth centres are Almere and Purmerend near Amsterdam; Zoetermeer near The Hague; and Houten and Nieuwegein near Utrecht.

Since the turn of the century, large cities are experiencing a revival in popularity, particularly among young people, who move towards the cities for educational or employment reasons. The influx of young people is continually increasing, even during the economic crisis that began in 2008. In contrast, the number of young families leaving the cities is declining.

Today, over 50% of the global population is living in cities, but the Netherlands reached this milestone already in the previous century. In 1950, around 55% of the Dutch population was already living in urban areas, and in the 21st century this is around 85%.

1.4 / DISTORTED PYRAMIDS

In 1950, the age construction of the Dutch population was pyramid-shaped. For quite some time already, the population pyramid has changed its shape; by 2040 the age construction of the population is projected to be more pillar-shaped. The shape of the population pyramid often reflects the main historical and social developments. For example, the baby boom

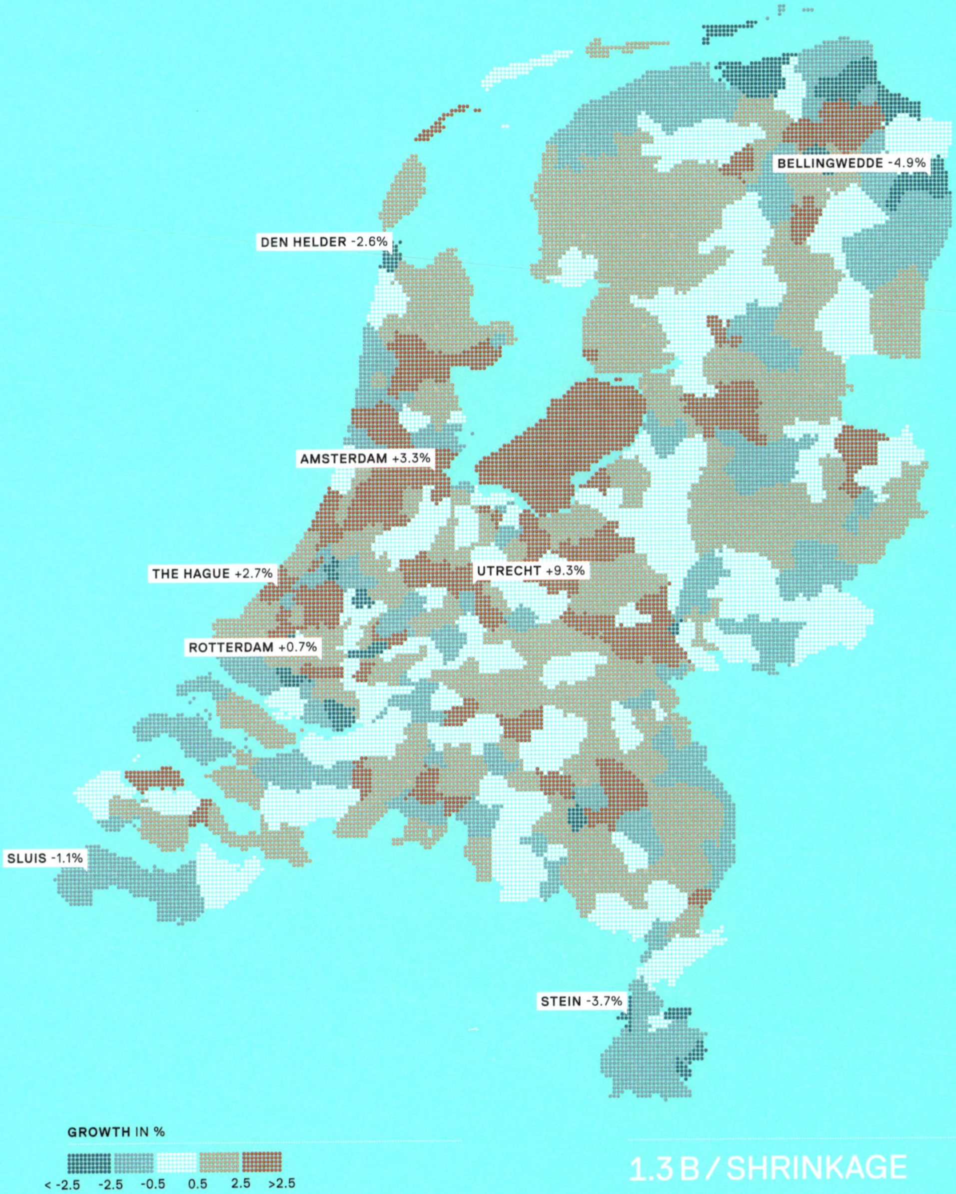

1.3 B / SHRINKAGE VERSUS GROWTH

Although the Dutch population keeps growing, this certainly does not apply to all municipalities. Particularly along the country's borders, various towns are shrinking; here, death rates are often high and birth rates low. Young people move away to the big cities. Particularly Utrecht and Amsterdam are growing rapidly.

Source: CBS

POPULATION PYRAMIDS FOR AMSTERDAM, HOUTEN AND DELFZIJL IN 1980–2010–2040, IN THOUSANDS

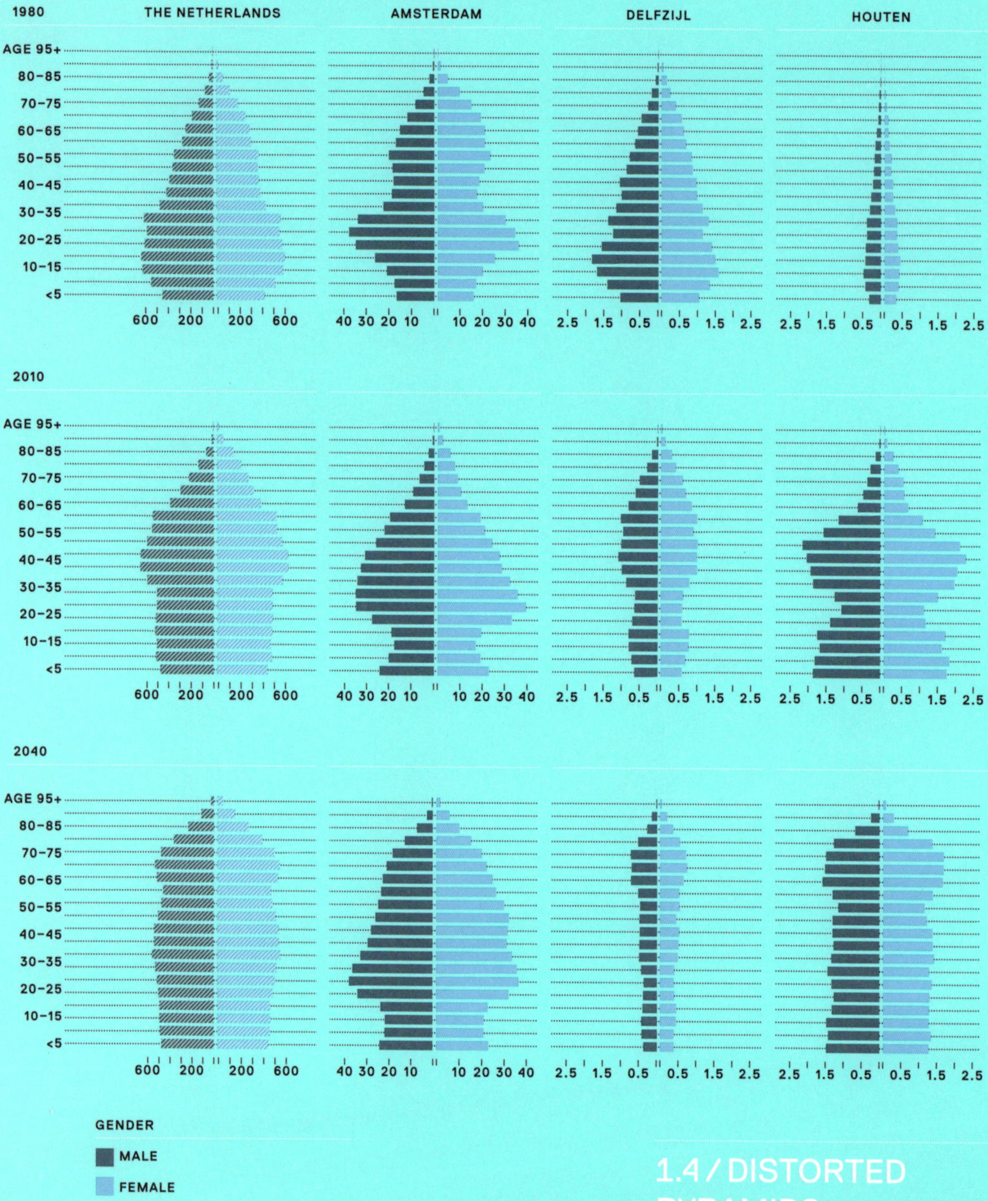

1.4 / DISTORTED PYRAMIDS

Population pyramids illustrate population development over several generations. The Dutch baby boom after World War II shows on the 1980 pyramid as a wide base, in 2010 as a 'fat belly' and in 2040 as a wide top. There are striking differences between the population pyramids of different municipalities, due to differences in birth, death, immigration and emigration rates.

Source: PBL/CBS

following the Second World War can be seen in 1980 as a thickening of the bottom of the pyramid, in 2010 as a wide mid-section and in 2040 as a relatively broad top.

Population pyramids can differ strongly between municipalities. Large cities, such as Amsterdam, have a wide mid-section; they have relatively many inhabitants between the ages of 20 and 40. These people moved to the city following their secondary education to study or follow courses and often they found their first jobs there. Of late, they have been found to continue living in those cities, increasingly more often. This in contrast to the situation of the late 1990s; at that time, people in their thirties often moved away from large cities to the growth centres and other surrounding municipalities. Houses were bigger there, and cheaper, and there was more greenery; an environment they deemed suitable for raising a family.

Another group of people in their twenties and thirties consists of immigrants, who mostly prefer a large city because of more employment opportunities, or because they already have family living there.

For municipalities in areas of shrinkage, the pyramid is becoming ever smaller, such as the one for Delfzijl, staying relatively wide only in the middle and on the upper end. These wider areas, in 2010, represent the ageing baby boomers.

A third noteworthy pyramid shape is that of the growth centres. The one of Houten has a wider base and middle, because over the past decades many young couples moved there and started a family. Their children are expected to move away at some point in the future, with the parents remaining there, which means Houten will be faced with a more than average ageing population.

1.5 / THE MOVE TO THE CITIES

Today, the earth counts over 7 billion people; by 2050, this number will probably have increased to over 9 billion. In less than 40 years this means an increase of 2 billion people. This explosive growth will be concentrated mainly in South Asia and in Africa south of the Sahara. Fertility rates are high here,

GLOBAL DEMOGRAPHICS PER COUNTRY AND URBANISATION (2010–2050)

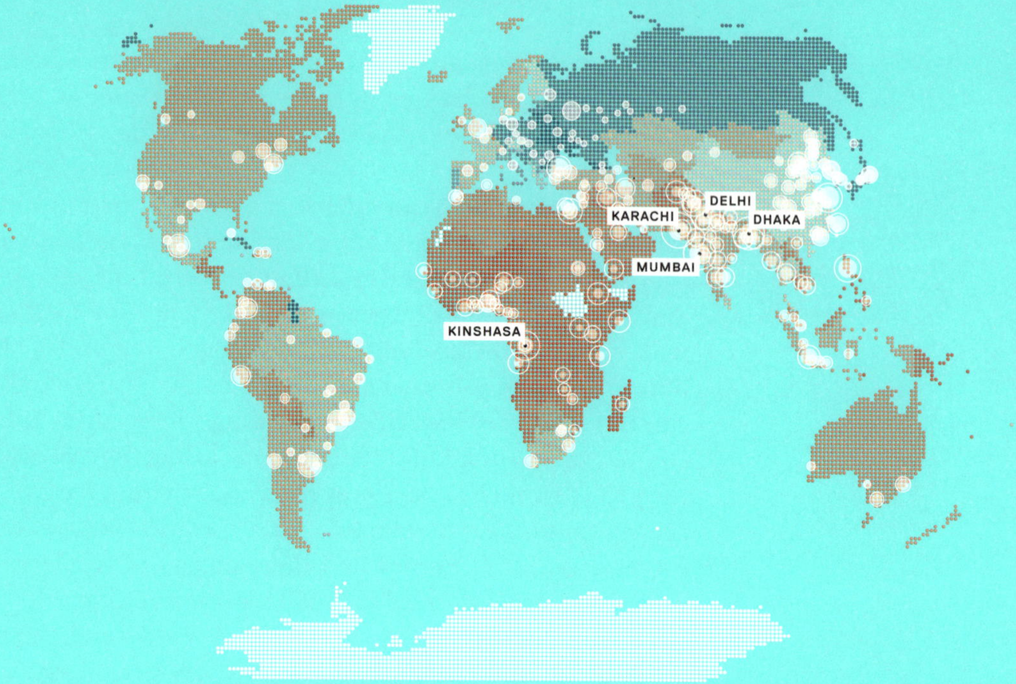

GLOBAL DEMOGRAPHICS, POPULATION PER REGION, IN BILLIONS

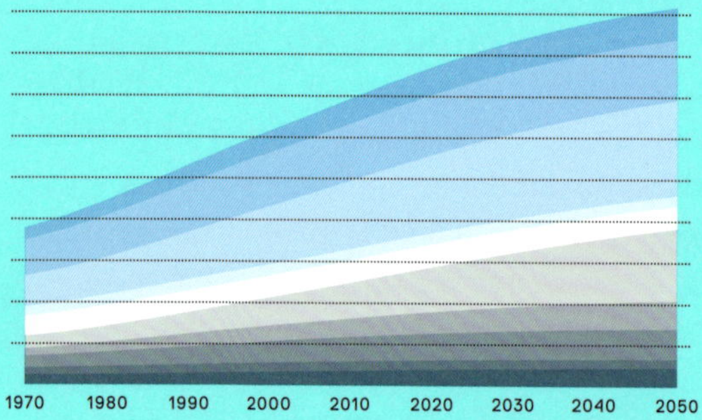

GLOBAL DEMOGRAPHICS, URBAN POPULATION PER REGION, IN BILLIONS

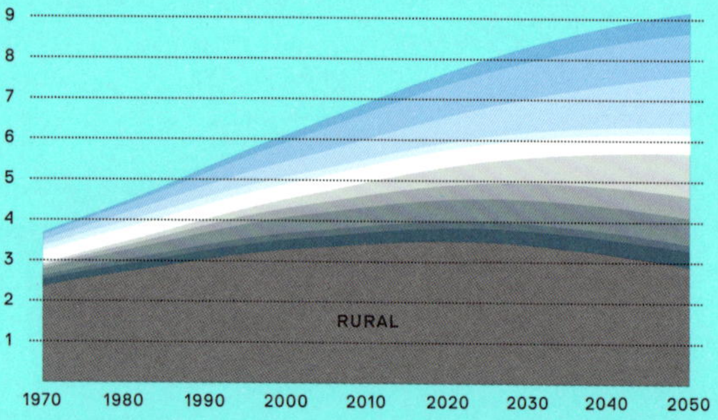

REGIONS

- SOUTHEAST ASIA
- CHINA REGION
- SOUTH ASIA
- RUSSIAN REGION AND CENTRAL ASIA
- WEST AND CENTRAL EUROPE
- SUB-SAHARAN AFRICA
- MIDDLE EAST AND NORTH AFRICA
- CENTRAL AND SOUTH AMERICA
- JAPAN, KOREA AND OCEANIA
- NORTH AMERICA

EXPECTED NATIONAL POPULATION GROWTH 2010–2050, IN %

-30 -20 -10 -5 0 5 10 20 30 40 50 100 200 300

NO DATA

POPULATION IN MAJOR CITIES, IN MILLIONS

30 10 5 1

2010

2050

MUMBAI • TOP 5 IN 2050

1.5 / THE MOVE TO THE CITIES

The global population is growing rapidly; from more than 7 billion now to probably well over 9 billion by 2050. This growth will be accompanied by strong urbanisation, particularly in Africa and South Asia. Rural populations will remain stable at about 3 billion. Not all countries will see population growth: considerable declines are projected for Russia and East Europe.

Sources: ESRI, PBL, UNEP

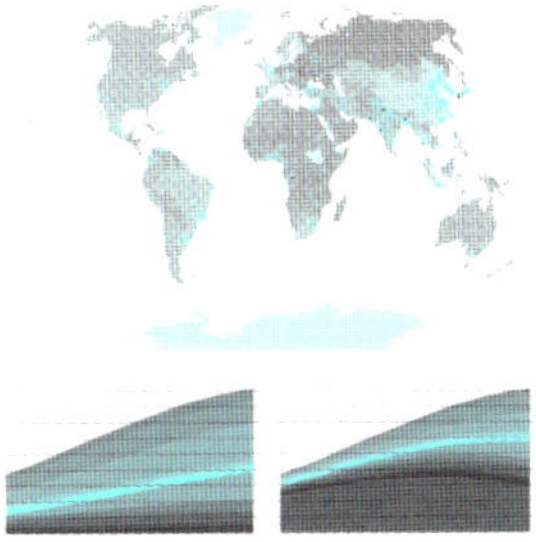

in part due to the lower level of education, hardly any emancipation of women and low levels of prosperity. Population growth, however, is by no means a certainty; for Russia and central and eastern Europe, a considerable degree of shrinkage is projected. Fertility rates there have been low after the Berlin Wall came down, partly because there is no longer any policy to stimulate people to have children.

Future population growth will only take place in urban areas, with the size of rural populations remaining stable. Close to 70% of the world population is projected to live in cities by 2050. Of all those living in cities, 15% will live in mega-cities, in 2050. Currently, this is 10%. Some mega-cities that currently have over 10 million inhabitants, such as Karachi in Pakistan and Mumbai in India, will see a population increase of, in some instances, twice the number of current Dutch citizens. Many more people, as they already do today, will live in middle-sized cities of less than 1 million inhabitants. Currently, this applies to around 60% of the urban population and, by 2050, this will still apply to around 50%.

The enormous population growth means cities will face large problems. All of the existing buildings and the infrastructure for the transportation of people and goods, and energy and water will no longer be sufficient. In addition, the urban economy will become increasingly more dependent on a continuing and undisrupted supply of affordable fuels, food, water and materials. This increases the vulnerability of cities, as climate change in fact is threatening to cause scarcity of important resources. In order to keep cities going and ensure they remain liveable, a drastic and sustainable transition is needed.

Air is a prerequisite for life. We take our oxygen-rich atmosphere for granted, but life on earth would not be possible without this unique property; it is what distinguishes our earth from other planets. Air is such a self-evident necessity of life that it usually does not get the appreciation it deserves.

Air is vital to humans, animals and plants, from the scale of microbes to that of the entire globe. In our homes, air is needed for heating and cooling. Combustion processes – whether in car engines, power plants or iron blast furnaces – cannot take place without the oxygen in the air.

Wind (which is simply air moving from one place to another) influences the weather, cools and warms, transports dust and sand, and provides energy through wind turbines. Roman architect Vitruvius already wrote about the importance of the prevailing wind direction for city design.

2.1 / AIR IS EVERYWHERE, AIR IS VITAL

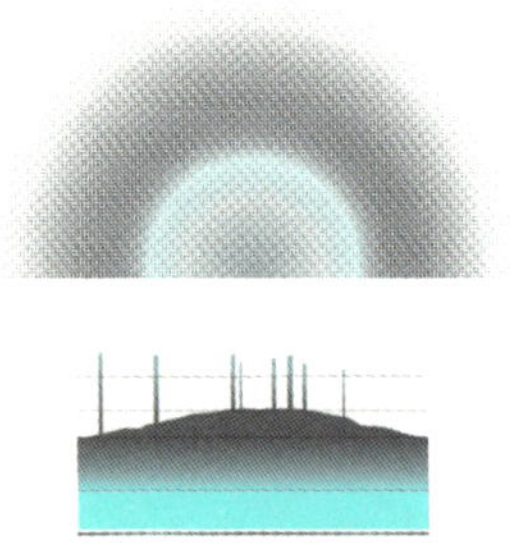

At every level, air is likely to be the one 'vital flow' that is most taken for granted – fortunately, there is more than enough of it.

An average adult breathes 6 litres of air per minute, taking up 300 millilitres of pure oxygen. This amounts to 8600 litres of air and 430 litres, or 0.43 cubic metres, of oxygen, per person, per day. Just by breathing, the entire world population of 7 billion people moves 60 billion cubic metres – or 60 cubic kilometres – of air per day, taking up 3 cubic kilometres of pure oxygen. In addition to humans and animals, combustion engines also require a fair amount of air; for example, a passenger car with an average fuel use, driving an average amount of kilometres per day, uses 24 cubic metres of air, per day, withdrawing 5 cubic metres of oxygen. Even if we add up the air breathed by all animals, this amount is still insignificant compared to the total volume of the atmosphere: 4.2 *billion* cubic kilometres.

Air and oxygen, therefore, can be said to be in abundant supply. Moreover, nature ensures that atmospheric oxygen levels remain sufficient. However, we do need to pay attention to air quality and composition. Humans, animals and plants tolerate air pollution only up to a certain point, and greenhouse gases may lead to climate change. It is therefore essential to monitor substances that have an acute or long-term impact on air quality and global climate, such as particulate matter and CO_2. Just as air is a prerequisite for life, air quality is a prerequisite for quality of life.

Buildings influence air flow and air temperature. In cities, this leads to local climates ('microclimates') with altered air flows – including air stagnation. Bricks and concrete, but also water bodies, absorb heat during the day and hold on to it during the night. In extreme cases, local temperatures soar and pollution accumulates. These effects are known as 'urban heat islands' and 'street canyons'.

In the Dutch climate, urban warming is usually considered a welcome side effect: outdoor cafés are thriving, and people are enjoying picnics in the parks. However, urban warming can lead to unpleasant conditions in warmer countries. The

AIR-RELATED ISSUES AT DIFFERENT SCALES

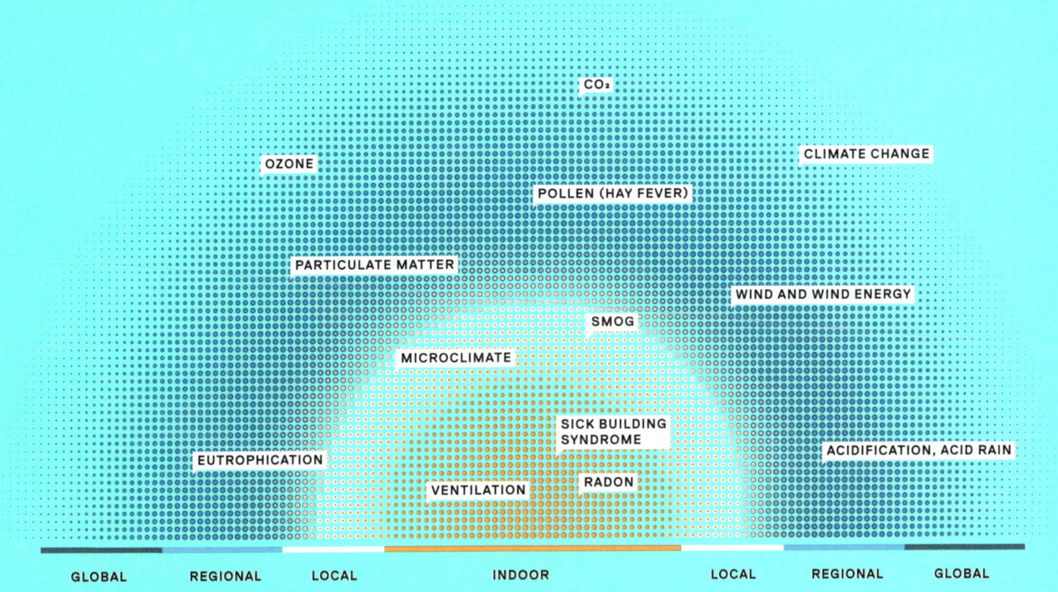

PARTICULATE MATTER (PM_{10}) BUILD-UP IN AND AROUND A TYPICAL DUTCH CITY (CROSS-SECTION)

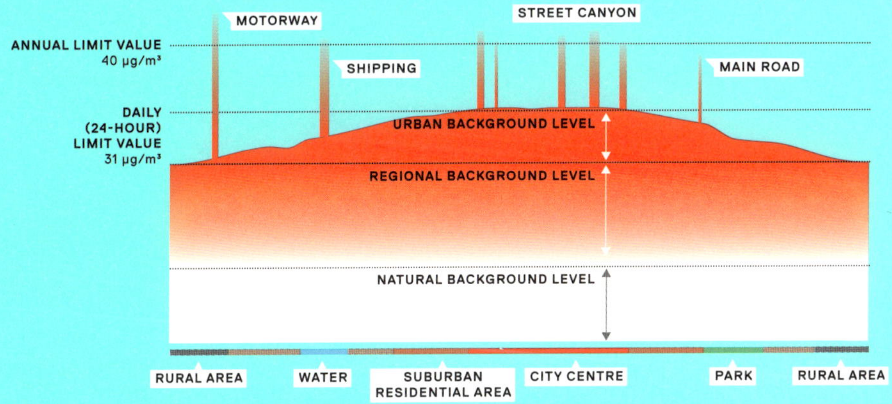

2.1 / AIR IS EVERWHERE, AIR IS VITAL

Humans, animals and plants need air to breathe. In our homes we need air for heating and cooling. Air also plays a key role in the global climate system. Clean air is a prerequisite for quality of life. However, air quality is sometimes seriously impaired by pollutants such as particulate matter.

Source: PBL (formerly MNP)

expected temperature rise due to climate change will further increase the occurrence and severity of such urban heat islands.

2.2 / PARTICULATE MATTER KNOWS NO BORDERS

The air in the Netherlands has relatively high concentrations of particulate matter (tiny particles suspended in the atmosphere). This is partly due to natural sources, such as salt spray from the North Sea and soil dust blown in from as far away as the Sahara. These sources account for 40% to 45% of particulate matter in the air, with annual fluctuations dependent on the weather. The remaining 55% to 60% comes from industry, road traffic, and shipping. Particulate matter is transported by wind, and does not stop at the borders. The particulate matter that is measured in the air above the Netherlands partly originates from the German Ruhr region and the industrial area around Liège, Belgium. Conversely, particulate matter emitted in the Netherlands is blown to neighbouring countries and seas. Overall, Dutch 'export' of particulate matter exceeds the 'import' by a factor of three.

2.3 / HUMAN ACTIVITY LEAVES TRACES IN THE AIR

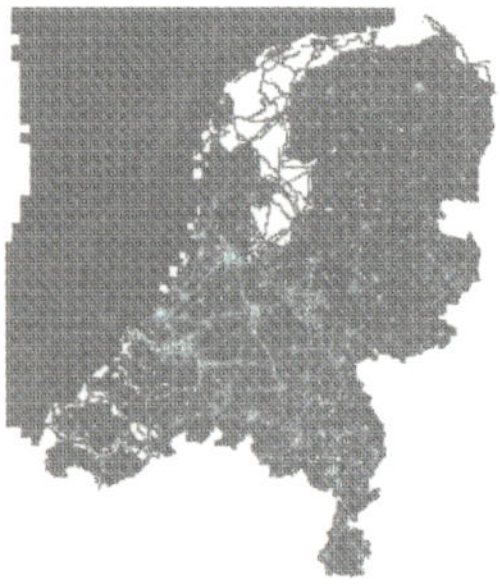

The production of particulate matter takes place on the ground, but the effect is found in the air. The air quality map of the Netherlands shows a striking pattern of elevated levels of particulate matter that reveal the course of roads and shipping routes. Elevated concentrations are also found in and around large cities, and in areas with intensive animal farming and high levels of industrial and shipping activity. The map also shows how local and transboundary flows come together; although emissions above sea cannot be measured as accurately as those above land, the map clearly shows the particulate matter footprint of busy North Sea shipping routes.

High particulate matter levels are harmful to human health, particularly to heart and lung functioning. Even at low

ORIGIN OF PM_{10} IN THE NETHERLANDS (2009)

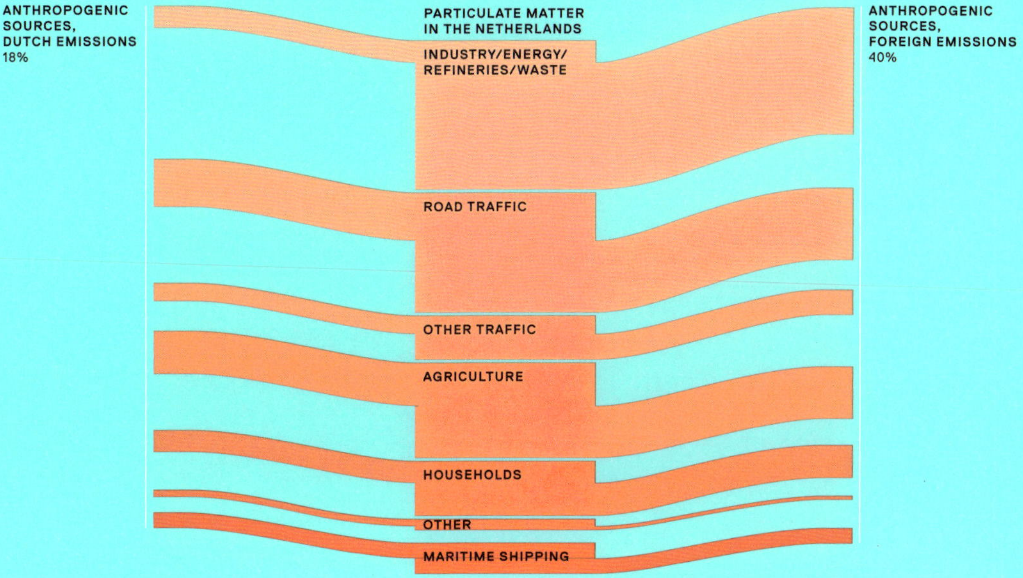

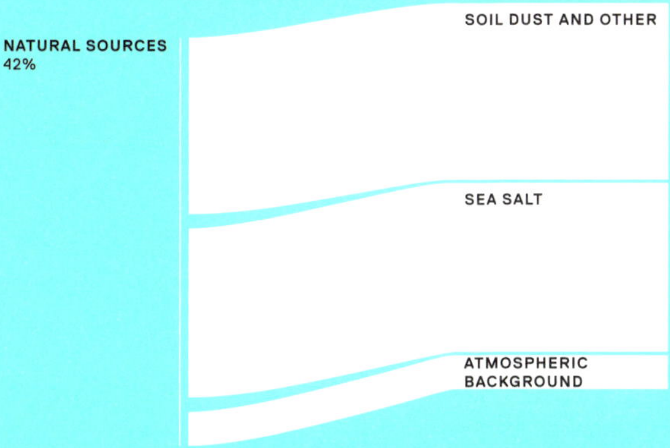

AVERAGE PM_{10} CONCENTRATIONS IN THE NETHERLANDS DUE TO ANTHROPOGENIC SOURCES, IN MICROGRAMS PER M³ (2009–2050)

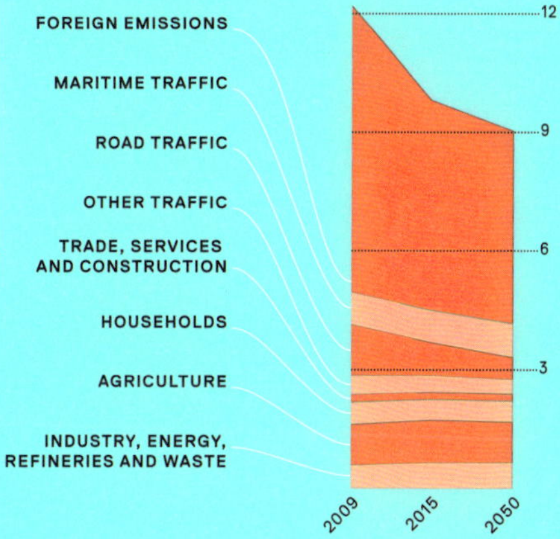

2.2 / PARTICULATE MATTER KNOWS NO BORDERS

Particulate matter levels in the Netherlands are relatively high. Natural sources account for almost 50%; the remainder comes from anthropogenic sources, domestic as well as foreign. Imported emissions are exceeded threefold by exported emissions. Thanks to measures such as particle filters, pollution levels have halved since 1990 and this trend is continuing.

Sources: PBL, RIVM

PM_{10} **EMISSIONS** (2011)

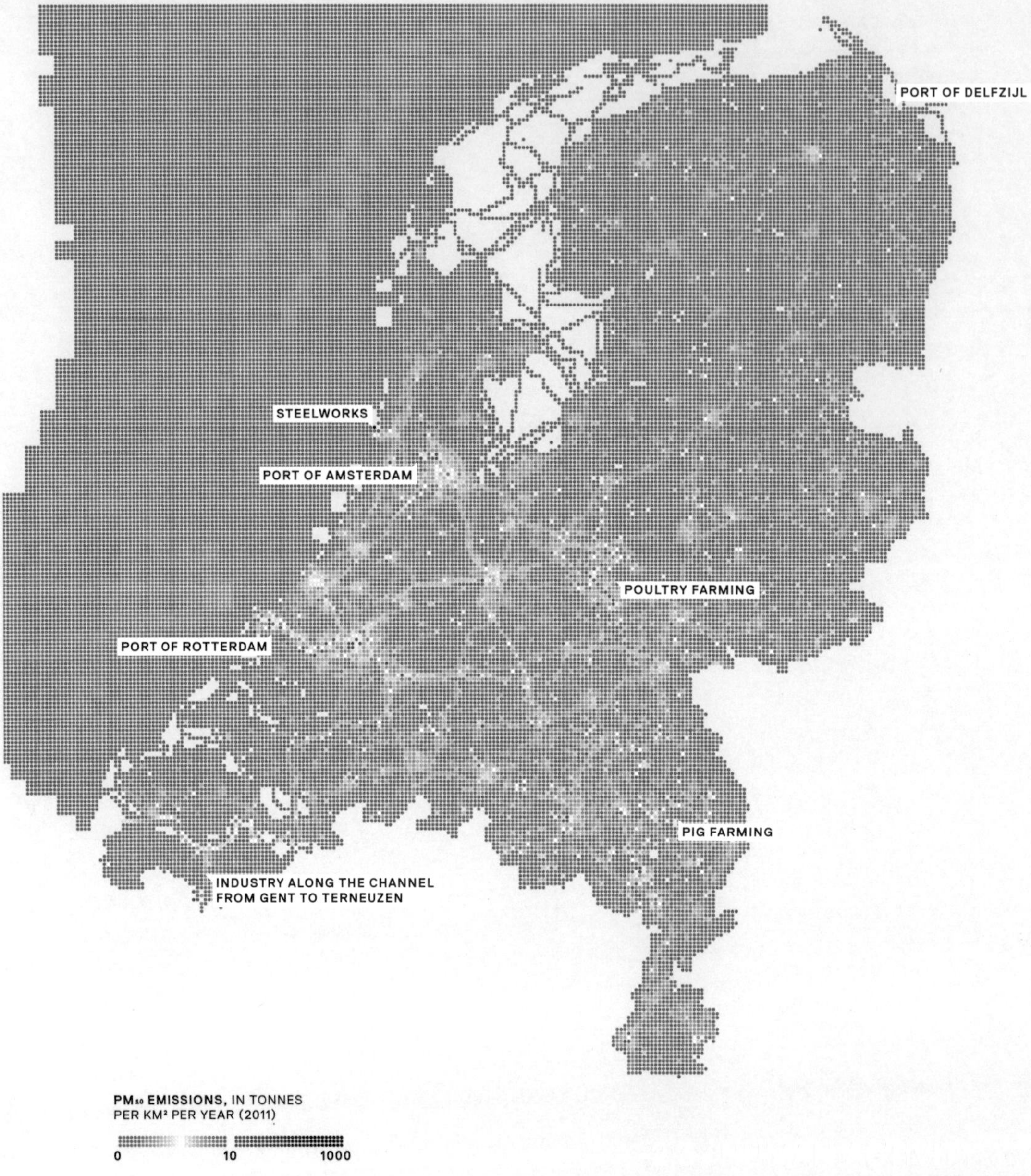

Emissions from cities, roads, shipping routes, livestock farming and industrial areas leave unmistakable traces in the air, as shown by the particulate matter map of the Netherlands and the North Sea. Particulate matter is harmful to human health; in the Netherlands it causes twice as much health damage as traffic accidents.

Source: RIVM

$PM_{2.5}$ EMISSIONS (2005)

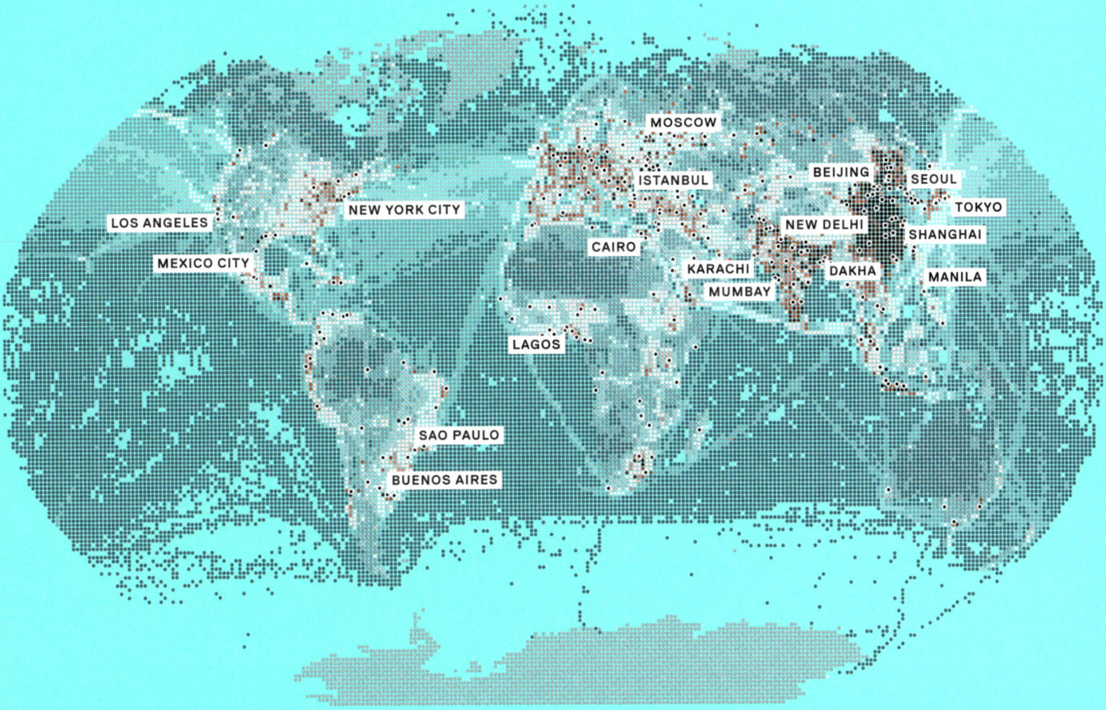

$PM_{2.5}$ EMISSIONS, IN TONNES PER 0.1 DEGREE × 0.1 DEGREE PER YEAR (2005)

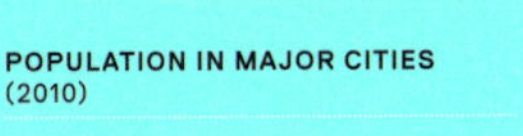

POPULATION IN MAJOR CITIES (2010)

• >1 000 000 >10 000 000

2.4 / THE SMOKESTACKS HAVE MOVED ELSEWHERE

A hundred years ago, Europe suffered from heavy industrial pollution. This problem has been solved thanks to cleaner production methods and relocation of industry to countries such as China and India. In the latter country, the recent rapid growth of cities, industry, traffic and energy consumption is causing extreme air pollution. International shipping also contributes to global air pollution.

Sources: JRC/PBL, PBL

concentrations, particulate matter increases the risk of detrimental health effects. In the Netherlands, the annual health damage from particulate matter is estimated at twice that from traffic accidents; it is the most important environment-related risk factor for public health.

In recent years, a number of measures have been taken to reduce particulate matter levels, such as installing particle filters in cars and establishing low emission zones (also known as environmental zones) in cities. Thanks to such measures, particulate matter concentrations in the Netherlands have been halved, compared to 1990 levels.

2.4 / THE SMOKESTACKS HAVE MOVED ELSEWHERE

Air pollution is a global issue, but levels vary between regions. Over time, the problem has also relocated. About a century ago, large parts of industrialised Europe, including the Netherlands, were suffering from heavy pollution. Air quality has dramatically improved since then; partly thanks to cleaner production methods, but also because the most polluting industries have relocated to countries outside Europe. Former industrial towns, such as Tilburg and Almelo in the Netherlands, are enjoying clean air again, as are Manchester and the Ruhr region. Today, the smokestacks are located in China, 'the factory of the world'.

In China and other Southeast Asian countries, the explosive growth in cities, industries, energy consumption (including oil-fired heating) and traffic is leading to extreme air pollution. Local populations suffer the most, but the rest of the world, including Europe, is also affected as the wind carries pollutants across the globe. In the more rural areas of the world, particularly in Africa, wood is still the most commonly used cooking and heating fuel, and this also leads to considerable air pollution. And last but not least, global shipping and air traffic also leave their traces, as the global map of particulate matter concentrations clearly shows.

AVERAGE PM$_{10}$ CONCENTRATIONS IN MAJOR CITIES,
IN MICROGRAMS PER M^3 (1990–2050)

PREMATURE DEATHS DUE TO PM$_{10}$ EXPOSURE,
DEATHS PER MILLION PEOPLE (1990–2050)

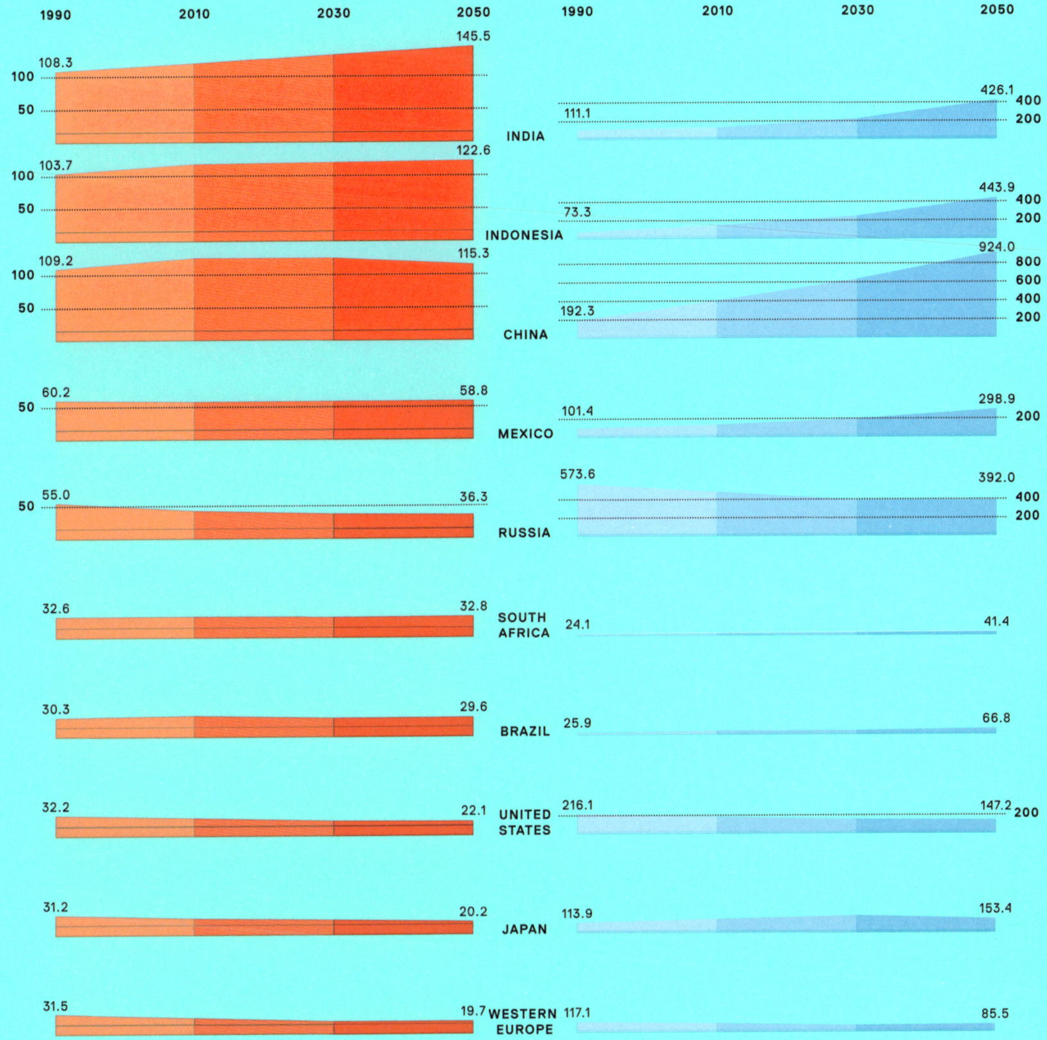

2.5 / PARTICULATE MATTER THREATENS HEALTH IN EMERGING COUNTRIES

Emerging countries, such as China, India and Mexico, pay for their explosive economic growth with heavy air pollution. This will increase mortality rates for decades to come, also because the populations of these countries are ageing. The elderly are more susceptible. Air pollution will soon present a greater health risk than bad sanitation, polluted water and malaria.

Source: OECD

2.5 / PARTICULATE MATTER THREATENS HEALTH IN EMERGING COUNTRIES

Although air pollution is being successfully controlled in Europe, it is still a major problem in the large cities of emerging countries. The smog (originating from the words smoke plus fog) that once suffocated London is now a major problem in cities such as Beijing. Here, on some days, concentration levels of particulate matter may reach 500 micrograms per cubic metre. This is more than 10 times the limit value of 40 micrograms advised by the World Health Organization (WHO) to prevent adverse long-term health effects.

Air pollution in these countries is so severe that it leads to increased mortality. The mortality rate impact is even greater in 'greying' countries, because elderly people are much more susceptible to the detrimental health effects of particulate matter. However, children are the most vulnerable in the long term, because they still have many years of breathing polluted air ahead of them.

The OECD is therefore of the opinion that particulate matter pollution in emerging countries presents a growing mortality risk, which is soon to surpass the health risks of bad sanitation, polluted water, malaria and poor indoor air quality.

The earth is a blue planet when looking at it from space, teeming with life, thanks to the abundant availability of water. Every creature on earth needs water – from a little to a lot – including us humans. By far the most amount of water on earth is the saline water of the oceans and seas; not even 3% of it is fresh water, which is the most precious to life on earth. Of all the fresh water on the planet, 99% is either frozen or groundwater; only 0.3% of the fresh water is located in the rivers and lakes and in the atmosphere.

3.1 / MANY TIMES HOME USE

Half of the human body consists of water. Adults have to take in 2.5 litres of water per day, through food and drink, to maintain their body fluid balance. Water is also required for basic needs, such as hygiene and food preparation.

All in all, domestic water use far exceeds the daily bodily requirement of 2.5 litres; the average Dutch citizen uses 120 litres of tap water, per day. Around twenty years ago this was even more, with 137 litres per day in 1995. Since then, overall water use has steadily decreased despite the increase in shower use. This reduction is mainly due to water-saving techniques, such as in washing machines and toilet flushing mechanisms. For the use of 120 litres of clean water, Dutch citizens pay 21 cents per day.

However, there is more to water consumption than the domestic use of 120 litres per person, per day. Through buying food and other products, households indirectly consume water that is needed to produce these goods. This indirect water consumption amounts to 146 litres per person, per day, for food and goods produced within the Netherlands, and more than 3000 litres per person, per day, for – mainly agricultural – imported products. These numbers include evaporation and water inclusion in products. In theory, water loss through evaporation is not a problem, because the evaporated water, eventually, will return in the form of precipitation elsewhere. However, in water scarce areas, evaporation and water export may have serious consequences.

3.2 / RIVER COUNTRY

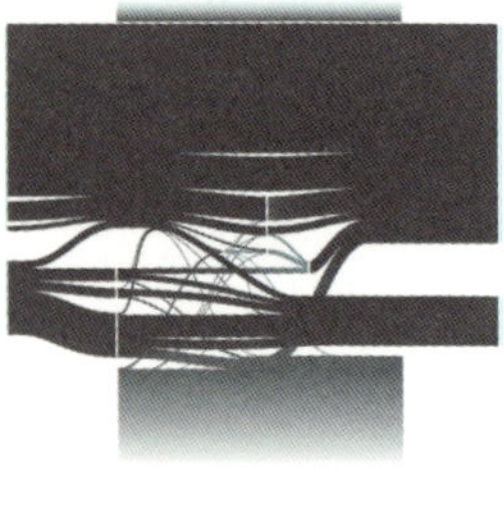

The Netherlands has an abundant supply of fresh water. In addition to an estimated 800 billion m³ of groundwater, the country has approximately 12 billion m³ of surface water – stored mostly in the IJsselmeer and Markermeer. On top of this, 110 billion m³ of fresh water enter the country every year through precipitation (25%), the Rhine (65%), and the Meuse and other rivers (10%). Sooner or later, most of this water (75%) flows out into the North Sea.

HOUSEHOLD WATER USE IN THE NETHERLANDS,
IN LITRES PER CAPITA, PER DAY

AVERAGE DAILY TOTAL WATER CONSUMPTION,
IN LITRES PER CAPITA, PER DAY (AVERAGE 1996–2005)

HOUSEHOLD WATER USE AND INDIRECT WATER CONSUMPTION

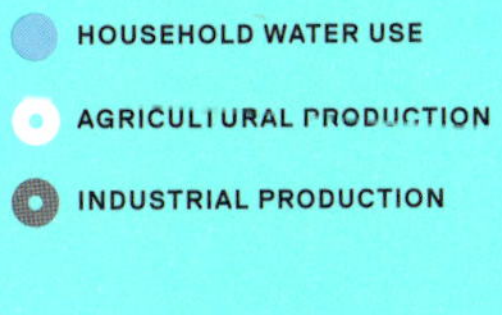

3.1 / MANY TIMES HOME USE

The average Dutch citizen uses 120 litres of water per day for drinking, cooking and washing. Far more water is used in the production of food and industrial goods; particularly for agricultural products imported from other countries. This may lead to problems in regions where water is scarce.

Sources: CBS/PBL/WUR, UNESCO-IHE

AVERAGE FRESHWATER FLOWS IN THE NETHERLANDS, IN MILLIONS OF M³ PER YEAR /
FRESHWATER RESERVES OF THE NETHERLANDS, IN MILLION M³

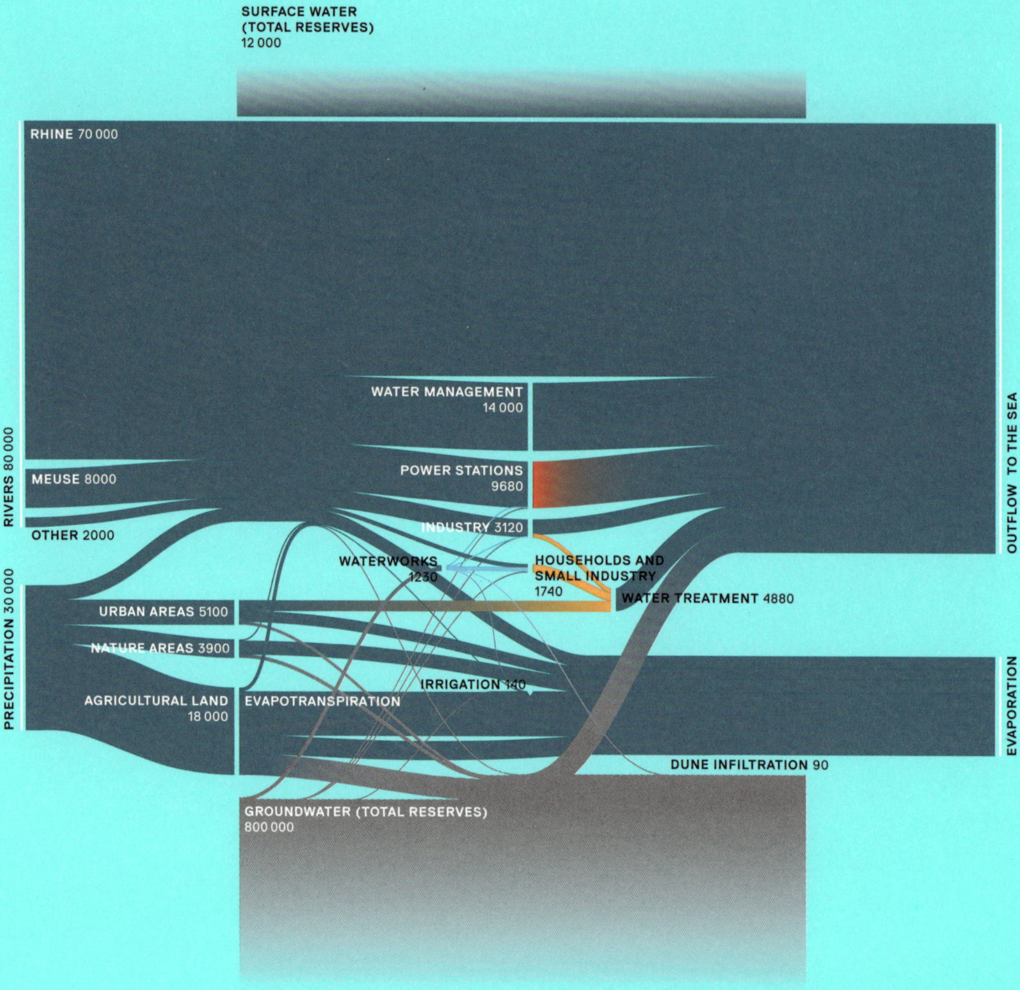

WATER TYPES

- SURFACE WATER
- PURIFIED WATER
- GROUNDWATER
- WARM WATER
- POLLUTED WATER

3.2 / RIVER COUNTRY

The Netherlands has abundant freshwater supplies in surface and groundwater. This water is used for many purposes, including agriculture, shipping, industry, drinking water, energy production and nature. Water distribution and availability is ensured by sophisticated water management. This 'water machine' requires continuous maintenance.

Sources: CBS, CBS/PBL/WUR, Deltares, STOWA, VEWIN

Only a fraction of the entire Dutch water suppy goes to drinking water production, agriculture and industry. Clean drinking water is sourced from groundwater (60%) and surface water (40%). Most of the used water is returned to surface water, via sewage systems and water treatment plants.

The Netherlands, thus, has plenty of water. The natural water system has been tailored to serve many purposes; in agriculture, shipping, cities, industry, energy production and nature. However, to keep this system running and to ensure water quality, water flows and supplies do require careful management. Furthermore, the reliability and controllability of the present flows and supplies cannot be taken for granted. Climate change is expected to have a significant impact on freshwater supplies in the Netherlands. Summers are likely to become drier, winters wetter, and river flows more unpredictable; moreover, in coastal areas, seawater may intrude further into the rivers and groundwater due to sea level rise and a reduced river flow in summer. Additional measures are needed to meet these challenges.

3.3 / TWEAKING THE WATER SYSTEM

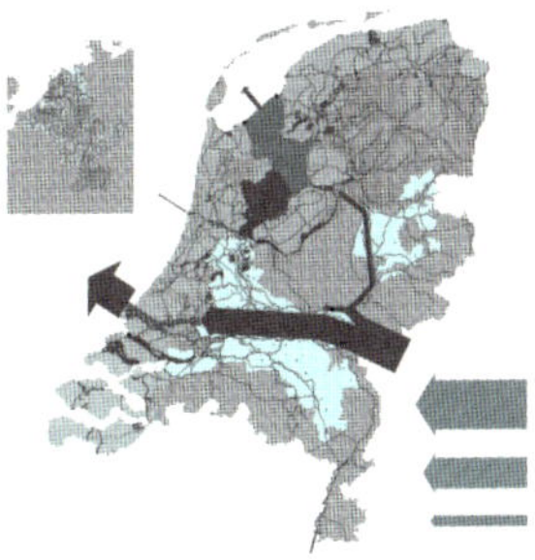

The Netherlands is located in a delta of four European rivers. The Rhine, Meuse, Scheldt and Ems rivers run through the Netherlands and discharge into the North Sea. The total area drained by these rivers is several times the size of the Netherlands. It covers Belgium and parts of Germany, France, Switzerland and Austria. Developments in these river basins will influence the freshwater supply downstream.

The Rhine plays a central role in the sophisticated water management system of the Netherlands. Of the incoming Rhine water, 90% is channelled to the west, to the Nieuwe Waterweg and the North Sea, while 10% is directed to the north, to the IJssel river and the IJsselmeer. This ratio is controlled by a series of weirs (Hagestein, Amerongen and Driel).

The water of the Rhine serves multiple purposes. By directing the main flow of the Rhine via the Waal and Lower Rhine/Lek rivers to the Nieuwe Waterweg, adequate water levels for shipping to and from Rotterdam are ensured. In addition, the river water serves to protect vital freshwater inlets of polders in the province of South Holland against salt water intrusion from the North Sea (known as the 'salt tongue'). Furthermore, the Rhine is the main source of fresh water for the west and north of the Netherlands. These parts of the country are mostly below sea level and thus have very limited fresh groundwater resources.

The Rhine water that is directed to the north (10%) also has an important function. The IJssel river drains into the IJsselmeer, supplying fresh water to the northern provinces for agriculture, salinisation control, drinking water production and refreshing of surface waters. Furthermore, in all low-lying areas of the north and west, river water is needed to manage groundwater and surface water levels, because too much fluctuation is unfavourable for agriculture and shipping, and will also damage pile foundations in urban areas.

Thus, both in the western and northern provinces, the water of the Rhine is used intensively for many different purposes. As a result, too little river water is left for the southwestern delta and the Haringvliet estuary. Here, the salt tongue threatens freshwater inlets for surface waters and drinking water production. The only way to halt this problem is to keep the sluices of the Haringvliet closed. As a consequence, the Haringvliet is much less dynamic than the Oosterschelde estuary, where tides and brackish/salt water move freely because, here, the sluices are closed only during storm surges. Thus, the abundant supplies of river water in the Netherlands are only relative; in managing and directing river flows, the country is forced to make choices that sometimes have far-reaching consequences.

For the Netherlands, the Rhine is a reliable source of fresh water, because it is a glacier river with predictable fluctuations. In spring and summer, when the ice is melting, water levels are higher than in autumn and winter. However, due to climate change, glacier rivers may gradually turn into rain-fed rivers. The latter are less predictable and have more extreme peak and low flows. This is likely to affect shipping, agriculture, energy production (cooling water intake) and flood safety. Thus, climate change and the increasing unpredictability of river flows may disrupt the carefully balanced water system that the Dutch have built up over the centuries.

The east and south of the Netherlands, which are above sea level and mostly consist of sandy soils, have their own water concerns. These areas depend much more on precipitation and groundwater because their surface water supplies are limited. Groundwater use has to be carefully managed to prevent depletion and soil desiccation. Most importantly, annual water consumption by agriculture, livestock farming and drinking water production has to be balanced with annual precipitation. Supplying these regions with water from the Rhine is a possibility, but this would require an elaborate pipeline network. In the absence of this supply, water saving and efficiency measures are vital.

In most built-up areas, rainwater runoff is drained into the public sewage system. The sewers must be large enough to deal with extreme precipitation events, and thus on most days will have overcapacity. To relieve the sewage system, excess water can also be drained in other ways; particularly by infiltration into the soil. In rural areas, this can be achieved by temporarily allowing higher water levels in ditches and canals; in urban areas, by using half-open pavement in parking lots and streets and encouraging the use of permeable surfacing in domestic gardens. Furthermore, temporary water storage in cities is possible in streets, 'water squares' and underground car parks: for example, the parking garage of the Rotterdam Museum Park has an underground basin able to store 10,000 cubic metres of water.

FRESHWATER FLOWS

RIVER BASINS

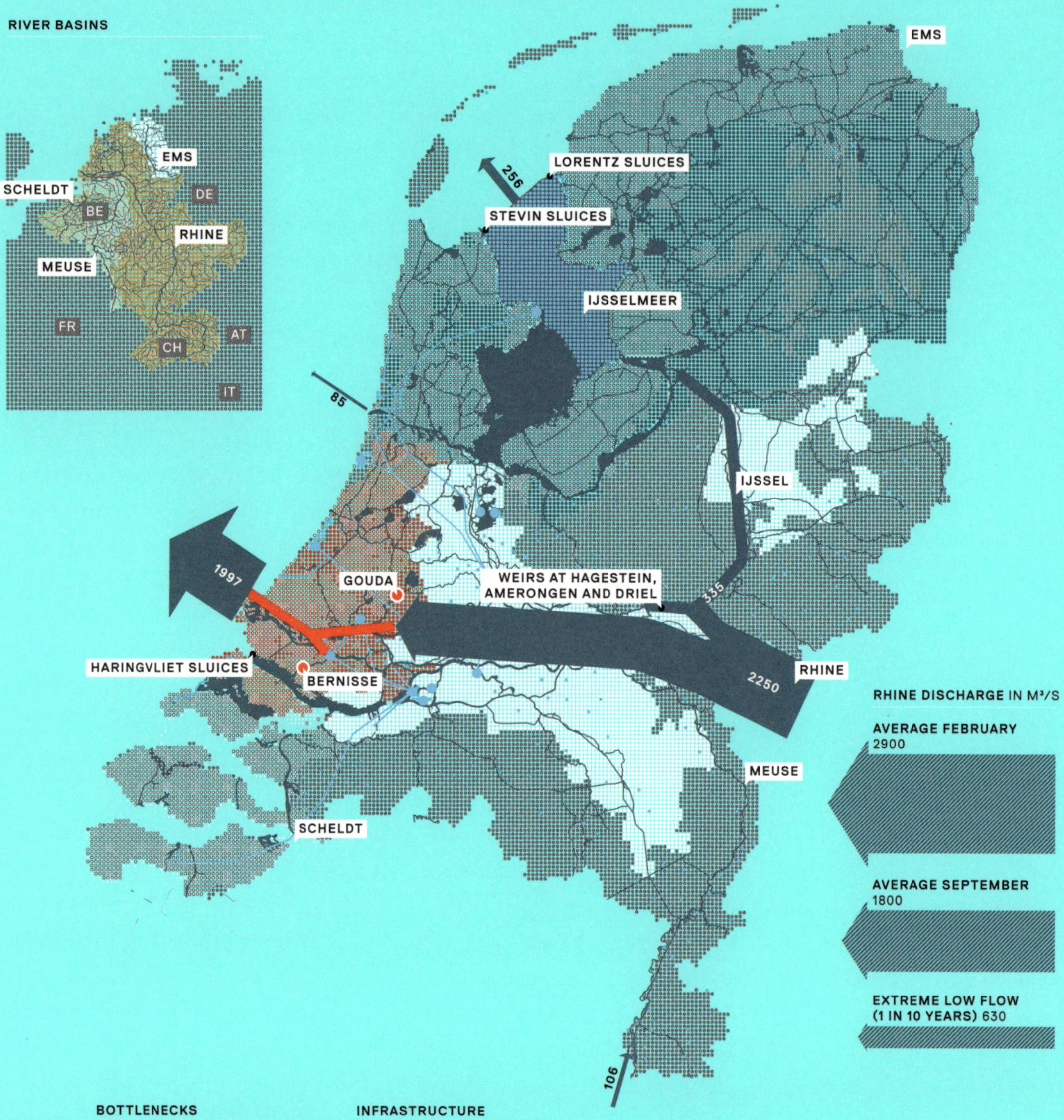

BOTTLENECKS

- SALT WATER INTRUSION
- RIVER FLOW IN AN AVERAGE YEAR (1967) IN M³/S
- AREA AT RISK OF SALINISATION VIA INTAKE POINTS
- AREA AT RISK OF SALINISATION VIA GROUNDWATER
- OVERDRAWN WATER BUFFER IJSSELMEER
- INADEQUATE RIVER WATER SUPPLY
- NO WATER SUPPLY FROM RIVERS

INFRASTRUCTURE

- WATERWAYS
- MAIN WATER SUPPLY PIPELINES
- WATER ABSTRACTION
  - >50 MILLION M³/YEAR
  - <50 MILLION M³/YEAR
- WATER RESERVOIR
- NATIONAL KEY CONTROL POINT
- INTAKE POINT

3.3 / TWEAKING THE WATER SYSTEM

The Rhine plays a central role in the water system of the western and northern Netherlands. However, the river flow is becoming less predictable due to climate change, leading to greater salt intrusion during extreme low flow. Therefore, measures are needed along the rivers and in river-sea transition zones.

Sources: Deltaprogramma, Eurostat, H+N+S Landscape Architects, Ministry of Infrastructure and the Environment, Noordhoff, PBL

WATER SCARCITY (1996–2005) / HOT SPOTS

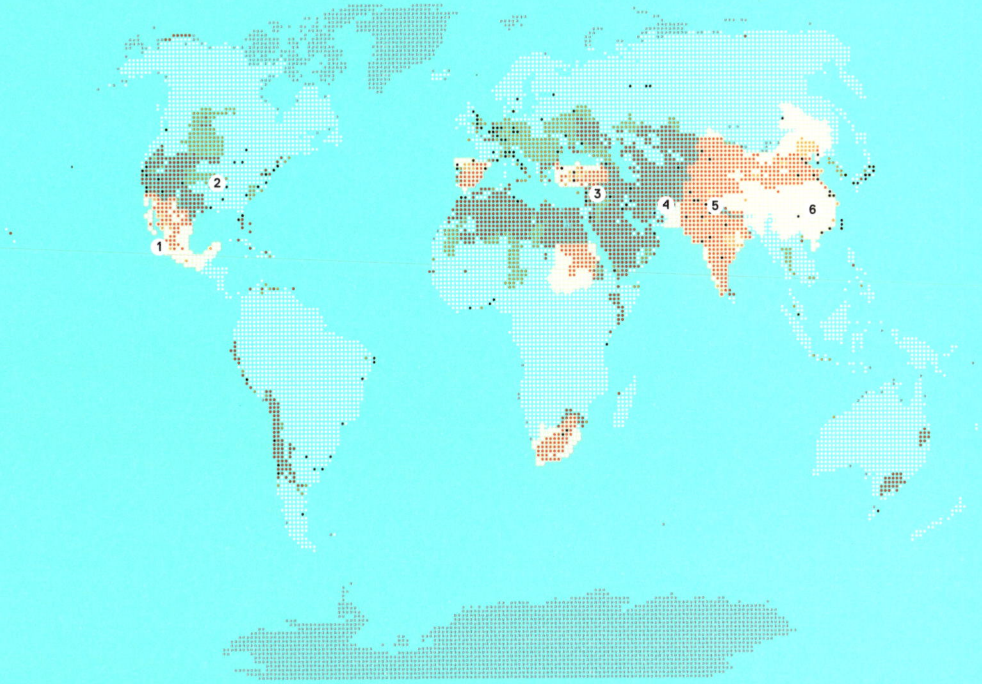

GROUNDWATER FOOTPRINT IN RELATION TO AQUIFER AREA: KEY REGIONS AND THEIR MAIN CROPS (2008)

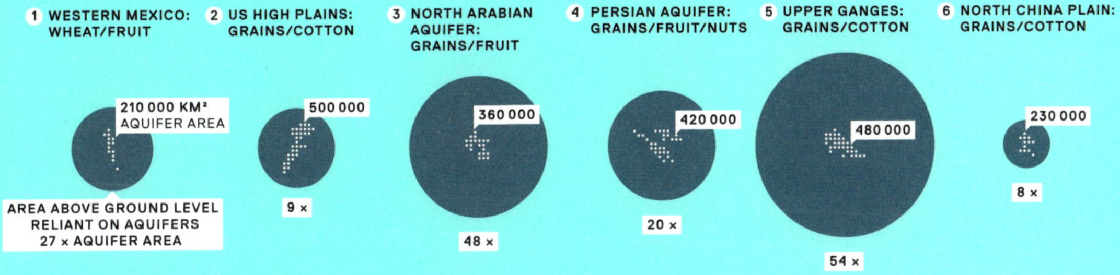

HOTSPOTS AND URBAN AREA

HOT SPOTS: COUNTRIES WITH WATER SCARCITY AND RELATIVELY HIGH WATER USE FOR AGRICULTURAL PRODUCTS IMPORTED BY THE NETHERLANDS

· URBAN AREA (2003)

LEVEL OF WATER SCARCITY (1996–2005)

- LOW
- MIDDLE
- HIGH
- NO DATA

3.4 / MORE PEOPLE, LESS WATER

Water scarcity is a growing problem in many regions of the world. Water use is rising due to population growth, economic growth and intensification of agricultural production for export. Overdrawn aquifers are gradually being depleted. These water problems increasingly lead to social and political conflict.

Sources: Gleeson et al., Natural Earth data, PBL, Utrecht University

3.4 / MORE PEOPLE, LESS WATER

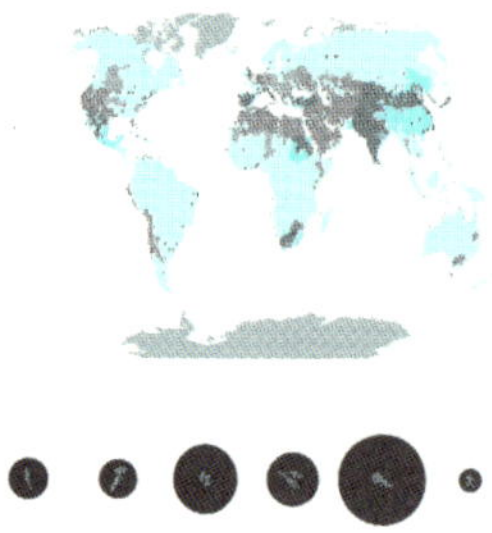

The Netherlands has enough water, an intricate water distribution network that ensures adequate water levels in practically every part of the country, a drinking water network that delivers water to every home, and a sewage network that carries off the waste water. Compared to many other countries, this is quite exceptional. In many river catchments around the world, water is scarce or severely polluted. There, reliable drinking water does not come from the tap, but has to be bought in bottles from the supermarket or in plastic bags from street vendors; and water available for washing and flushing is often not very clean.

The expected growth in the world population from 7.2 billion now to more than 9 billion by 2050 – and the likely increase in overall prosperity and living standards – will dramatically raise global demand for fresh water. Water supplies are in danger of depletion, and water scarcity is becoming a real risk in densely populated catchments. Not only surface water but especially groundwater supplies are running out. In some groundwater systems (aquifers), water extraction is dozens of times higher than the natural recharge by precipitation. In regions where water availability is limited, such as in the Middle East and parts of Africa, increasing scarcity may lead to social unrest and political conflict.

3.5 / RUNNING DRY

Water consumption keeps increasing, worldwide; particularly in the BRIICS countries (Brazil, Russia, India, Indonesia, China and South-Africa). Surprisingly, global water consumption for irrigation is decreasing. This is partly due to more efficient irrigation methods and precision agriculture, but also because there is simply less water available for agriculture than before, while domestic and industrial water demand keeps increasing. In some areas the bottom of the barrel is really in sight. The growing water shortage is likely to have negative consequences for economic development, agricultural production, local populations and ecosystems.

GLOBAL WATER DEMAND, IN KM³ PER YEAR (1 KM³ = 1 000 000 000 000 L)

OECD & BRIICS COUNTRIES (2012)

OECD → ORGANISATION FOR ECONOMIC CO-OPERATION AND DEVELOPMENT

BRIICS → BRAZIL, RUSSIA, INDIA, INDONESIA, CHINA, SOUTH AFRICA

PURPOSES

- ELECTRICITY
- MANUFACTURING
- LIVESTOCK
- HOUSEHOLDS
- IRRIGATION

3.5 / RUNNING DRY

Water consumption keeps increasing, worldwide particularly, in the emerging economies of the BRIICS countries. Remarkably, water use for irrigation is decreasing: food production loses ground to households and industry. Many Western companies are operating in water-scarce countries; they could contribute money and knowhow to help improve local water management.

Sources: OECD, Wada et al.

Internationally operating companies from the Netherlands and other Western countries influence the water situation in other parts of the world – directly, if they have local production facilities, or indirectly if they do business with local producers. Local water sources are used for irrigating agricultural and horticultural crops, as an ingredient in drinks, food and other products, and, on a large scale, in numerous industrial production processes. The textile industry in Asia, cotton production in Turkey, and fruit production in Spain and South Africa are notorious examples of water consumption and pollution. Most of these goods are produced for international markets. Thus, lifestyle and consumption patterns in the Netherlands and other rich countries have a significant influence on the water supply in other parts of the world.

Western companies may help to address local water problems by greening their business and taking on corporate social responsibility. They may also contribute money and know-how to improve local water infrastructure and water management. Furthermore, consumers may wield their influence by buying sustainably produced clothing and food products.

Without food there can be no life. Food is the source of energy for all our bodily functions and the supplier of vitamins and minerals. Adults need 2000 to 2500 kilocalories in food energy per day; this is as much energy as there is in about a quarter litre of petrol.

However, food is more than just a source of nutrition. Eating is a social phenomenon. It offers pleasure and comfort, and it both unites and distinguishes people. German philosopher Ludwig Feuerbach was not far wrong when he wrote: 'Der Mensch ist, was er ißt'. You are what you eat.

4.1 / DUTCH HOME CUISINE

What foods are served at the Dutch table? The main ingredients in the ever more varied diet consist of dairy, grain and potato products, vegetables and meats. The annual groceries, per Dutch household, add up to 1350 kilograms; around 800 kilograms in food and nearly 550 kilogram in drinks. Per household, the average annual food bill comes to 5000 euros, which, for the average-income households, is 15% of their disposable income. There is an abundance of food, these days, in prosperous countries such as the Netherlands. The Dutch eat an estimated 10% more than their required calorie intake.

A whole world lies hidden behind the plate of food on the table. Food production requires large quantities of land, water, fertiliser and energy. Supplying one Dutch household with sufficient food for one year requires more than 8800 square metres of land for agriculture, horticulture, livestock and feed crops. This represents a food footprint that is the size of three quarters of a soccer field, per person. In order to meet the demand for food, each year large nature areas are being converted into highly productive agricultural areas. Thus, 60% of global biodiversity loss is caused by agriculture.

Food production not only requires large amounts of land, it also needs over 200,000 litres in irrigation water, per year. Although in itself this water use does not have to be a problem, it is problematic if production takes place in areas of water scarcity.

Growing food crops, in addition, requires fertilisers such as nitrogen and phosphorous, while animals and plants also are treated with antibiotics and pesticides to combat certain diseases. Per household, this involves for example 67 kilograms of nitrogen and 13 grams of antibiotics. This means that the animals in intensive livestock systems receive 4 to 5 times the amount of antibiotics that the average Dutch person receives.

Water drainage, pollution of both water and soil by over-fertilisation, and the application of chemicals have a large impact on ecosystems and biodiversity. In addition, intensive livestock farming also has an impact on public health; excessive use of antibiotics may cause antibiotic resistance in certain bacteria. Furthermore, infectious animal diseases may also be passed on to humans, as for example has been the case for Q fever.

Finally, each step in the production chain also costs energy, which is largely being supplied using fossil fuels. The total energy use comes to 35 to 40 gigajoules, per household, per year. Every calorie consumed by humans as food energy will have required five times that amount of energy in fossil fuel, for the food to be grown, processed, wrapped, refrigerated and transported.

In addition to CO_2, food production (e.g. livestock and rice crops) also emits the very powerful greenhouse gases of methane and nitrous oxide. Food production, all in all, involves the emission of over 6400 kilograms of greenhouse gases, per household per year, or 18 kilograms per day. This is 15% to 20% of global greenhouse gas emissions.

4.2 / THE TRAVELS OF FOOD

The entire world is represented in the supermarket. Pizzas, curries and burritos have become everyday dishes. Ingredients come from all over the world. The food industry involves advanced logistics and a road map that stretches across all continents. Products such as hazelnut paste (Nutella) contain hazelnuts from Turkey, palm oil from Malaysia, cocoa from Nigeria, sugar from Brazil and Europe, and vanilla from China; the only local product is the milk. Moreover, the packaging of glass, plastics and paper also has come from far and wide. The Netherlands occupies a special place in this global food network. Traditionally, it is a trade and transit country. From the perspective of financial value, the Netherlands is even the second largest exporter, globally, of food and agricultural products, following the United States.

The degree of success of the Dutch 'agri and food' sector has three explanations. First, its fertile soil and favourable climate enable high production levels. Second, Dutch agriculture and horticulture is both knowledge-intensive (education, research

FOOD AND DRINK PURCHASES, IN KILOS PER HOUSEHOLD, PER YEAR, WITH THE CORRESPONDING PRODUCTION FOOTPRINT PER DUTCH HOUSEHOLD (2010)

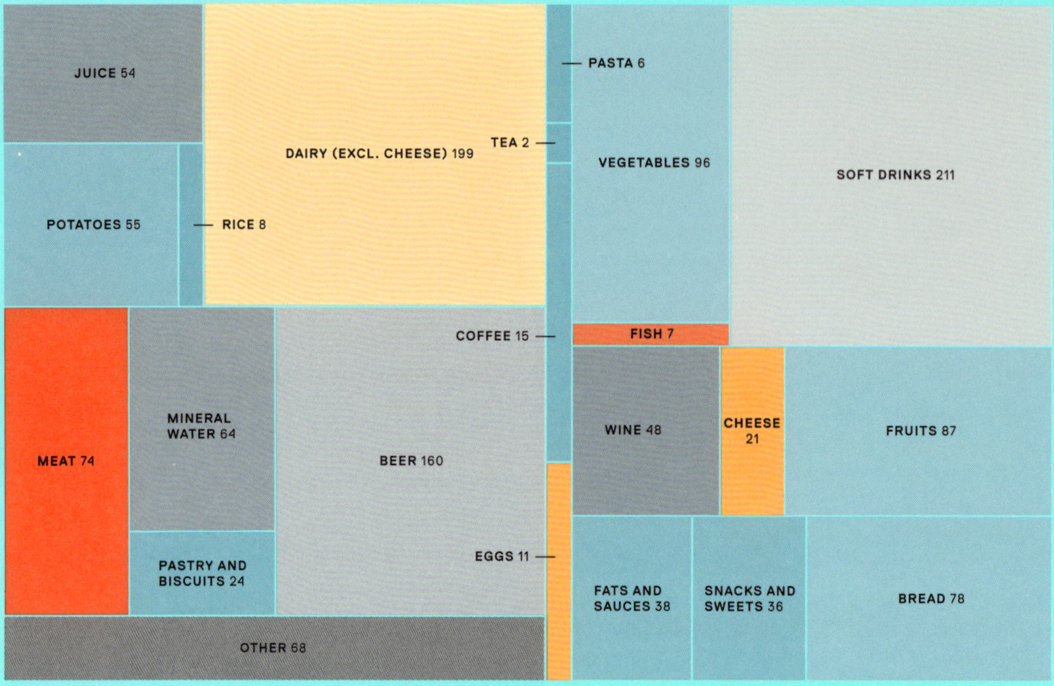

8800 M²	226000 L	6400 KG	67 KG	13 G
LAND	WATER	GREENHOUSE GASES (IN CO_2 eq)	NITROGEN	ANTIBIOTICS

4.1 / DUTCH HOME CUISINE

The average Dutch household buys more than 1350 kilograms of food and drink per year. The production of these groceries requires nearly a hectare of farmland, plus large quantities of water, energy, fertilisers, pesticides and antibiotics. Moreover, it causes an invisible by-product: 18 kg of greenhouse gases per day, or more than 6400 kilograms per year.

Sources: GfK/RIVM/Milieucentraal, PBL, UNESCO-IHE – all adapted by PBL

FOOD PRODUCTION, CONSUMPTION, IMPORT AND EXPORT, IN MILLION TONNES (THE NETHERLANDS, 2009)

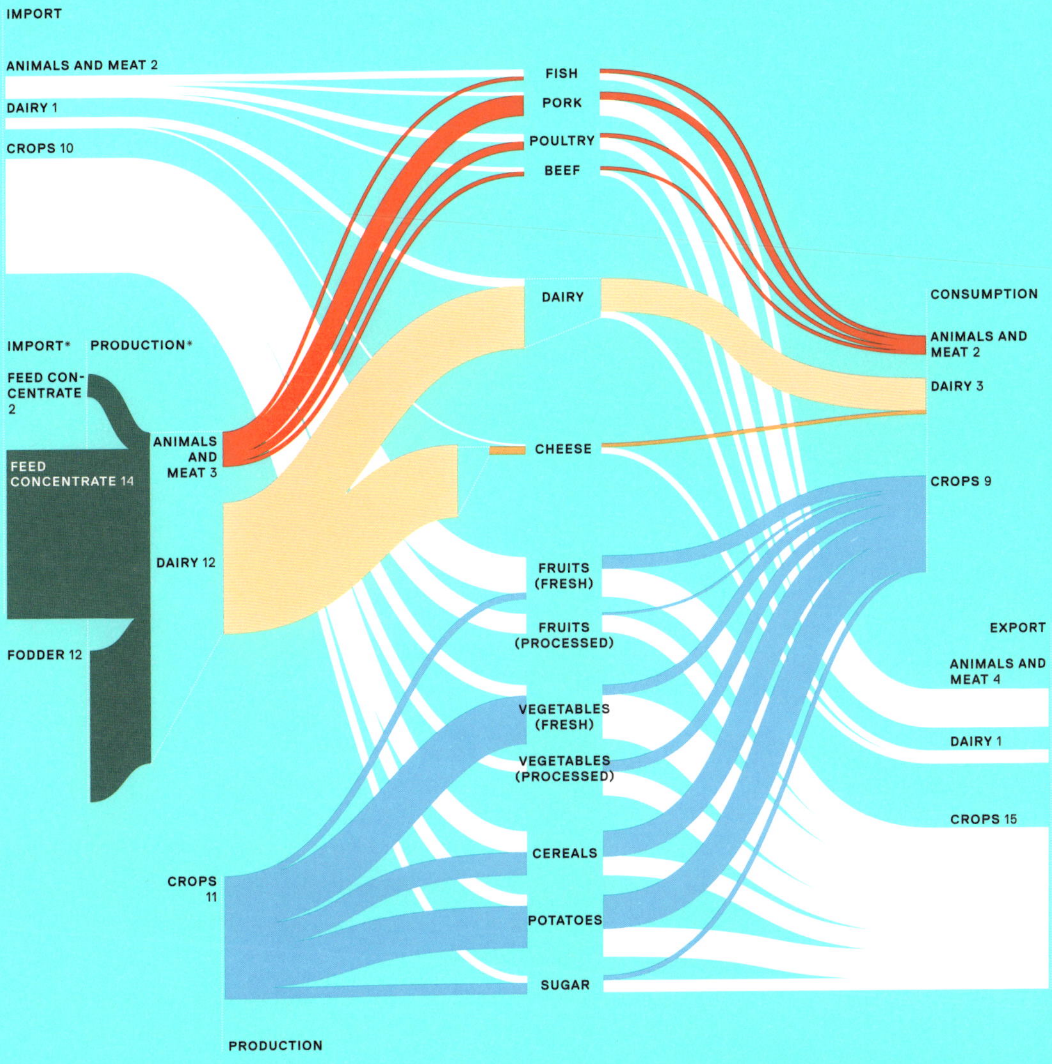

*DRY MATTER

4.2 / THE TRAVELS OF FOOD

Food is a global market, with products and ingredients travelling over long distances. The Netherlands occupies a special position within this global food network; the country is a high-tech agricultural superpower that makes maximum use of its favourable agricultural conditions and its strategic position in international trade and freight distribution.

Sources: CBS, LEI, PDV, PZ – all adapted by PBL

and innovation) and capital intensive (large investments). This also causes high yields per hectare, with products such as sowing seeds, bulbs and flowers, and a high added value for this sector. The third explanation is the way the Dutch food sector utilises its strategic position in the international trade network. Amsterdam Airport Schiphol and the Ports of Rotterdam and Amsterdam are nodes in the global logistics of crops and animal products, semi-finished products and finished products. This means it is attractive to import and process raw materials into the Netherlands and to subsequently trade the resulting high quality products.

Dutch agriculture can more than meet the domestic demand for many everyday products, such as pork, dairy, potatoes, vegetables and sugar. Fruit, which is imported in large quantities, is one of the exceptions.

4.3 / FARMERS SHAPE THE LANDSCAPE

For centuries, agricultural developments have been determining the Dutch landscape. Intensification, mechanisation, expansion and industrialisation of arable farming have changed the landscape over the past century. The agricultural area has expanded due to reclamation and cultivation, and shrunk by urbanisation. Currently, it covers a little over half the country's land surface.

Until far into the 19th century, agriculture was strongly related to soil fertility; potatoes and onions grew in the clay of Zeeland, fruits grew in the river region, and livestock was kept on the arid sandy soils. The international agricultural crisis of 1880 – 1895 led to a drastic reorientation. From then on, the government stimulated knowledge gathering, intensification, innovation (artificial fertiliser, greenhouses) and exports. Before the Second World War, the Netherlands already had one of the most intensive agricultural systems in the world.

After 1945, this course was stepped up and pursued further. The landscape changed; plots of land were combined, water levels were lowered, and small-scale elements, such as wooded banks, were removed.

Rationalisation also meant an increased specialisation per region; dairy in Friesland, Gelderland and the Green Heart; chickens in the Gelderse Vallei; pigs in northern Limburg and eastern North Brabant; and high grade export crops, such as flowers and greenhouse vegetables, were grown in the west, near Amsterdam Airport Schiphol and Rotterdam.

The rise of intensive livestock farming in the Netherlands was stimulated by the proximity of the Port of Rotterdam, which enabled the cheap importation of feed. Distribution took place via the network of canals that had already been dug for the transportation of peat, among other things. Along these canals, feed production companies were established.

The landscape continues to undergo change. In the 21st century, urbanites are discovering the countryside as a place to live and spend their leisure time, and are in search of the desired, picturesque landscape. A Dutch culinary culture has emerged, with an eye for food quality, traditional methods and regional flavours. Farmers respond to this culture by introducing new regional products (e.g. Beemsterkaas, Mariënwaerdt). Other things that also influence the landscape are nature developments, agricultural nature management and the emergence of new forms of 'mixed' farms, such as camping and care farms. The landscape variety became less in the post-war years of rationalism, while in the 21st century a new form of diversity has been forming.

4.4 / LAND TO FEED BILLIONS

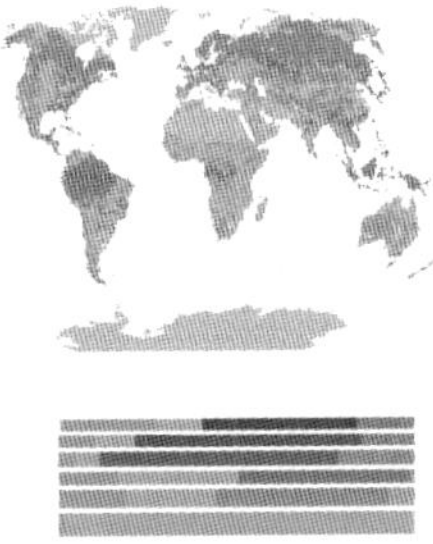

Today, in order to feed 7.2 billion people, a global amount of 38 million km² of agricultural land is being used. If the world population grows to over 9 billion by 2050, this will need to expand to over 42 million km²; an increase of 4 million, equalling a land area of 120 times that of the Netherlands. In order to eradicate world hunger, however, even more would be needed. The question is where all these additional millions of square kilometres must be found, and what would be the impact on biodiversity and greenhouse gas emission levels.

AGRICULTURAL LAND USE AND THE FOOD-PROCESSING INDUSTRY (2012)

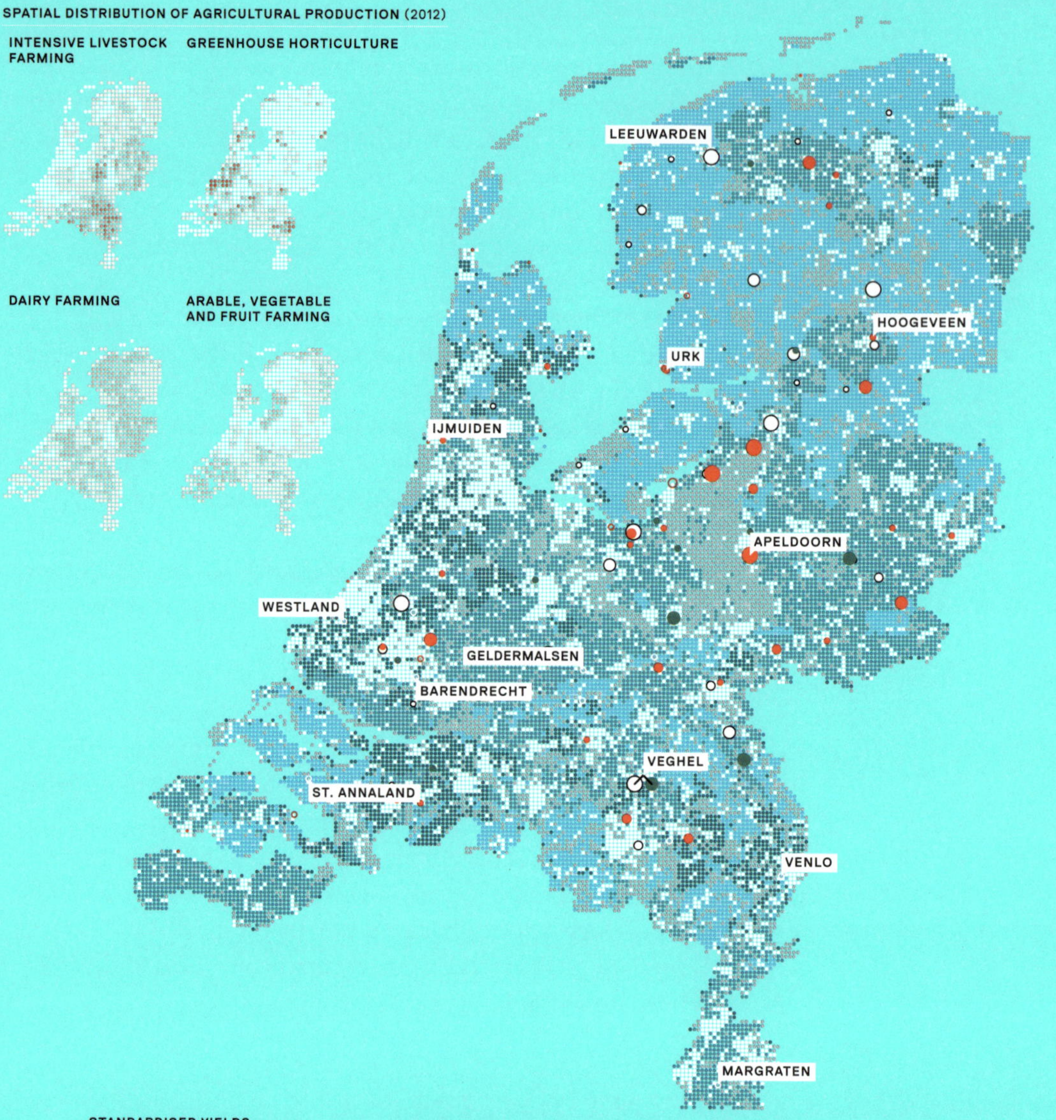

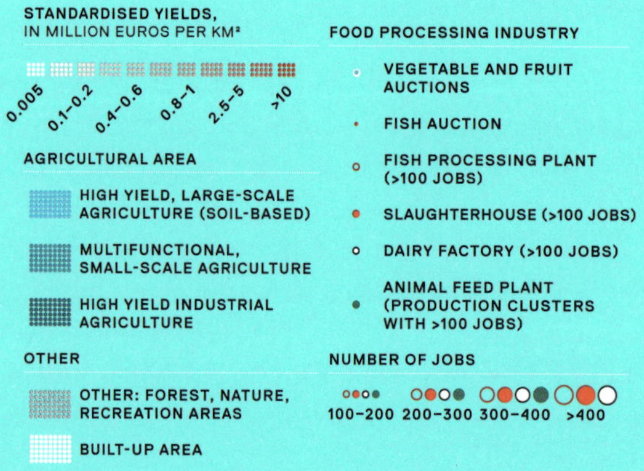

4.3 / FARMERS SHAPE THE LANDSCAPE

Present-day agriculture has changed the Dutch countryside into an ultra-modern production landscape, where farming businesses work together in internationally operating regional production clusters of, for example, greenhouse horticulture or hog farming. This far-reaching rationalisation is counterbalanced by renewed public interest in food quality, nature and landscape quality.

Sources: Alterra, CBS – adaptation by LEI, LEI, LISA – all adapted by PBL

GLOBAL LAND USE (2000-2050)

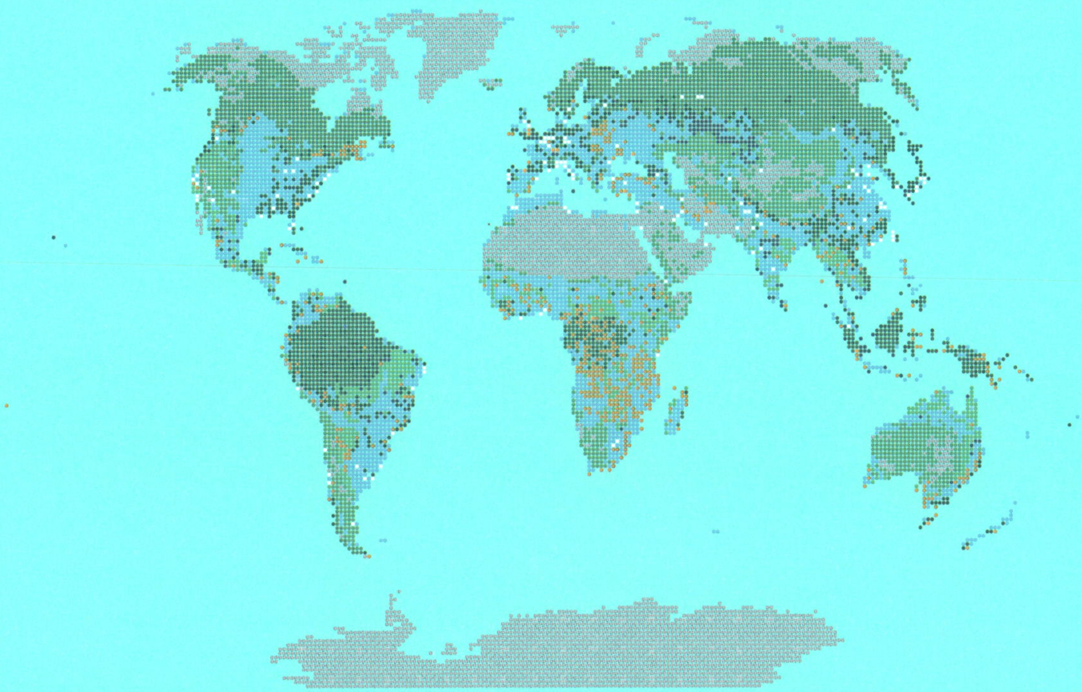

GLOBAL LAND USE PER ECOSYSTEM TYPE (2010)

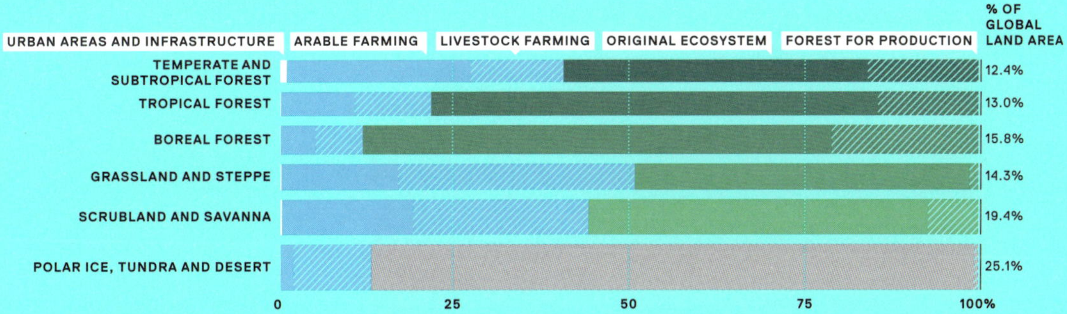

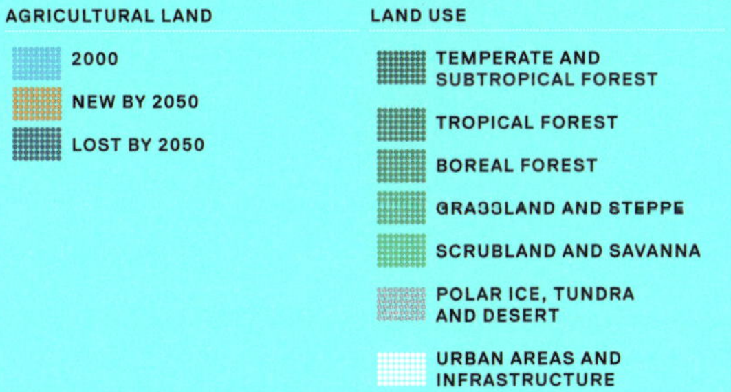

4.4 / LAND TO FEED BILLIONS

Global agricultural land area, presently, totals 30 million square kilometres. To feed the growing world population, at least 4 million square kilometres more will be required by 2050. New farmland will be created mostly in areas with relatively high plant and animal diversity, such as tropical and subtropical forests, and savannas.

Sources: FAO – adaptation by PBL, PBL

Large areas on earth are not or hardly suitable for agriculture or livestock farming, because the climate is either too hot, too cold or too hilly. The most suitable areas, including delta areas such as in the Netherlands, are all being used already. Expansion of the agricultural area is the most logical in locations where vegetation is already growing: by clearing forests. In the past, over 40% of the original forest land was converted into agricultural land. Today, an estimated 37 million km^2 remain. Around a third, 12 million km^2, consists of production forests and forest plantations, supplying products such as timber and palm oil. Moreover, the forest areas that would be the most suitable for agriculture are the very areas with the highest levels of biodiversity. This concerns subtropical and tropical rainforests, savannahs and transitional scrubland. Therefore, the downside of the increase in agricultural area and in food for the growing population is particularly the loss in ecosystems and biodiversity.

The increase in food production requires more than additional land alone. The amounts in other production factors, such as water, energy, fertiliser and pesticides, also would be higher than they are today. Greenhouse gas emissions will increase by more, relatively speaking, due to the release of greenhouse gases during deforestation and drainage of wetlands. Eutrophication of surface waters also increases. In 2010, amounts of 9.4 million tonnes of nitrogen and 1.3 million tonnes of phosphorous were being discharged in household waste water. This is only 20% of the total; 80% of these substances come from agriculture. These discharges disturb the ecological balance of the water; they lead to harmful algal growth rates and deoxygenation of the water. The water could be purified, but many countries do not have the appropriate installations at their disposal.

The demand for agricultural land may even be greater than it is today, if increasing numbers of people adopt a rich, 'Western' high protein diet. In contrast, demand may also end up being smaller, if agriculture could be intensified. However, to date, there is no large-scale application of a form of agriculture that can supply larger amounts of food, on a global level, without using more land, fossil energy and other resources.

4.5 / THE POWER OF THE MENU

The production of food represents an onslaught on the earth. It is, therefore, necessary for our food supply to become more sustainable. Consumers have the power to influence the 'food-print' via their menu, simply by eating healthy. The Dutch consume over 20% more saturated fats than would be good for them. A menu with a healthy amount of saturated fat would have a footprint that is 18% smaller and would lead to 6% less greenhouse gas emissions. The reason for this is the smaller amount of meat on this menu. The production of 1 kilogram of pork requires over 5 kilograms of vegetable foods; for chicken meat this is 3 kilograms and for beef 15 kilograms are needed.

Compared to a meat menu, a vegetarian menu that uses dairy as a substitute for meat uses 36% less of the available land and leads to 21% less greenhouse gas emission. In addition, the use of antibiotics required for such a vegetarian menu is only 13% of that of an average meat menu. A 100% vegetarian menu is best for the environment, but also a partly vegetarian menu – a so-called flexitarian menu – is already less of an onslaught on the earth.

Nevertheless, it is not always easy to determine what would be best. Whether organic food is better or worse for the environment than regular food, is debatable. Organic seems better, as it does not involve chemical pesticides, artificial fertilisers or preventative antibiotic applications, and it requires less energy. However, organic farming is less productive; yields per hectare are 20% lower than under conventional farming practices. Thus, to feed the world, organically, would require more land – something that is unsustainable. But the footprint could be reduced by more efficient food consumption – in other words, by reducing wastage. A Dutch household annually discards 105 kilograms of food, which is nearly 15% of the total amount of groceries, equalling a value of 340 euros. Businesses (e.g. food industry, shops, restaurants) also waste food. The total annual amount of food wastage in the Netherlands is between 1.4 and 2.5 million tonnes. These Dutch data are relatively favourable; because of effective food

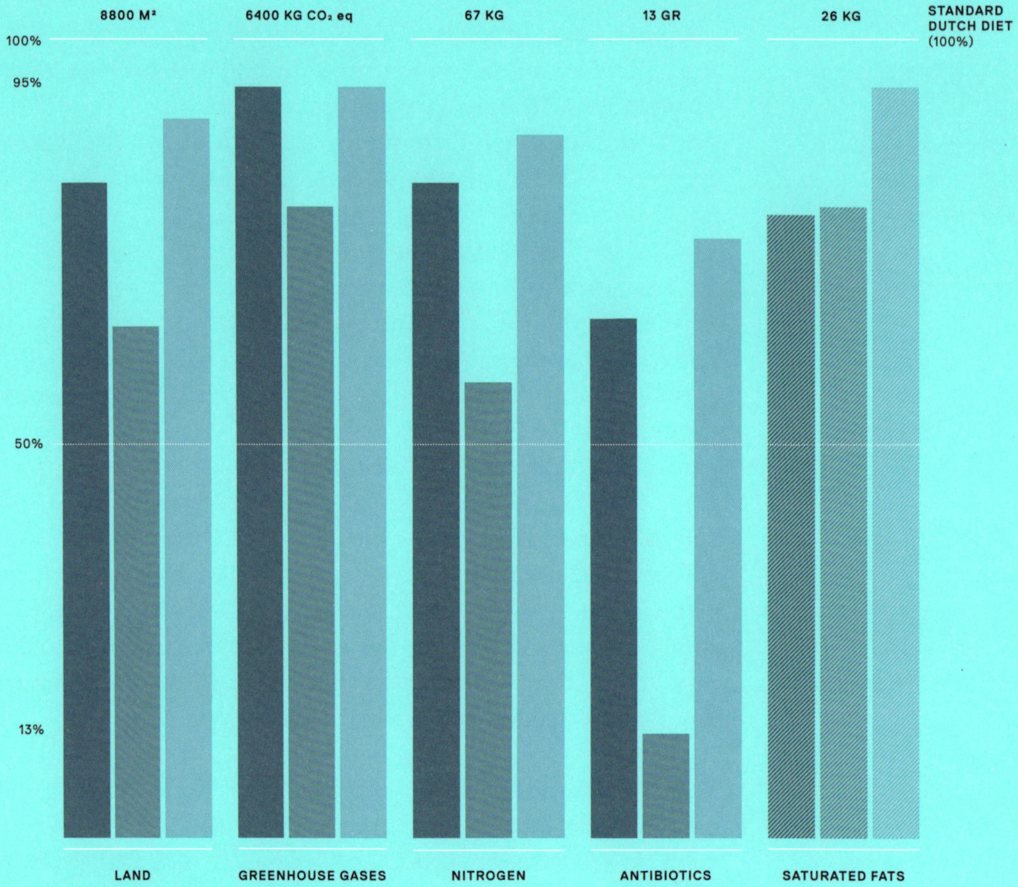

DIET

- HEALTHY DIET BASED ON NATIONAL NUTRITION GUIDELINES
- VEGETARIAN DIET (NO MEAT OR FISH)
- FLEXITARIAN DIET (VEGETARIAN 2 DAYS A WEEK)

4.5 / THE POWER OF THE MENU

The ecological footprint of food consumption in the Netherlands can be reduced if more people switch to healthier diets; particularly, if they cut back on meat. It takes 5 kilograms of animal feed and 8 to 15 m² of farmland to produce 1 kilogram of pork. Shifting to a more plant-based diet will also help to reduce fertiliser and antibiotics use and greenhouse gas emissions.

Source: PBL

logistics, not much food is lost along the way 'between soil and plate'. On a global level, losses are far more dramatic; each year 1.3 billion tonnes of food are lost – over a third of the global food production.

05 BIOTA

Nature is of vital importance to man, and to urban communities. We cannot live without nature; directly or indirectly, all human activities are made possible by the underlying natural processes.

In daily language, 'nature' can mean many different things. Some people reserve the term for unspoilt wilderness, while others use it to describe a meadow or dandelions growing through the cracks in the pavement. Some make a strict separation between 'us' and 'nature', while others argue that nature determines human behaviour.

This chapter discusses 'nature' from a practical point of view. In analogy with the service economy, we here consider nature as a service-providing system that offers a large array of goods and services which humans need and use. This analysis is intended as an invitation to recognise and appreciate the natural processes that are right below the surface of our daily existence. Similar to the other flows discussed in this book, these natural services ('ecosystem services') take place at various scales, including the global scale.

5.1 / THE SERVICES OF NATURE

Inhabitants of the Netherlands benefit from ecosystems both nearby and far away. Some examples. Dutch forests produce about 8% of the wood used in the Netherlands; the other 92% is produced by forests in other areas of the world. One fifth of the Dutch coastline and riverbanks is protected from flooding by natural barriers, such as coastal dunes; the remainder must be protected by dykes, engineering works, and other alternatives to nature. Nature also plays a key role in the supply of clean drinking water. The Dutch landscape contributes to human health and well-being by offering pleasant surroundings – in varying degrees of naturalness – for bicycle rides and other leisure activities.

Nature provides food, wood and biomass. Among nature's many services are soil erosion control and soil fertility improvement, carbon sequestration, crop pollination, agricultural pest and disease suppression, water purification and flood protection. In addition, nature contributes to human well-being by offering recreational opportunities, cultural and spiritual inspiration and diversity.

People and nature often work closely together; for example, in the production of food. However, for many services we are completely dependent on nature; for instance, in the case of crop pollination by wild bees. Even so, these bees also depend on us, in the sense that their habitat is influenced by humans.

5.2 / THE NETHERLANDS IS MAN-MADE

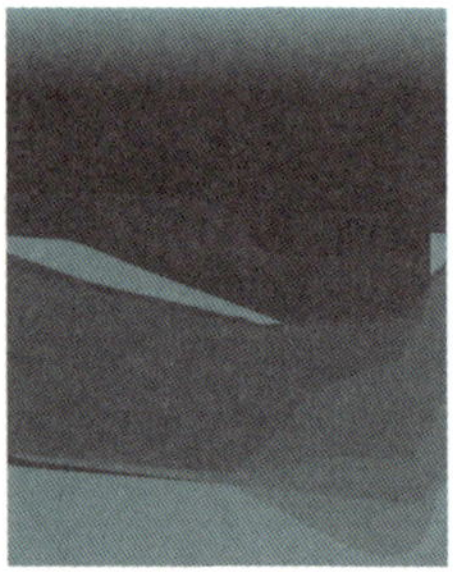

For centuries, the Dutch have actively changed and managed their land. They cultivated the wilderness, cleared primeval forests, changed boggy peat and poor sandy soils into fertile fields and meadows, reclaimed land from the sea, and brought water levels under control with windmills, steam engines and electrical pumps. Today, the country is filled with roads, canals, railways, villages, towns and cities, harbours and airports. In raked-over Netherland, every square metre is taken care of by one policy or another.

The North Sea is also used intensively: for shipping, fisheries and extraction of sand, oil and natural gas, for recreation, (wind) energy production and aquaculture, and in the future probably also for carbon dioxide storage in empty gas fields.

However, nature is ever present, even in man-made Netherlands. For one thing, water will always play a decisive role, since the country is located in a river delta, partly below sea level. As for flora and fauna, habitat conditions may change due to human interference, but species may be able to adjust if these changes are gradual enough; in other words, nature will move along. Humans are but one of the causes of the perpetual change of landscapes – even though human impact has increased spectacularly.

Again some examples. The Dutch hunger for land and energy changed the vast marshlands into treeless landscapes of pastures and ditches, drawing new animal species. The arrival of artificial fertiliser also had a dramatic effect on the landscape by reducing the demand for manure for poor sandy soils. The moorlands which were grazed by sheep for this purpose lost their function and were replaced with Scots pine plantations for the production of shoring timber for the mining industry. Black-tailed godwits and peewits were not at all common in the Netherlands before the wilderness was cultivated, but they thrived on the extensively managed farmlands that became the dominant land use. As for doves and herons, they have perfectly adjusted to the urban landscapes of today.

The Dutch cleared forests and marshland to generate income and feed a growing population. However, as prosperity increased, the appreciation of nature grew, as did concerns over its destruction. Out of a moral sense, but also out of self-interest, nature conservation became a growing priority. Today, the practice of nature restoration goes one step further; if we create the right conditions, nature will return. The Oostvaardersplassen nature reserve is the most famous example of nature restoration in the Netherlands; this extensive wetland area was established in the late 1960s in a location where once there was marshland, followed by a natural lake, inland sea, artificial lake, polder, and planned industrial park.

SUPPLY OF GOODS AND SERVICES BY DUTCH ECOSYSTEMS RELATIVE TO DOMESTIC DEMAND, IN %

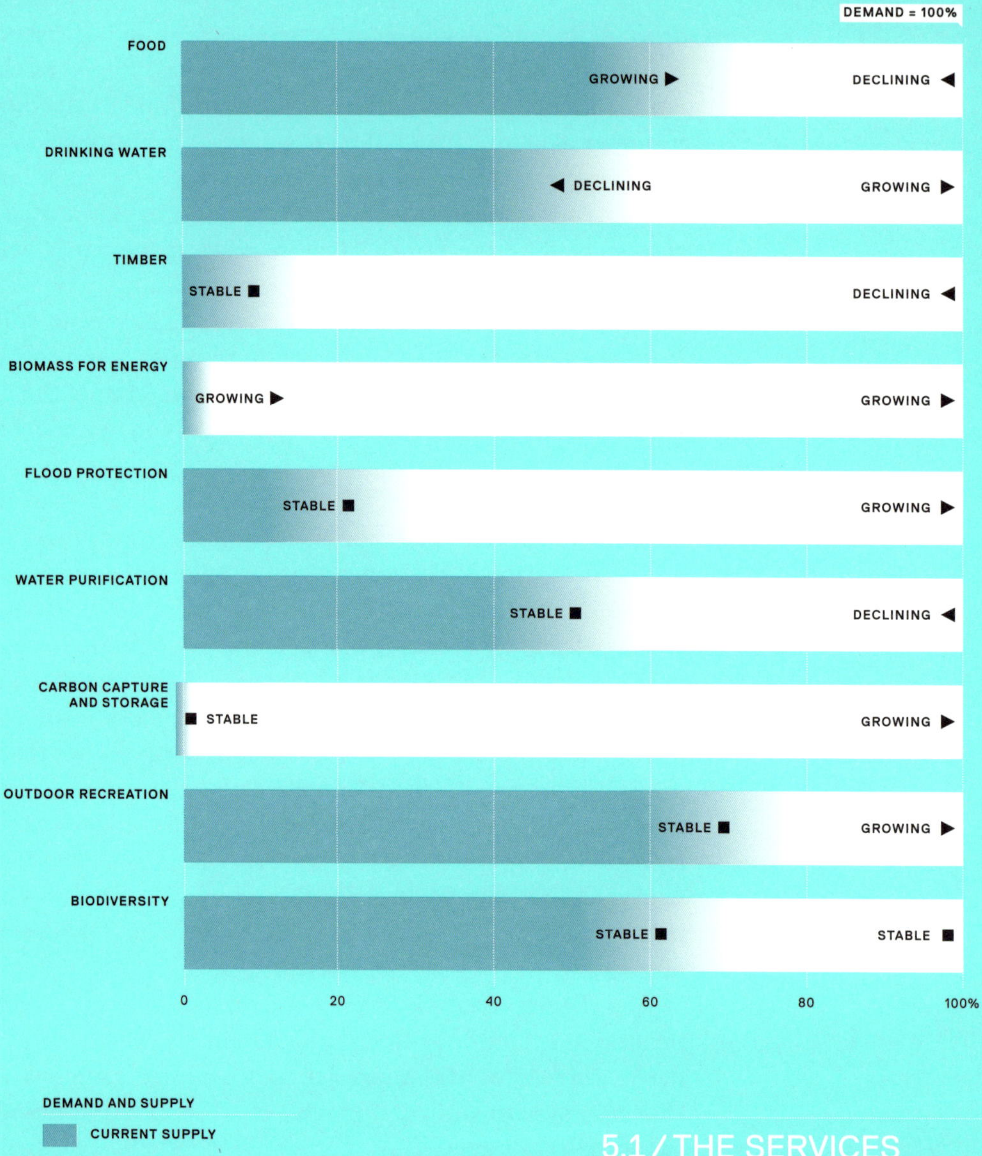

5.1 / THE SERVICES OF NATURE

Nature is of vital importance to man. We may view nature as a service providing system that delivers services such as water purification, food production and coastal protection. For example, one fifth of the Dutch coastline and riverbanks is protected from flooding by natural barriers, such as coastal dunes. The remainder has to be protected by dikes and engineering works.

Source : PBL/WUR

DUTCH LANDSCAPE CHANGES

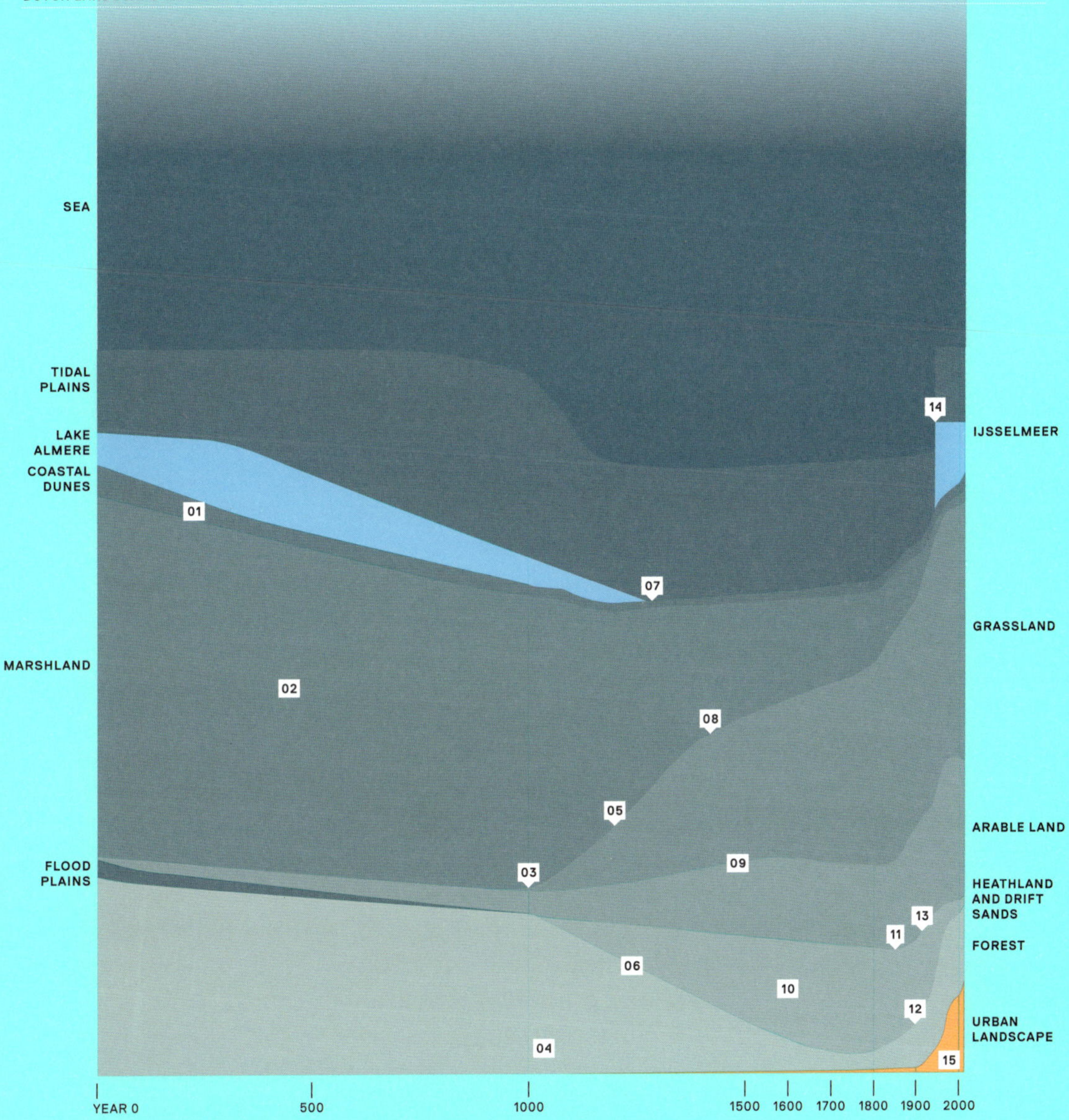

01 Throughout the centuries, the coastal dunes have protected the land against sea floods

02 Large parts of the Netherlands used to be marshland

03 A period of massive land clearing in the late middle ages

04 Cities start to influence the Dutch landscape

05 The first water boards are founded, marking the start of Dutch consensus-based collaboration (known as 'polderen') to keep the land dry

06 Forests are cut down for fuel and shipbuilding wood, and to grow crops

07 St. Lucia's flood hits the Netherlands and creates the Zuiderzee

08 St. Elisabeth's flood hits the Netherlands and paves the way for the Biesbosch wetland

09 The demand for food increases due to population growth

10 Agricultural overexploitation of sandy soils results in heathland and drift sand formations

11 Heathland is no longer needed as a nutrient source and sheep grazing land, due to the arrival of artificial fertiliser and the collapse of the wool industry

12 Forests are planted to provide timber for the mining industry and to control sand drifts

13 Rise of nature conservation; heathland and drift sands are no longer cleared for cultivation

14 The IJsselmeer lake is created with the construction of the Enclosure dam (Afsluitdijk)

15 Industrialisation leads to rapid urbanisation

5.2 / THE NETHERLANDS IS MAN-MADE

The Netherlands has no virgin wilderness; the country has been cultivated for centuries. But natural forces – climate and river delta dynamics in particular – still play an inevitable role in shaping the land. Where possible, flora and fauna will adjust to habitat changes, no matter whether these are due to human activity or natural causes.

Sources: Alterra, HES, TNO

Nature restoration may be regarded as a gift from urbanites to nature; cities have used the services of nature for centuries, and now return the favour by giving nature more space.

5.3 / NATURE'S WORKSHOP

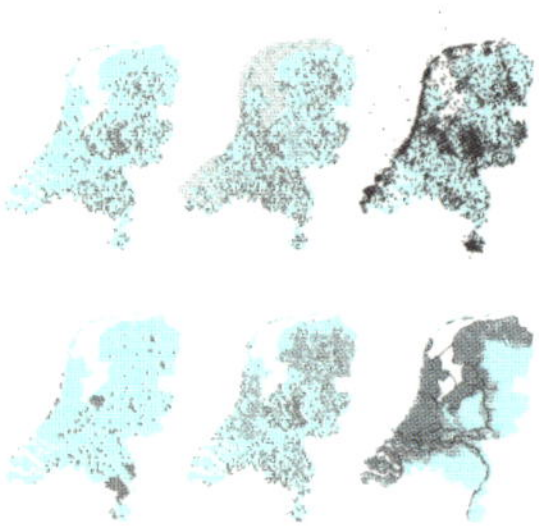

The Netherlands is too small and too densely populated to leave much room for natural forces. Spatial planning is a complex balancing act to accommodate multiple requirements and stakeholders. Often, the best solution is to combine various user functions in one area. In this process, nature is always an important factor. Sometimes, it is the main 'user' or objective, but more often it is the means to an end, or a favourable side effect.

The Dutch coastal dunes are an excellent example of an ecosystem delivering multiple services. This internationally unique system contributes to coastal flood defence and water purification, offers room for recreation, and accommodates many rare plant and animal species. On higher ground, the forests of the Veluwe and Utrechtse Heuvelrug also provide a wide range of ecosystem services. Most nature areas offer 'recreational services'. In military training areas, nature mainly serves as a useful backdrop.

Nature is everywhere, and all over the country we make use of its services. We could give something in return: firstly, by making generous room for nature areas, since biodiversity requires large interconnected areas with ample room for natural processes; and secondly, by making sure that man-made structures and human interventions can also be of use to nature. For instance, through smart design and ecological management it is possible to attract and increase specific species. Measures may range from using moss-friendly lime mortar and establishing nature-friendly banks and roadsides, to combining river sand and gravel extraction with riparian ecosystem development.

5.4 / HOMO SAPIENS IS THE DOMINANT SPECIES

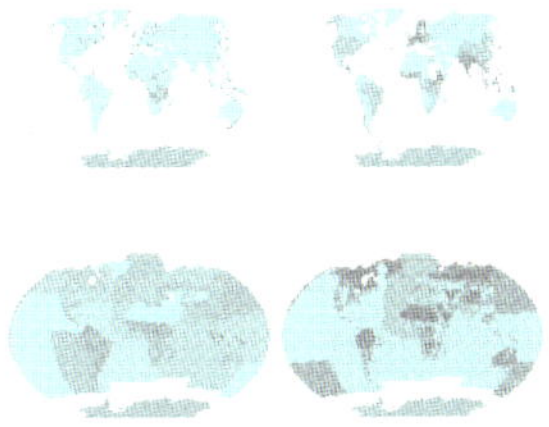

Our influence on nature is noticeable, worldwide. Homo sapiens has spread all over the world, leaving no biotope untouched.

We are changing the natural environment to build homes, produce food, extract raw materials and travel around; in short: to increase our quality of life. This invasion of nature follows the same general pattern, everywhere; resulting in a significant decrease in natural landscape diversity.

Furthermore, we are transporting and introducing plants and animals to areas where these species would not be able to migrate themselves. As a result, natural communities are becoming less and less unique and diverse. Although the introduction of non-native agricultural crops has lead to more varied diets (e.g. potatoes and corn in Europe), exotic species have also caused devastating infestations (e.g. rabbits and brambles in Australia, or the fungal Panama disease threatening banana plantations worldwide).

The growing world population also makes abundant use of ecosystem services. However, it is clear that the service providing capacity of nature is not endless. In a number of areas, ecosystems are in danger of being overtaxed and exhausted. The resulting loss of ecosystem services will also affect us, because without these services it will be harder to increase our quality of life or even maintain the status quo.

Our food supply is mainly based on agriculture, but also on hunting, gathering and fishing. The food supply from these last three is threatened by overhunting and overfishing. Biodiversity is steadily declining. Although plants are able to absorb CO_2, all the vegetation of the world together can barely keep up with the increase in CO_2 emissions caused by human activity. Dammed and 'tamed' rivers are barely able to transport enough sand to low-lying delta areas; cconomic profit from hydropower production upstream is given more priority than natural sand accretion and coastal flood protection downstream.

The question is when does 'ecosystem services' become a euphemism for our exploitation of nature.

TIMBER (2009)

BIODIVERSITY (2007)

FAVOURITE LOCATIONS (2011)

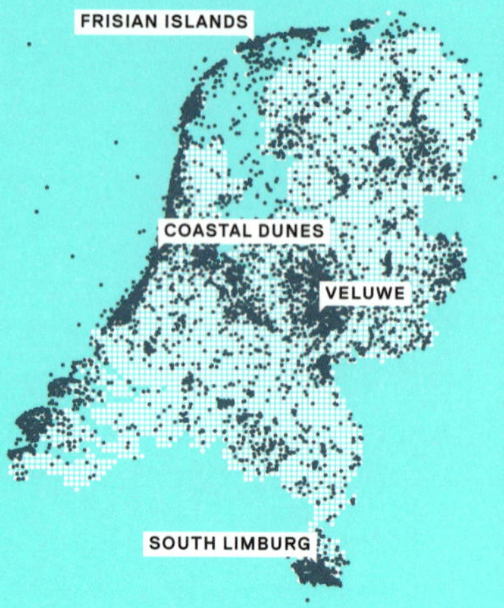

DRINKING WATER (2008)

CARBON SEQUESTRATION (2009)

FLOOD PROTECTION (2009)

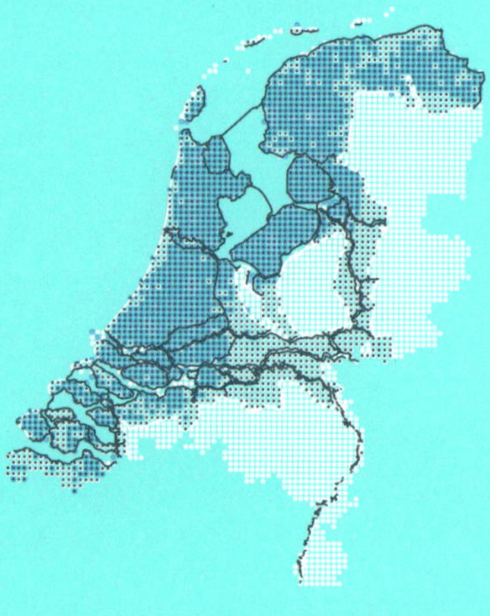

TIMBER

- TIMBER

BIODIVERSITY

- NATIONAL ECOLOGICAL NETWORK
- EUROPEAN PROTECTED NATURE AREAS

FAVOURITE LOCATIONS

- FAVOURITE LOCATIONS OF 4000 DUTCH CITIZENS

DRINKING WATER

- DRINKING WATER PROTECTED AREAS

CARBON SEQUESTRATION

- FOREST (CARBON SEQUESTRATION)
- PEATLAND (CARBON EMISSION)

FLOOD PROTECTION

- DYKE PROTECTED AREAS
- AREAS BELOW SEA LEVEL
- NATURAL FLOOD PROTECTION
- MAN-MADE FLOOD DEFENCE STRUCTURES

5.3 / NATURE'S WORKSHOP

In the Netherlands, smart multifunctional land use is key to accommodating multiple stakeholders and spatial requirements. Ecosystems are multifunctional by nature. For example, coastal dunes provide flood protection, water purification, unique biodiversity and room for outdoor recreation. In return, we can try to make sure that nature also benefits from our interventions.

Sources: AHN, Alterra,
Ministry of Agriculture, Nature and Food Quality, PBL, RUG/PBL/Alterra, RWS

GLOBAL DISTRIBUTION OF ECOSYSTEM SERVICES

CARBON CAPTURE AND STORAGE

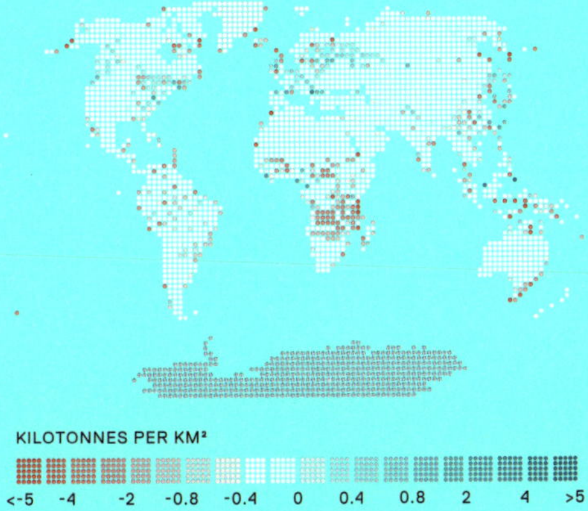

TIMBER PRODUCTION

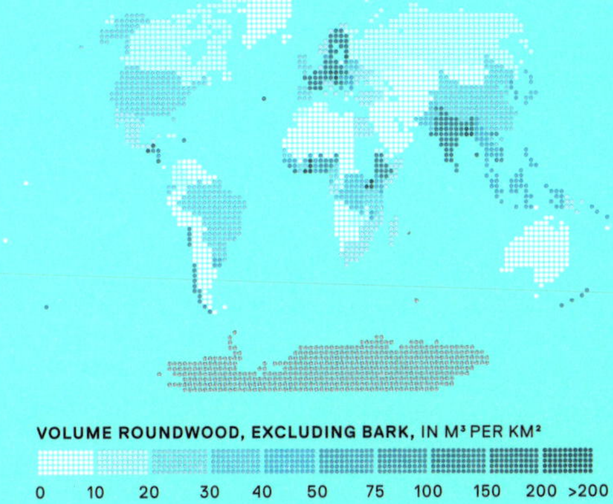

FOOD HARVESTED FROM NATURAL ECOSYSTEMS

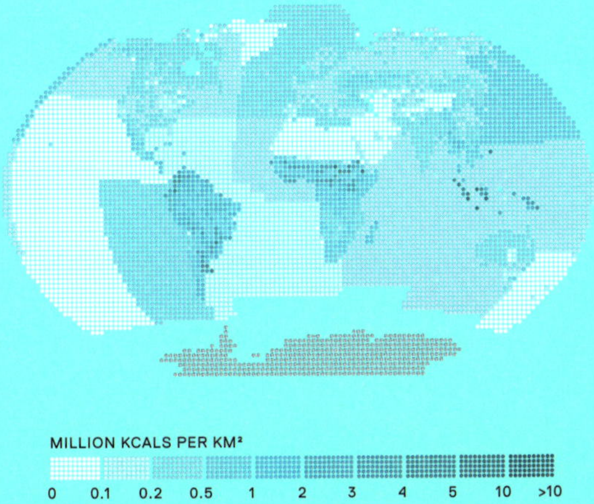

BIODIVERSITY

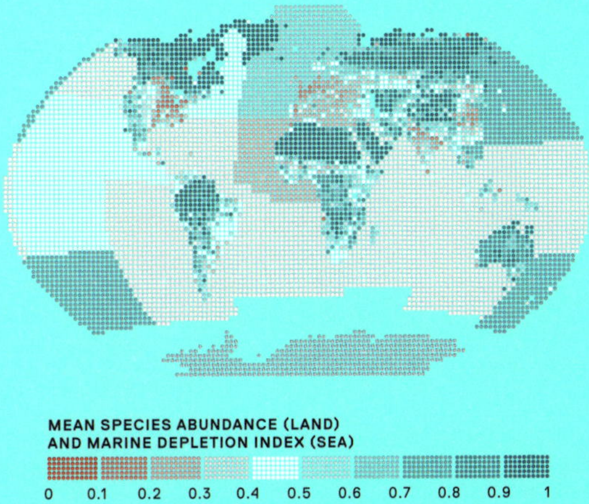

NO DATA

5.4 / HOMO SAPIENS IS THE DOMINANT SPECIES

Homo sapiens have spread all over the world and dominate every biotope. Biodiversity is decreasing; natural areas are becoming more and more uniform. The service-providing capacity of nature is not endless. The question is where does natural resource utilisation end and overexploitation begin?

Sources: FAO, PBL, PBL/UBC

5.5 / NATURE AS AN URBAN DWELLER

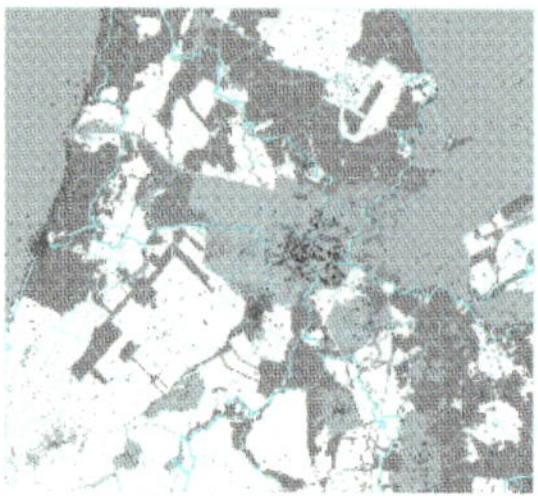

Nature and cities are often regarded as mutually exclusive, as two opposites that cannot go together. In fact, they are closely interlinked. Cities offer a diversity of habitat conditions that favour particular species. Most nature lovers among homo sapiens actually also live in cities. Historical city centres have much to offer to nature, and this is even more true for the larger urban landscape. In the Netherlands, species richness in urbanised areas is often larger than in rural areas where monoculture farming dominates.

For example, the city of Amsterdam not only accommodates 800,000 inhabitants and millions of tourists, but also a variety of ecosystems with many different plants and animals. Most of these species move freely across city borders to use the habitat possibilities offered by the greater Amsterdam metropolitan area. This area extends from the North Sea coast (between Zandvoort and Bakkum) into the Flevopolder, and from Waterland to Amsterdam Airport Schiphol and beyond.

Urban areas provide a suitable habitat for a range of species, thanks to the presence of surface water, microclimatic differences, monumental trees, food, and an enormous diversity of structures and building materials. Species living within the municipal boundaries of Amsterdam include the grass snake, the peregrine falcon and rare wall ferns, such as the rustyback, hart's-tongue fern and black spleenwort.

Hence, cities not only serve as centres of human society, but also offer a relatively new and dynamic landscape with many habitat opportunities for other species. In cities, nature is not a distant stranger but a fellow inhabitant.

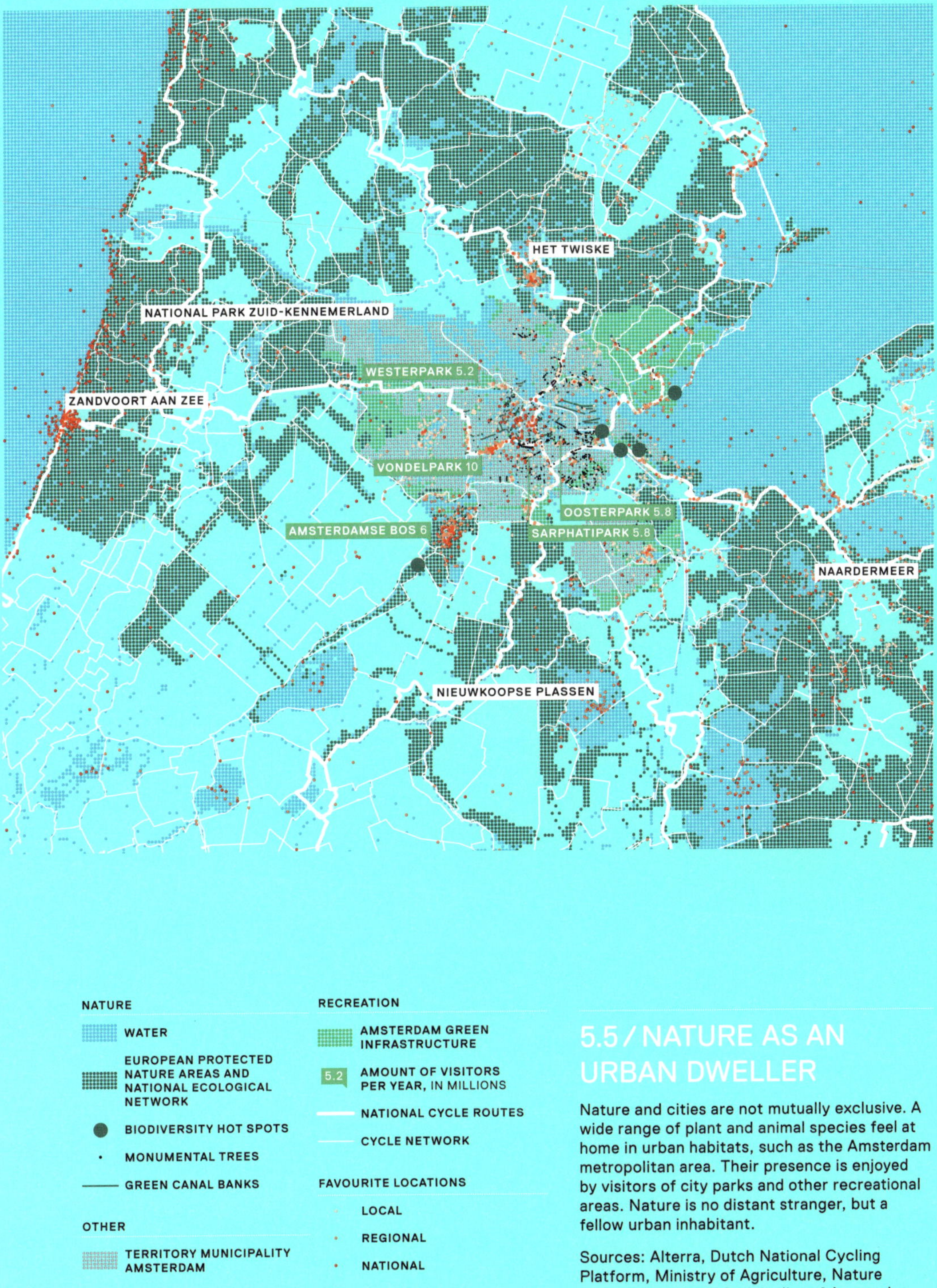

5.5 / NATURE AS AN URBAN DWELLER

Nature and cities are not mutually exclusive. A wide range of plant and animal species feel at home in urban habitats, such as the Amsterdam metropolitan area. Their presence is enjoyed by visitors of city parks and other recreational areas. Nature is no distant stranger, but a fellow urban inhabitant.

Sources: Alterra, Dutch National Cycling Platform, Ministry of Agriculture, Nature and Food Quality, Municipality of Amsterdam, PBL, RUG/PBL/Alterra

Human beings are social 'animals' who need contact with other human beings. The foundation for people's well-being, their culture and prosperity of society rests on social interaction. This requires distances to be traversed – either small or large, even to the other side of the world. With increasing prosperity comes more mobility, but this also leads to greater complexity for travelling and to more questions, for example, about the safety and environmental consequences.

6.1 / THE ERA OF THE CAR

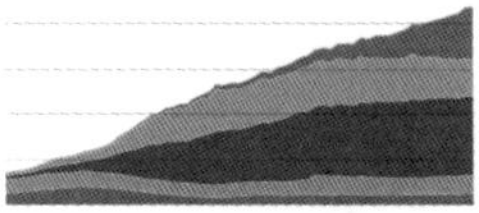

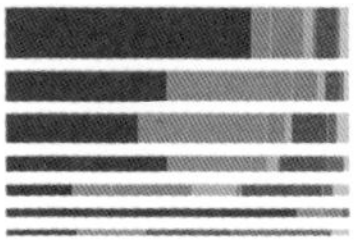

Over the past century, the amount of travel by the Dutch has steadily increased. Today, they travel an average 42 kilometres, per person, per day (including air travel). This is twice the amount of 1970 and six times that of 1950. However, the time they spend travelling has hardly changed over the years; since 1985, people in the Netherlands spend around one hour per day travelling.

Travelling more kilometres within the same amount of time became a possibility with the arrival of the car. The number of passenger vehicles increased from less than 150,000 in 1950 to 8 million today. The car, currently, is used in three quarters of all journeys within the Netherlands, and usually the driver is the only occupant. Leisure trips most frequently include passengers.

The car is used in more than half of all business and commuting trips. For trips to school, university or other educational purposes, cycling, public transport and walking are the most common ways to travel. The use of public transport, over the years, has remained relatively stabile, with an impulse early in the 1990s due to the introduction of the student travel card. On average the Dutch travel around 4 kilometres per day by public transport, 75% of which by train.

Bicycle use steadily increased up to 1960, followed by a steep decrease in favour of the passenger car, with national levels having remained relatively stable since the late 1970s. Bicycles have become more popular again, in recent times; on average, the Dutch travel around 2.5 kilometres by bicycle, per day. This is a lot, from an international perspective.

Air travel, in particular since 1990, has increased spectacularly, as a result of cheap air fares and a growing economy. The Dutch fly an average of more than 3500 kilometres per year, which is close to 10 kilometres per day.

6.2 / BACK AND FORTH

People are creatures of habit. They move according to certain patterns: from home to school or work and back again. And, from time to time, they make trips back and forth to, for example, city centres, fun parks, furniture malls, airports and beaches. The best-known pattern is that of the commute; many people travel to work around the same time in the morning, and return home again, en masse. This is not a new pattern; for centuries, a steady flow of workers twice a day has been lining the streets. What has changed since the arrival of the car is the radius within which commuter traffic takes place. In the past, people tended to live and work in the same city, whereas today residential and employment locations are often much further apart. The area in which citizens operate – the *daily urban system* – is more extensive than ever before.

Commuters in cars, on average, spend half an hour getting to work (or going home again). For those travelling by public transport, travel times are longer, for cyclists they are shorter. Commuters, on average, travel around 18 kilometres, twice a day. The Randstad (conurbation in the Netherlands, consisting of the four largest cities of Amsterdam, Rotterdam, The Hague and Utrecht, and their surrounding areas) takes in an exceptional position among commuter patterns. A large share of employment is concentrated in the Randstad, which is why commuter flows are far larger here than elsewhere in the country. If their employment is located near an inter-city railway station, people tend to travel by public transport. About twenty per cent of the kilometres travelled within the Randstad is by public transport and between the four large cities this share is close to 50%. Outside the Randstad, the public transport share is around 10%.

However, there are also large differences within the Randstad. For example, in the northern part, Amsterdam, being the main employment city, draws people from the entire region, while in the Southern part of the Randstad there is not much difference between the main cities Rotterdam and the Hague, which are very similar as employment locations. Utrecht, however, because of its central location within the

DAILY DISTANCE TRAVELLED PER DUTCH INHABITANT, BY MAIN TRANSPORT MODES

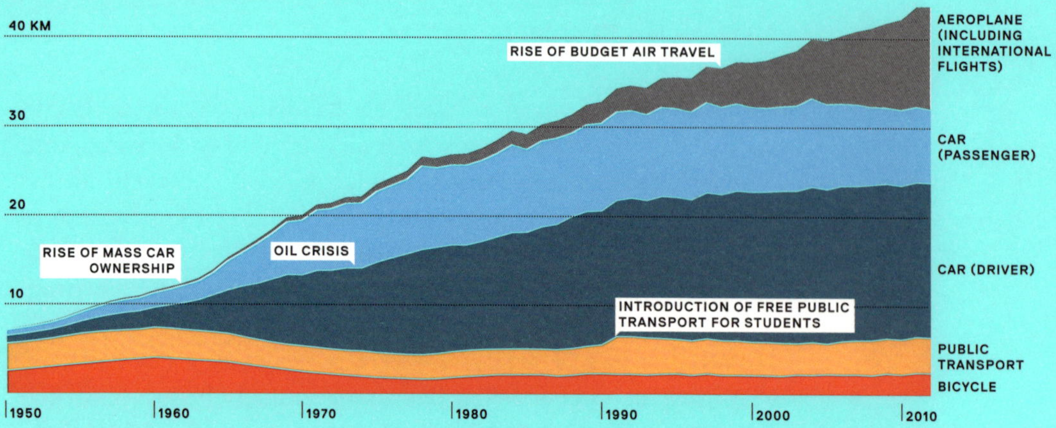

DISTANCE TRAVELLED PER PERSON, PER DAY, BY PURPOSE AND BY MODE OF TRANSPORT (2012, AIR TRAVEL EXCLUDED)

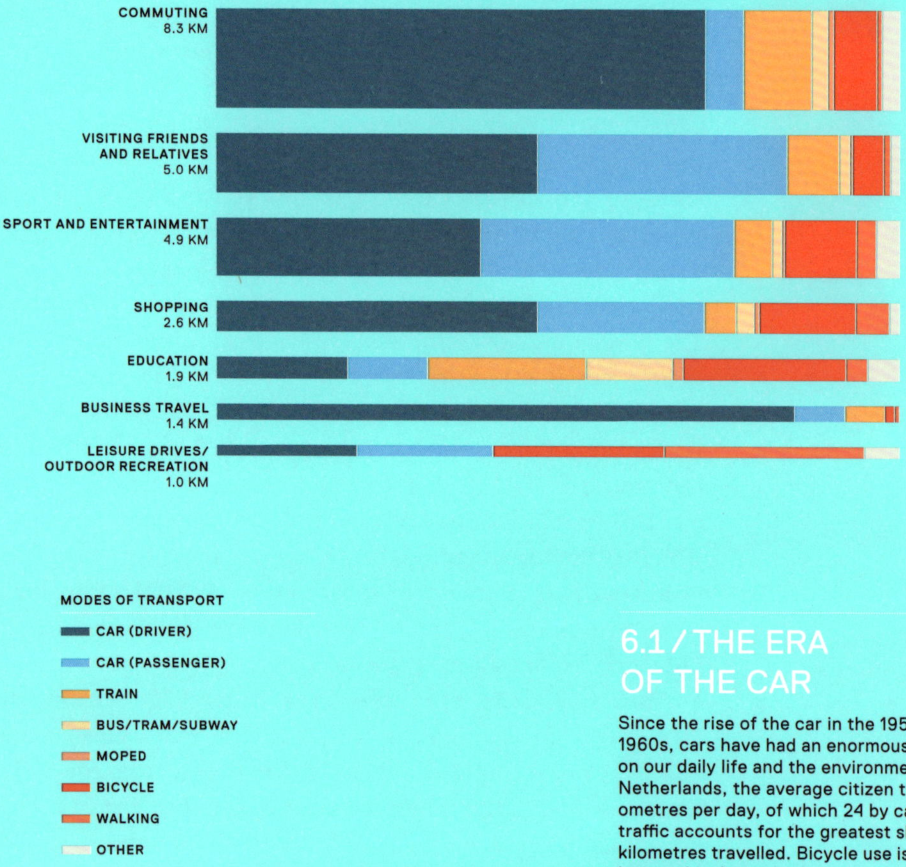

6.1 / THE ERA OF THE CAR

Since the rise of the car in the 1950s and 1960s, cars have had an enormous influence on our daily life and the environment. In the Netherlands, the average citizen travels 42 kilometres per day, of which 24 by car. Commuter traffic accounts for the greatest share of the kilometres travelled. Bicycle use is high, by international standards.

Sources: Amsterdam Airport Schiphol, CBS, KiM, RWS

AVERAGE ANNUAL COMMUTER TRAFFIC BETWEEN MUNICIPALITIES (2004–2012) / **PERCENTAGE OF COMMUTERS, BY MUNICIPALITY OF RESIDENCE** (2011)

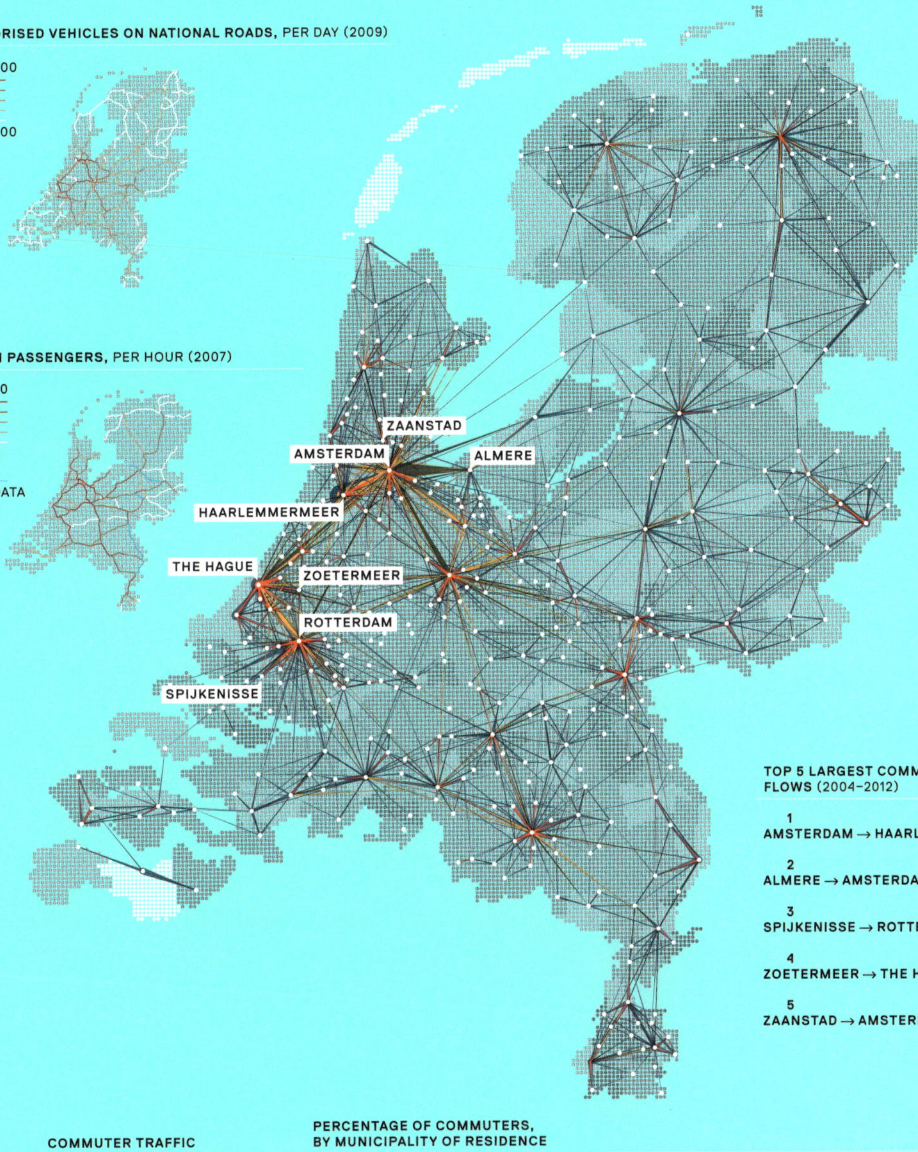

MOTORISED VEHICLES ON NATIONAL ROADS, PER DAY (2009)

>80 000

<20 000

TRAIN PASSENGERS, PER HOUR (2007)

>2000

<250

NO DATA

TOP 5 LARGEST COMMUTER FLOWS (2004–2012)

1
AMSTERDAM → HAARLEMMERMEER

2
ALMERE → AMSTERDAM

3
SPIJKENISSE → ROTTERDAM

4
ZOETERMEER → THE HAGUE

5
ZAANSTAD → AMSTERDAM

COMMUTER TRAFFIC

- 150 000 JOURNEYS, PER YEAR
- 5.5 MILLION JOURNEYS, PER YEAR
- CENTRE OF MUNICIPALITY
- HOME
- WORK
- CAR
- PUBLIC TRANSPORT
- SLOW (NON-MOTORISED) MODES

PERCENTAGE OF COMMUTERS, BY MUNICIPALITY OF RESIDENCE

0 25 50 75 100%

6.2 / BACK AND FORTH

Travel movements largely follow fixed patterns, such as the daily trips to work and school. The commuting map of the Netherlands clearly shows high traffic intensities around the larger cities and in the Randstad conurbation. Public transport connections between cities are also used intensively.

Sources: CBS, Deltarail/Prorail, Goudappel Coffeng/RWS – adaptation by PBL railway system, attracts relatively many commuters from further away.

A number of large, relatively young cities in the Netherlands have a notably large share of commuters. Examples are Spijkenisse and Zoetermeer, which were originally developed as growth areas for Rotterdam and The Hague, respectively. Another one of these *new towns* is Almere that, together with Zaanstad, is focused on Amsterdam. Furthermore, there is the commuter flow between Amsterdam and Haarlemmermeer (Amsterdam Airport Schiphol), which is one of the largest in the country.

6.3 / EVER-DENSER WEBS

Mobility has increased enormously, over the last century; partly as the result of a spectacular expansion of infrastructure. The motorway network grew from less than 500 kilometres in 1960 to over 2300 kilometres in 2010. More recently, although the network is hardly being expanded in length, lanes are being added. Well-known example is the A2 between Amsterdam and Utrecht, which was recently widened from three to five lanes in both directions.

The railway network has grown considerably less, since 1960. Some railway lines, stations and rail types (Hanzelijn, HSL, metro, Randstad rail) were added, but other disappeared, such as the rail service to IJmuiden and the lines between Apeldoorn and Dieren en between 's-Hertogenbosch and Lage Zwaluwe.

In total, today, there are 3268 kilometres of national roads (motorways and national highways), 6713 kilometres of provincial roads, 3013 kilometres of railways (including for freight), 612 motorway exits, and 406 railway stations.

City and infrastructure are closely interwoven. Infrastructural expansions and increase in the number of motor vehicles has enabled a different urban and spatial development. Distances between homes and employment locations, shops and other facilities were able to become larger, as these could easily be reached by car. In the 1950s and 1960s, new suburbs along the edges of cities were designed with the passenger car in mind: parking spaces very close to residences, wide streets and access roads. From the 1970s onwards, attempts were made to give cars a less dominating position within residential areas, in order for children to play outside more safely. The 'woonerf' is a well-known example of this.

Inner cities, which previously had been adapted to create space for the busy traffic, changed their traffic policies in the 1970s in a counter movement to turn these inner cities back into pleasant areas for people to be in. Car access was reduced via pedestrian zones, car-free squares and shopping streets, traffic circulation plans, and paid parking areas. Where possible, parking was moved underground or in parking buildings.

In contrast, many motorways have become more 'urban' in character. Up to the 1970s, motorways mostly were endless stretches of lanes that cut through rural green areas, at a fair distance from cities. To a large degree, these green areas have since been built-up. Motorways have become popular locations for companies, shops, schools and hospitals; there are no other locations where employment has increased as much as near motorway exits. Over the past decade, employment increased the most around the Oudenrijn motorway junction (A2/A12), along the A2 at Veldhoven, the A9 at Amsterdam Zuidoost and along the A4 at Amsterdam Riekerpolder.

Railway stations are also changing their appearance. From being purely a place where travellers pass through, they are changing to become a mixed urban environment with a large variety of shops, restaurants and bars, companies and services. The immediate vicinity of the larger stations is also changing. Industry and transport – traditionally located close to the railways – are giving way to office buildings ('s-Hertogenbosch), hospitals (Leiden) and government (The Hague Central Station).

Furthermore, the airport infrastructure has also expanded, considerably, since 1960. Amsterdam Airport Schiphol has added a new runway, nearly every decade, and substantially expanded its terminals. Since the early 1990s, also regional airports, such as Eindhoven Airport, are experiencing

INFRASTRUCTURE DEVELOPMENT

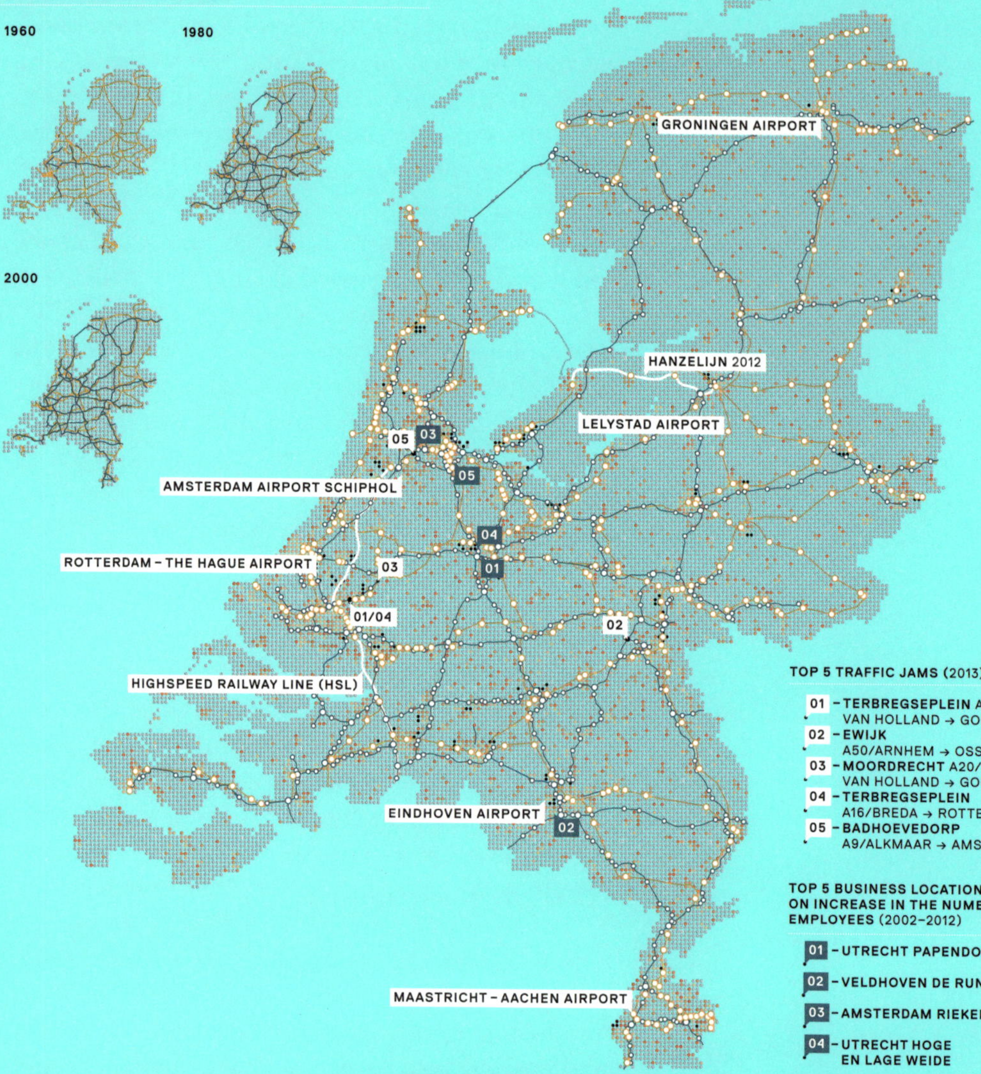

TOP 5 TRAFFIC JAMS (2013)

01 – **TERBREGSEPLEIN** A20/HOEK VAN HOLLAND → GOUDA
02 – **EWIJK** A50/ARNHEM → OSS
03 – **MOORDRECHT** A20/HOEK VAN HOLLAND → GOUDA
04 – **TERBREGSEPLEIN** A16/BREDA → ROTTERDAM
05 – **BADHOEVEDORP** A9/ALKMAAR → AMSTELVEEN

TOP 5 BUSINESS LOCATIONS, BASED ON INCREASE IN THE NUMBER OF EMPLOYEES (2002–2012)

01 – **UTRECHT PAPENDORP**
02 – **VELDHOVEN DE RUN**
03 – **AMSTERDAM RIEKERPOLDER**
04 – **UTRECHT HOGE EN LAGE WEIDE**
05 – **AMSTERDAM ZUIDOOST**

INFRASTRUCTURE

- RAILROAD
- NEW RAILROAD
- TRAIN STATION
- MOTORWAY
- MOTORWAY EXIT
- MOTORWAY JUNCTION

URBANISATION

GROWTH URBAN AREA

1960 1980 2000 2010

INDUSTRIAL/ BUSINESS AREA (2010)

URBAN EXPANSION AREA (VINEX)

6.3 / EVER-DENSER WEBS

Mobility could grow over the last century, among other things, because of an expanding infrastructure. Since 1960, the Dutch motorway network has grown by some 2000 kilometres, while lanes also were added. A growing number of urban activities are located around sliproads, railway stations and airports. Regional airports are more and more popular with low-cost carriers.

Sources: Alterra – adaptation by PBL, CBS, LISA, PBL, RWS

spectacular growth. Because of the implementation of one European airspace, regional airports, because they are relatively cheap, became more attractive to the smaller airlines.

6.4 / FROM 1 TO 3 BILLION CARS

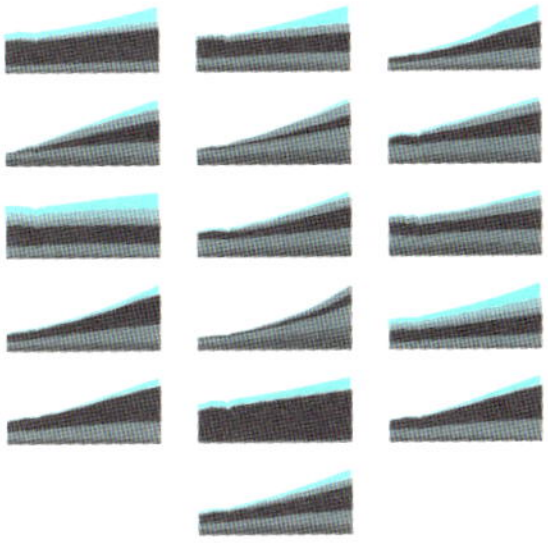

For decades, the car's popularity only increased. This unbridled rise seems to have come to an end in Western countries. Many city councils are striving to provide more room for bicyclists and public transport. New York City has constructed special bicycle paths along main roads, Paris is developing the 'Green Seine' and London has futuristic plans to develop elevated 'SkyCycle' bicycle routes above the city.

All these efforts, however, pale in comparison to the ongoing increase in the number of cars on a global scale. In Asia, cars are on the march, and a comparable growth may be expected in Africa. Car use is also strongly increasing in Central and South America. On a global level, the bus is also a popular transport mode with a stable growth rate, and high speed rail also has an important position, particularly in Western Europe, Oceania and Japan.

The global number of cars is projected to increase from 1 billion today, to 2.5 to 3 billion around 2050. Together, these cars will travel an estimated 50,000 billion kilometres per year, more than double the current amount. In 2013, Dutch cars together travelled close to 100 billion kilometres.

Growth takes place particularly in urban areas; not in the last place because, by 2050, two thirds of the world population is expected to be living in those areas. Similar to the situation in Europe, the rise of automotive transportation will also have substantial impacts on the functioning and appearance of cities elsewhere. Individual freedom of movement is increased, and allows urban areas to expand and stretch out. As a result, these areas increasingly will be faced with the consequences, in the form of congestion, parking problems, fuel use, CO_2 emissions and air quality issues.

TOTAL DEVELOPMENT OF MOBILITY, IN TRILLION PERSON KILOMETRES PER YEAR

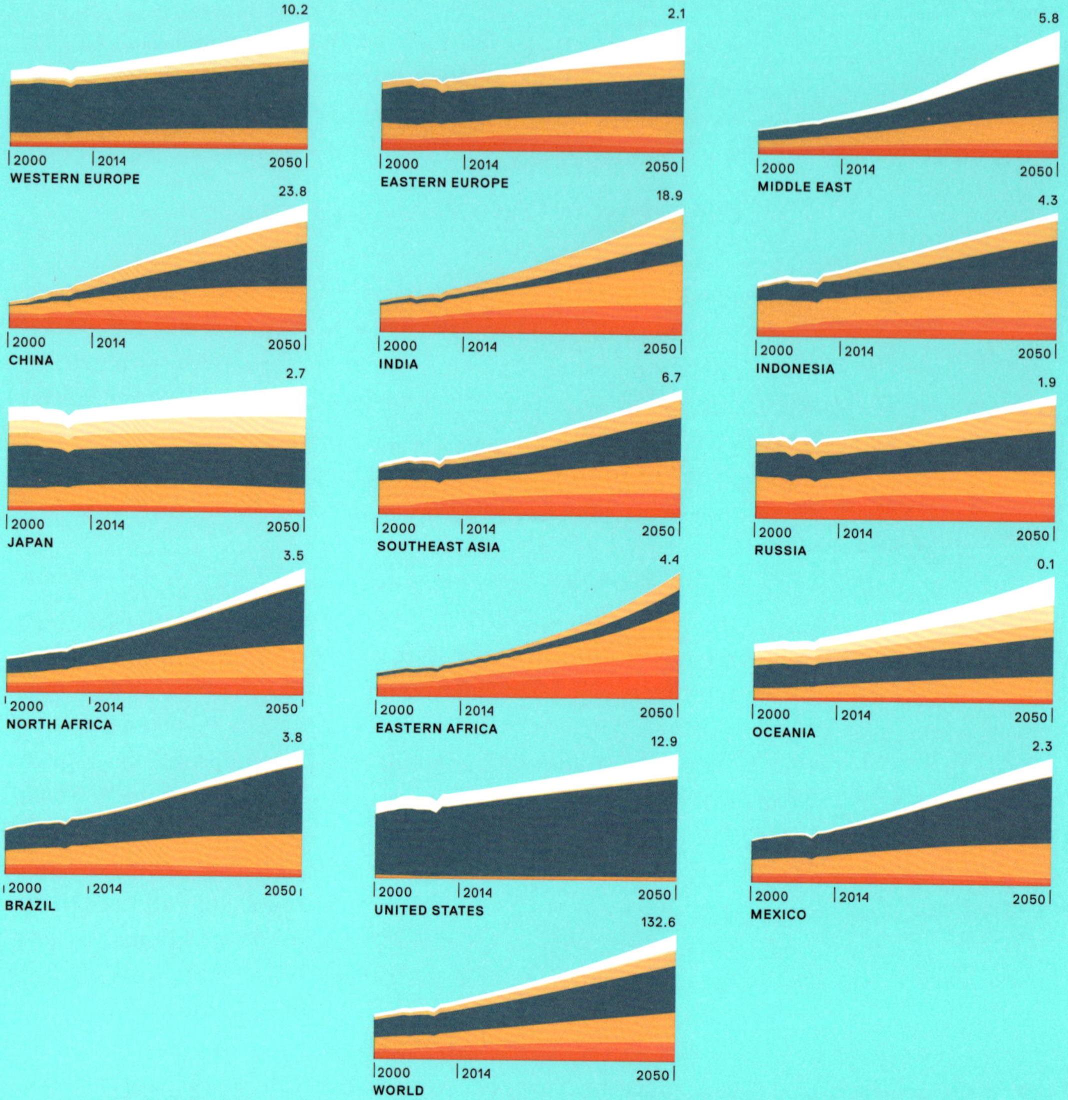

MODES OF TRANSPORT

- AEROPLANE
- HIGH SPEED TRAIN
- TRAIN
- CAR
- BUS
- BICYCLE
- WALKING

6.4 / FROM 1 TO 3 BILLION CARS

Western cities are trying to curb car dominance in city traffic, but elsewhere cars remain on the rise as a symbol of progress. The global car fleet is expected to triple from one billion today to three billion by 2050, and so are the issues related to environment and accessibility.

Source: OECD

ACCESSIBILITY AS A FUNCTION OF PROXIMITY AND TRAVEL SPEED (2008)

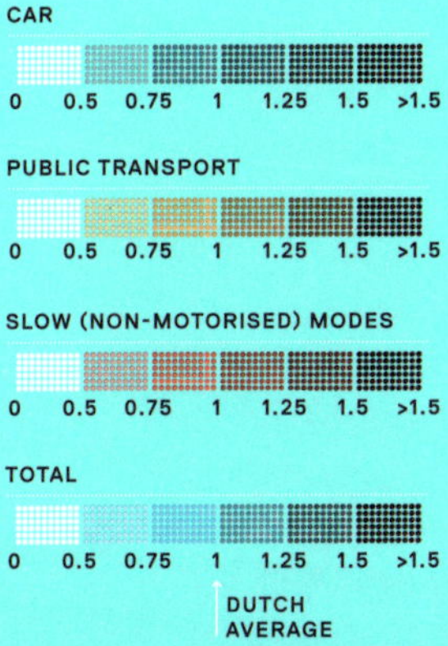

6.5 / GETTING TO WHERE YOU ARE GOING

Travel speeds are lower in the Randstad conurbation than elsewhere in the Netherlands, but within the same timespan, five times as many jobs can be reached. Viewed this way, the mobility of Randstad residents is greater. When considering both travel speed and proximity to destinations, new possibilities emerge for improving accessibility.

Source: PBL

6.5 / GETTING TO WHERE YOU ARE GOING

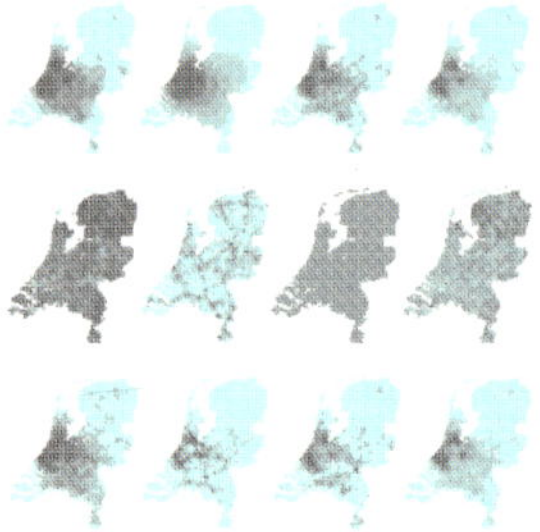

People wish to travel from A to B, preferably as fast as possible. This can be done with a fast car along a road without traffic jams or traffic lights. But short travel times can also be achieved if A and B are located close together.

In the Randstad conurbation, for example, cars are less able to speed up than outside this region; on average, travel times are around 15% shorter than in the Randstad for car travellers in the Dutch provinces of Groningen, Friesland, Drenthe and Zeeland. On the other hand, in the Randstad, compared to elsewhere, there are up to five times the number of employment opportunities close by. In addition, shopping centres and theatres also are close by. The close vicinity of a variety of destinations is an important factor in the economic power of the Randstad; the somewhat slower travel speeds hardly alter that fact.

Over the past decades, accessibility policy has mainly focused on solving congestion on main roads; thus, on improving travel speeds. Substantial investments in this area have led to good results, but also to added mobility and even to new congestion, often at other locations.

However, if not only travel speed but also the vicinity of destinations is taken as a measure, new options emerge for improving accessibility. Having housing, employment and facilities nearby would improve accessibility of these destinations and help reduce vehicle kilometres travelled. Infrastructure connecting all these places, of course, is essential. This would offer people a wider range of choices; not only in destinations but also in modes of transport. They would be able to walk or cycle from A to B more often, or have the option of using high quality public transport, such as trams and metros. Added advantage would be a reduced dependence on the car, in everyday life.

Cities have always been nodes in trade networks. They developed and prospered near road junctions, river fords, sea coasts and strategic halting places along trade routes. In their market squares, goods from nearby or far away, such as food, fuel and building materials, were sold to traders and citizens. And in their harbour warehouses, stocks were stored to be shipped at the most profitable moment.

Today these patterns can still be recognised, even though the nature and volume of goods transport have changed radically, just like the nature and size of cities. The function of market squares has been taken over by international commodity exchanges; large seaports and airports have become the central nodes in a trade network gone global. The Netherlands, one of the most urbanised countries in the world, occupies a special position in this network, thanks to its strategic location in the delta of the Rhine and Meuse rivers.

7.1 / 273 KG OF CARGO PER PERSON PER DAY

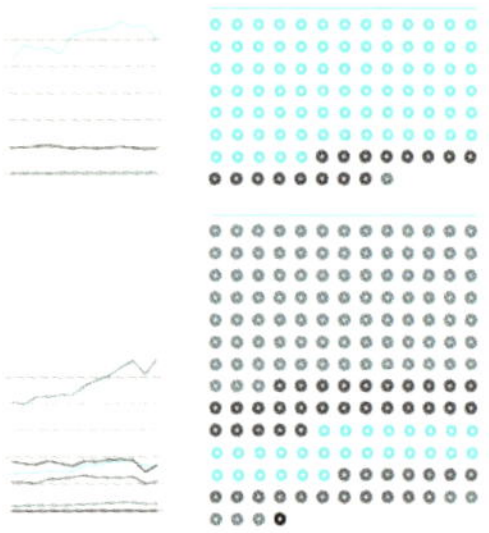

Each year, 1.6 billion tonnes of cargo are transported across Dutch territory. This is equal to 4.5 million tonnes per day, or 273 kg per capita per day. Of this amount 100 kg stays within the borders, while 173 kg either enters or leaves the country as import, export or transit goods.

The market for domestic transport is dominated by road transport, which carries 500 million tonnes per year. Sea and inland shipping play a major role in international transport, moving 570 million and 170 million tonnes of cargo per year, respectively. Compared to these volumes the tonnage transported by air is negligible; Schiphol Airport handles only 2 million tonnes of cargo per year.

In economic terms, however, air transport is a heavyweight; it generates 17% of the value added in the transport and storage sector as a whole. In 2010, the total value added in this sector was 52 billion euros, 21 billion of which was generated by road transport, 9 billion by air transport, and 5 billion by water transport. The remaining 17 billion was earned with logistical, postal and courier services.

Cargo transport is inextricably linked to economic development in general and global trade in particular. This was clearly shown by the sharp decline in international shipping in 2009 as a result of the economic crisis. The crisis also caused a significant drop in domestic road transport in the Netherlands in 2010.

7.2 / A GLOBAL DISTRIBUTION HUB

The Netherlands is eminently suited for cargo distribution. Situated in a delta of large rivers in a strategic corner of western Europe, the country is an important node in international cargo flows. Its geographical location is ideal for transhipment, the transfer of cargo between sea and inland shipping. Favourable tax rates and other measures also contribute to an attractive trading environment.

DOMESTIC CARGO,
IN MILLION TONNES PER YEAR

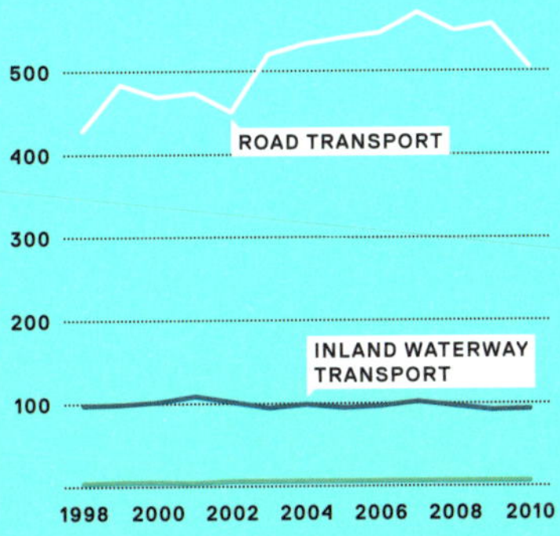

CARGO TRANSPORT IN THE NETHERLANDS, IN KG PER CAPITA, PER DAY (2010)

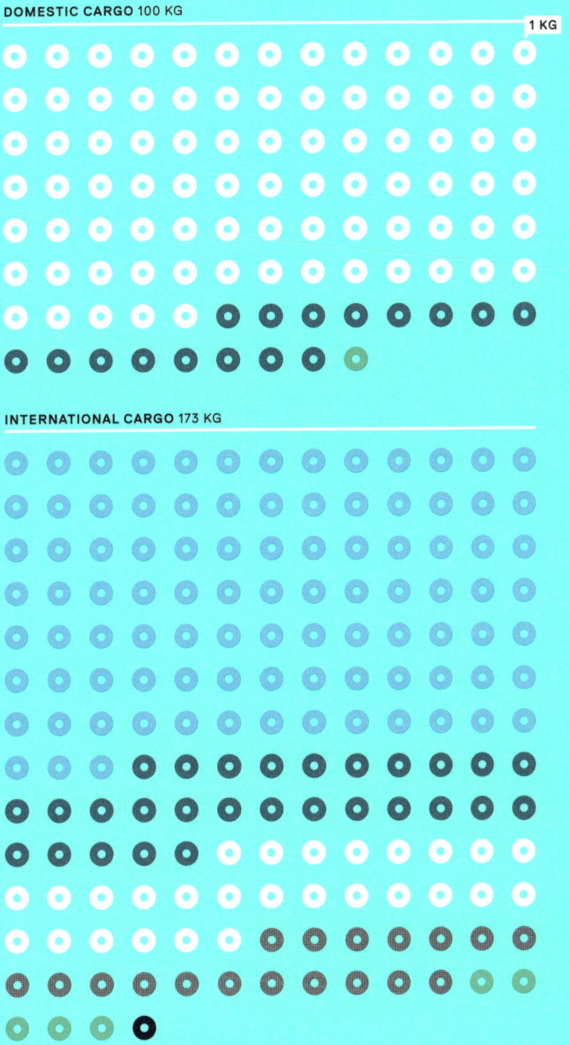

INTERNATIONAL CARGO,
IN MILLION TONNES PER YEAR

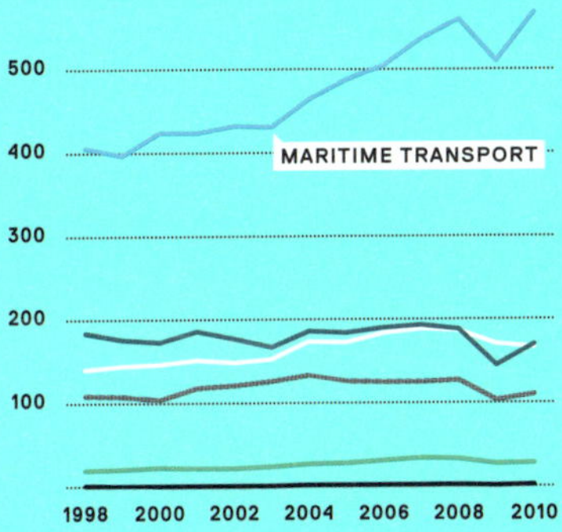

TRANSPORT MODES

7.1 / 273 KG OF CARGO PER PERSON PER DAY

Each year, 1.6 billion tonnes of cargo are transported across Dutch territory. Domestic cargo is moved mostly by road; international cargo mostly by boat. Air cargo is modest in volume but significant in economic terms. The amount of cargo fluctuates in response to the economic climate, as the drop after 2008 shows.

Sources: CBS – adaptation by PBL, CBS/PBL/WUR

IMPORT AND EXPORT IN THE NETHERLANDS, IN MILLION TONNES (2010)

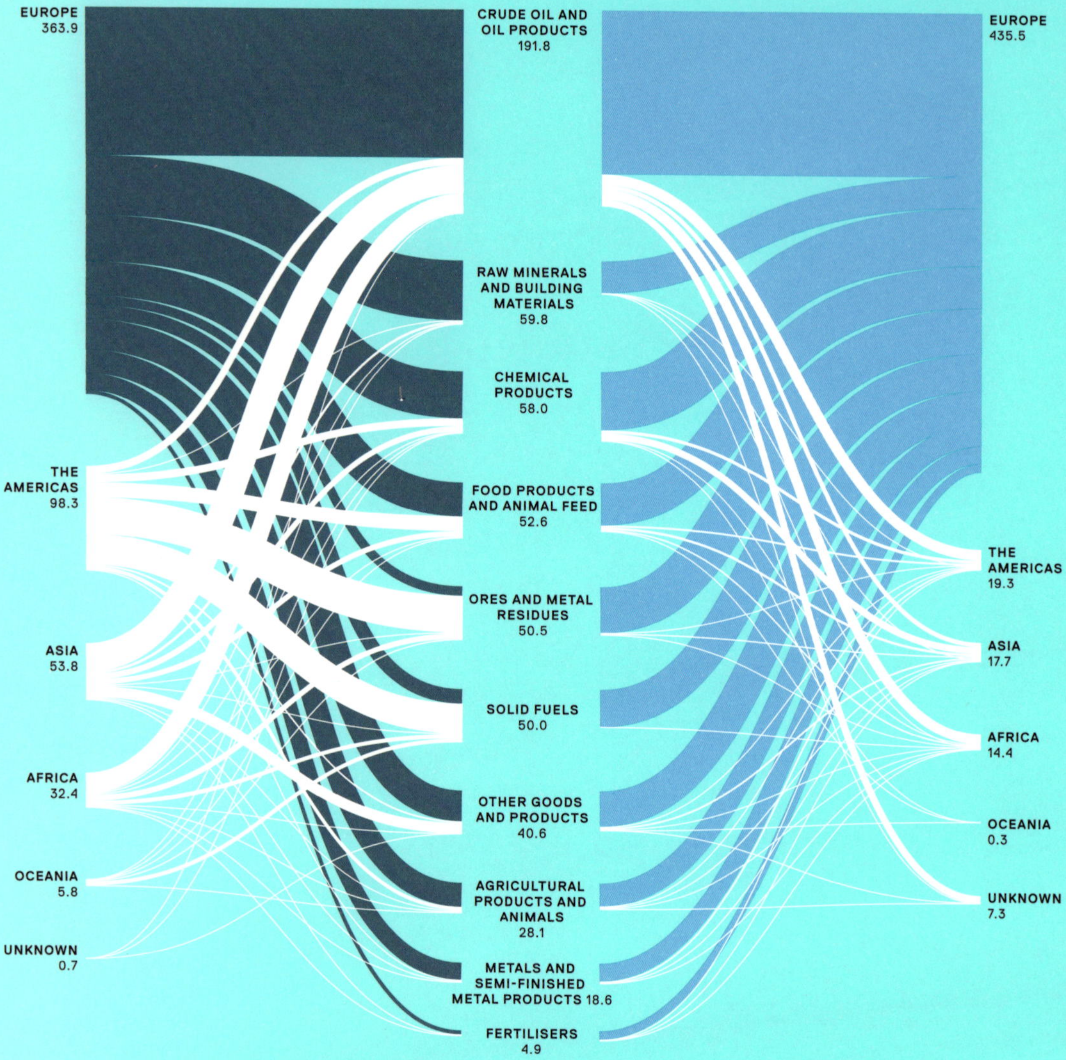

7.2 / A GLOBAL DISTRIBUTION HUB

The Netherlands is eminently suited for cargo distribution. Thanks to its strategic location, the country is an important node in global cargo flows. Many goods are forwarded immediately. Other goods are processed first and then re-exported. To maintain its competitive position, the Netherlands has invested heavily in cargo hubs ('mainports') and infrastructure.

Source: CBS – adaptation by PBL

The Low Countries already took advantage of this geographical position back in the fifteenth and sixteenth centuries, at the time of the Baltic trade. In the following centuries new trade opportunities continued to open up, for example in the nineteenth century when the German Ruhr region industrialised.

Today the Dutch economy still depends to a significant degree on the import, export and transit of goods and raw materials, particularly petroleum and solid fuels. Cargo from all over the world arrives in the Dutch ports, to be transported on to other European countries. Some goods and raw materials are refined or processed first before further transport takes place.

Just like in the past, the Dutch government plays an active role in promoting and improving the strategic trading position of the Netherlands. In the 1980s it launched a national investment policy under the motto of "The Netherlands, distribution country". As part of this policy, significant investments have been made in infrastructure and major cargo hubs such as the Port of Rotterdam and Amsterdam Airport Schiphol (known in the Netherlands as 'mainports').

7.3 / TRANSPORT CALLS FOR INFRASTRUCTURE, AND VICE VERSA

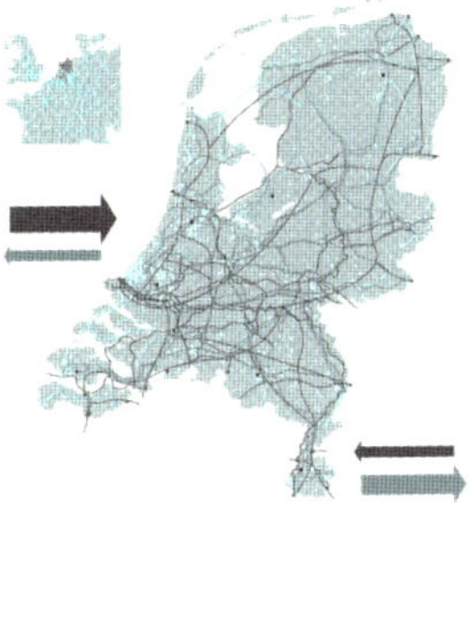

The Netherlands takes advantage of its favourable position as gateway between the European hinterland and the rest of the world. The Port of Rotterdam is Europe's largest port; Schiphol is the third largest cargo airport.

The logistic performance of these 'mainports' hinges on the Dutch infrastructure of roads, railways and waterways. From the 1980s, major infrastructure investments have been made in anticipation of – and as an incentive for – future cargo growth. Projects included the construction of a freight railway from Rotterdam to Germany (the Betuwelijn), the rerouting of the Zuid-Willemsvaart canal near the city of Den Bosch, the construction of a new port and related infrastructure on reclaimed land (Maasvlakte 2), the widening of the A15 motorway, and the construction of a new runway at Amsterdam Airport Schiphol (the Polderbaan).

MAIN INFRASTRUCTURE FOR CARGO TRANSPORT (2010)

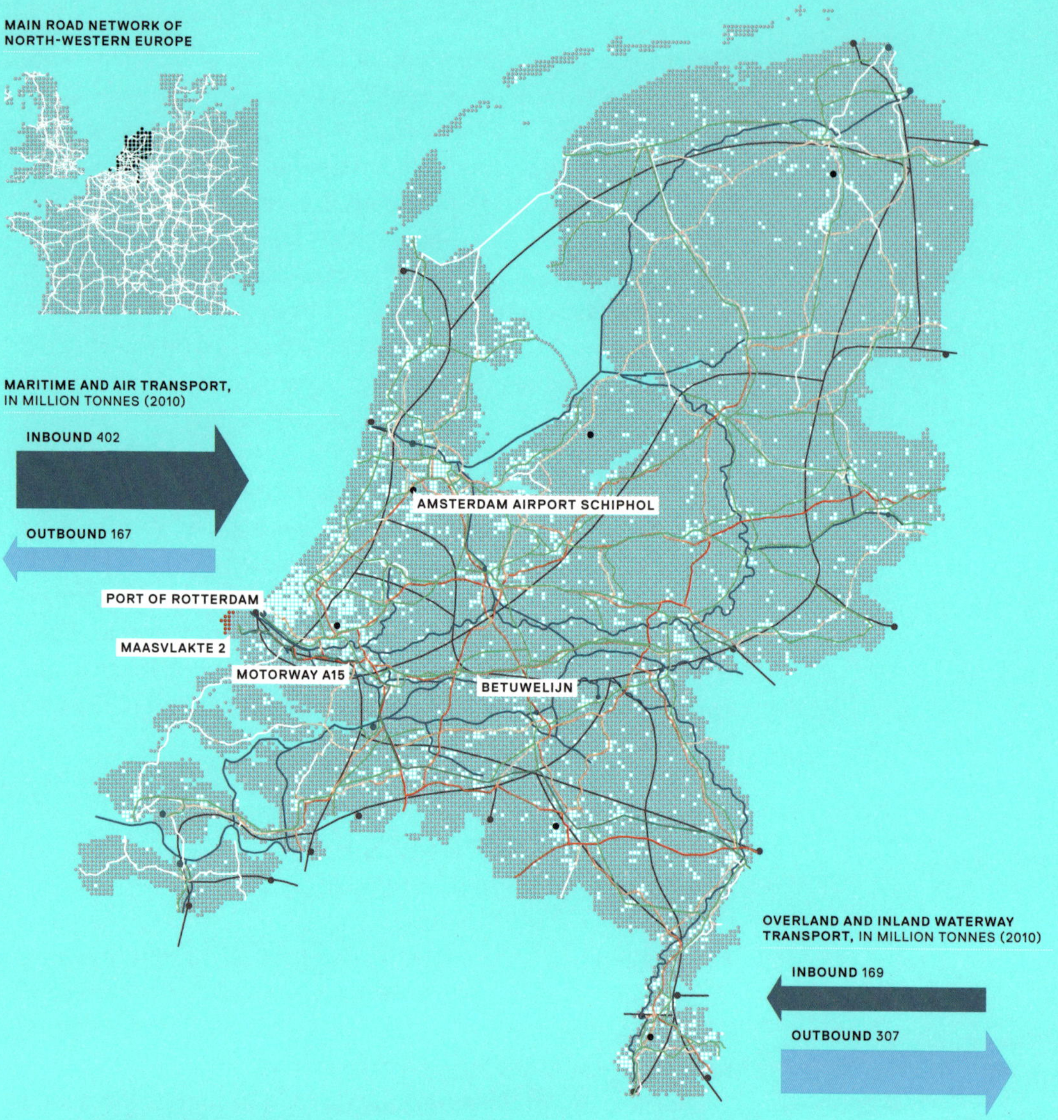

MAIN INFRASTRUCTURE FOR CARGO TRANSPORT (2010)

- AIRPORT
- SEAPORT
- INLAND PORT
- WATERWAY
- GAS PIPELINE
- GAS ENTRY POINT

ROAD AND RAIL FREIGHT TRAFFIC, IN VEHICLES PER DAY (2007)

ROADS

0 1000 2000 3000 4000 5000 >5000

RAILROADS

0 1000 2000 3000

OTHER

URBAN AREA

7.3 / TRANSPORT CALLS FOR INFRASTRUCTURE, AND VICE VERSA

Good transport links to the European hinterland are vital for the Dutch 'mainports' (Port of Rotterdam, Amsterdam Airport Schiphol). Significant infrastructural investments have been made to stimulate further economic growth and further enable cargo transport. The Dutch landscape between the 'mainports' and their hinterland has one of the densest infrastructures in Europe.

Sources: CBS, Deltarail/Prorail, Eurostat RWS – all adapted by PBL

These investments are based on the assumption that cargo transport will keep growing, and that improved infrastructure will attract additional economic and transport activity. The social return of these investments thus depends on the extent to which growth is actually realised. This in turn depends on factors over which the Netherlands has no control. The difficulties surrounding the connection of the Betuwelijn to the German rail network are a case in point.

Infrastructure has an enormous spatial impact. The landscape between the Port of Rotterdam and the east and south of the Netherlands already had one of the densest infrastructures of Europe, and this has only intensified. The improved infrastructure does enable smooth and efficient transport of goods, but the environmental impact – noise, air pollution, spatial fragmentation – is considerable.

7.4 / DISTANCE BETWEEN PRODUCTION AND CONSUMPTION

Cargo transport is increasing worldwide. This is not only the result of economic growth and global trade expansion, but also due to innovations within the transport sector. Thanks to scaling-up and efficiency improvements cargo transport has become progressively cheaper. The most spectacular results have been achieved in shipping. Shipping costs have decreased so much that their influence on the price of many products has become negligible. Today, transport costs make up only 3% of the price of consumer goods. Hence, in Dutch supermarkets, apples produced in New Zealand (20,000 kilometres away) cost the same as apples produced in the Dutch province of Zeeland (200 kilometres away). Because of decreasing transport costs, manufacturing has gradually moved to countries with low wages and less stringent environmental regulations, during the last fifty years. As a result, the geographical distance between production and consumption has grown considerably.

Global trade promotes economic development and international relations, but also has its downsides. Goods imported

DUTCH IMPORT AND EXPORT OF GOODS (2012)

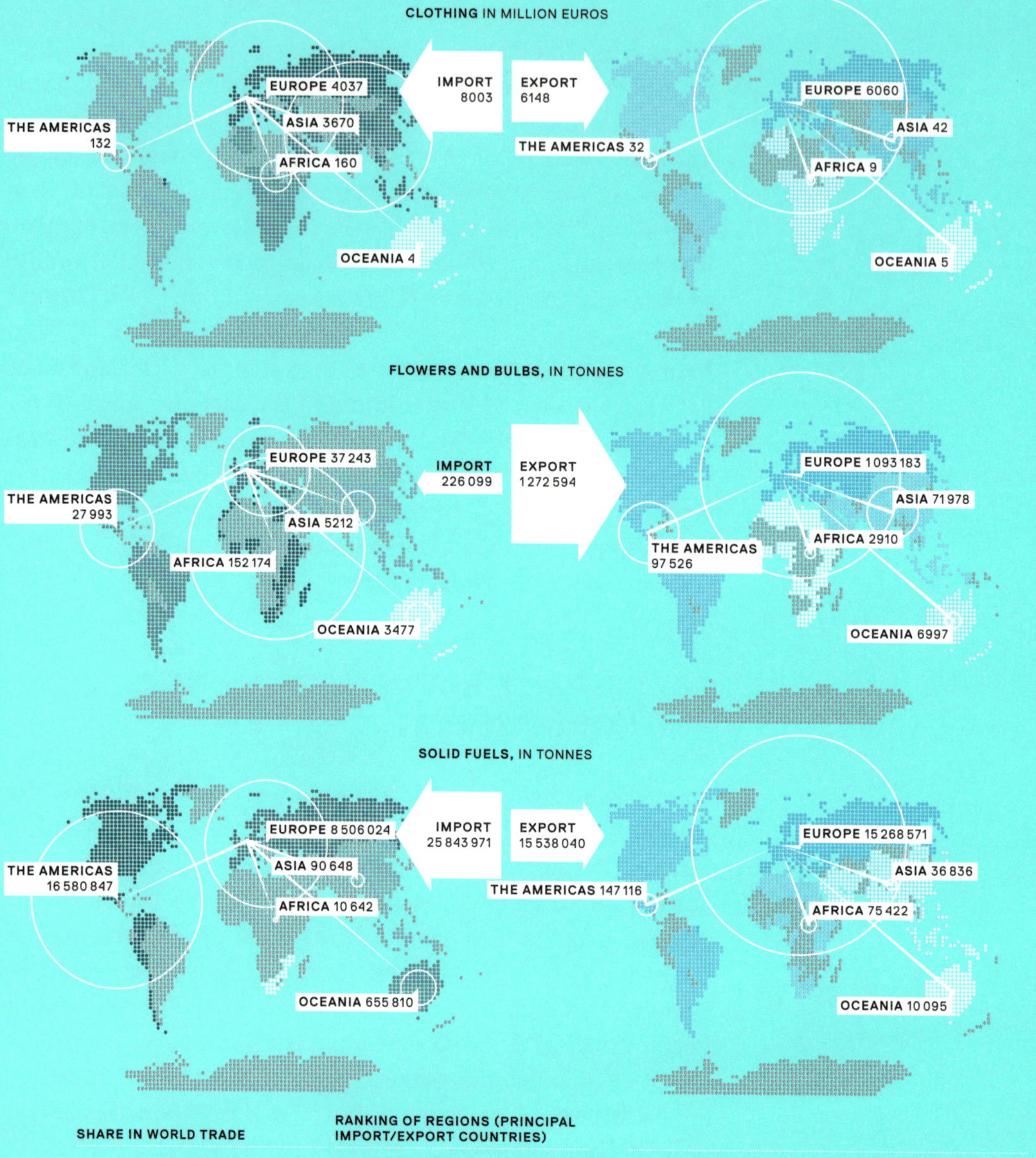

7.4 / DISTANCE BETWEEN PRODUCTION AND CONSUMPTION

Cargo transport has become ever cheaper, worldwide. Maritime transport costs, in particular, are now almost negligible. This is one of the reasons why manufacturing has moved to low-wage countries. Global trade stimulates economic development, but also has its downsides; local labour conditions are sometimes poor, and the environmental costs of freight transport are high.

Source: CBS – adaptation by PBL

INTERCONTINENTAL CONTAINER TRANSPORT ALONG MAJOR TRADE ROUTES, IN MILLION TEUs (TWENTY-FEET EQUIVALENT UNITS)

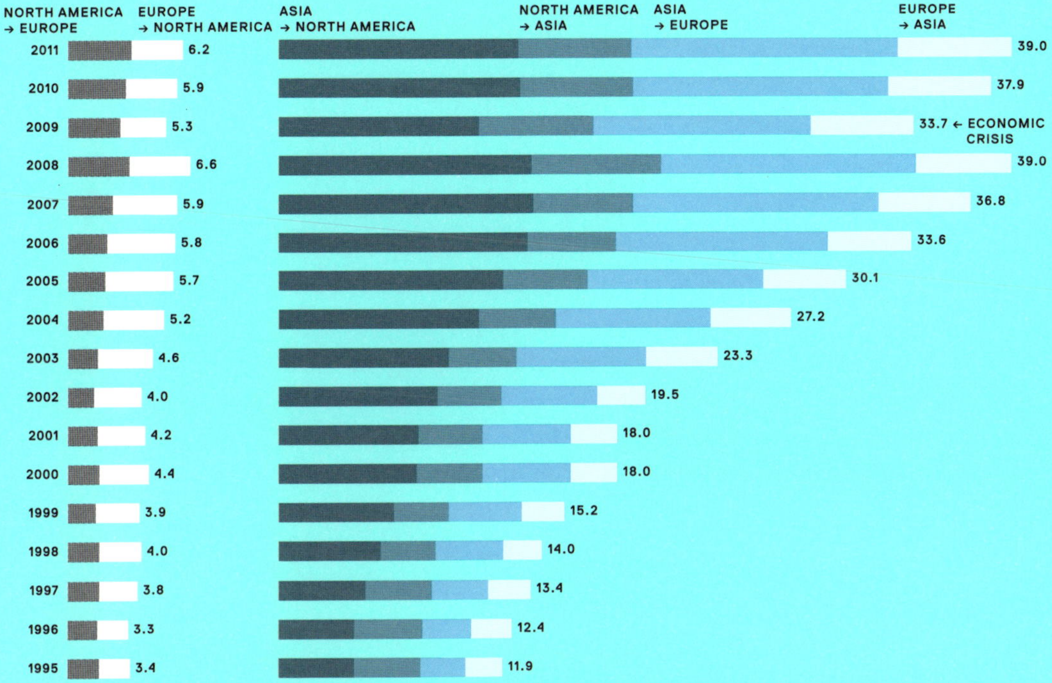

CONTAINER THROUGHPUT AT PORT OF ROTTERDAM, IN MILLION TEUs (2011)

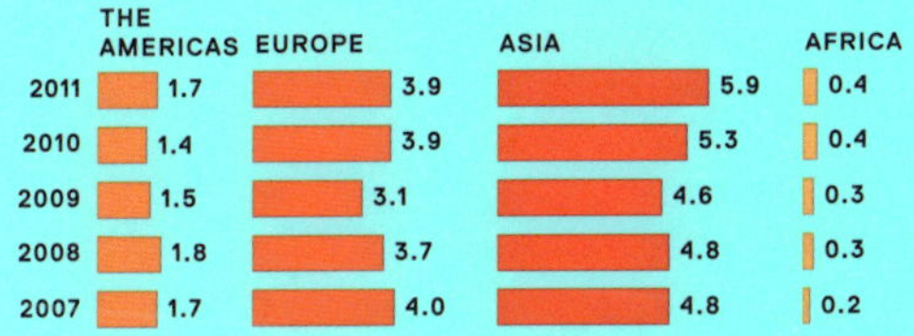

7.5 / CHANGING CARGO FLOWS

Intercontinental cargo flows are growing and shifting. Transport to and from Asia, in particular, has grown spectacularly. Asian megacities are investing heavily in seaports and airports to increase their share in international trade. The Port of Rotterdam maintains a solid position. Uncertainties for the future include vulnerable shipping routes (Panama, Suez) and growing fuel costs.

Sources: Port of Rotterdam, UNCTAD – adaptation by PBL

by prosperous countries may have been manufactured under poor labour conditions; a notorious example is budget clothing produced in Bangladeshi sweatshops. Furthermore, global cargo transport has a significant impact on human health and the environment. In Europe, the traffic and transport sector is responsible for 25% of greenhouse gas emissions. Of this amount, more than 70% is emitted by road transport (of which 40% is for cargo transport) and 23% by international shipping and aviation. The latter are the fastest growing sources of greenhouse gas emissions in the EU. Despite international agreements and technical innovations, greenhouse gas emissions by the traffic and transport sector keep increasing, due to the strong growth of the sector.

7.5 / CHANGING CARGO FLOWS

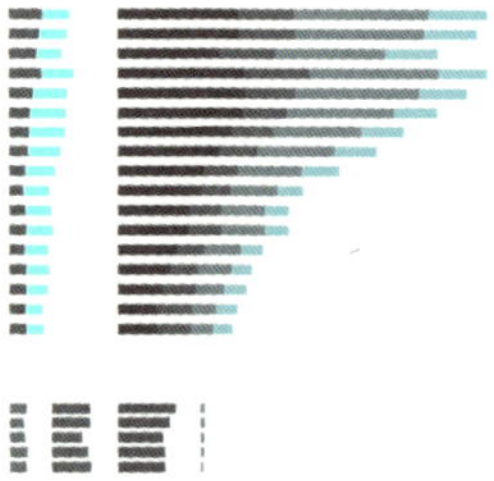

Global cargo flows not only keep growing, but they are also shifting. Since 1995, the number of containers transported between Europe and North America has doubled, while it has quadrupled between Europe and Asia. Asian megacities are investing heavily in the construction and extension of seaports and airports, aiming to increase their share in the global trade turnover.

The question is whether these Asian investments will pay off. The future course of globalisation is currently unclear. The growing problem of piracy, the vulnerability of existing shipping routes (Panama, Suez) and the possible opening of new routes via the Arctic contribute to this uncertainty. Furthermore, the rising costs of raw materials and fuel may change the cost structure of products, such that the share of transport costs may increase relative to labour and production costs. Another uncertain factor is the possible implementation of a carbon tax (CO_2 tax) on shipping and aviation, which would result in higher transport costs.

Hence, the apples from Zeeland may one day again be cheaper than the ones from New Zealand.

Houses have an air of permanency. Immovable, they appear like everlasting structures; particularly, when compared to their dynamic urban surroundings in which everything else moves and changes. However, they are not as static as they seem. Every house and building is part of a larger dynamic; that of the immense flow of building materials. This manifests itself at least twice during a building's lifetime; when it is built and when it is demolished; but also when is is being maintained, renovated and/or modified in-between.

8.1 / A HOUSE IS MADE OF MORE THAN BRICKS

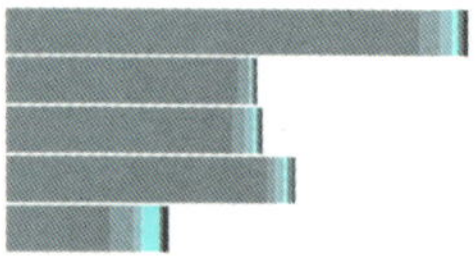

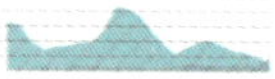

The amount of building material required to build a new house varies per construction method and housing type. For example, a terraced house of concrete construction with brick outer walls requires about 75% more building material (in weight) than a timber frame construction with wooden facade; and a detached house takes about twice as much material to build as a flat. In the Netherlands, an average, newly built terraced house contains over 100 tonnes of building material. Sand, gravel and cement (the principal components of concrete) account for more than 75%; the remainder includes bricks, gypsum, timber, steel, glass and insulation material. Soil, sand, gravel and tiles for the garden are not included in this amount. Nor is the fill sand for the foundation, which, in low-lying areas of the Netherlands, amounts to an average 450 tonnes of sand for each new building plot. Furthermore, about 10% of building material is 'lost' during construction; for example, because it is damaged or left over.

Over the last hundred years, the per-capita consumption of housing construction materials has risen considerably. The average Dutch home has increased in size, while the number of occupants per house has decreased. In addition, the amount (weight) of building material per square metre has risen, due to an increased use of concrete construction. Altogether, the current Dutch housing stock of 7.3 million homes contains an estimated 1.2 billion tonnes of building materials.

In addition to the massive amount of building materials needed for housing construction, about twice this amount is required for the construction of offices, schools, businesses, dykes and infrastructure. Of all concrete used in 2010, 28% went to housing construction, 35% to non-residential construction, 24% to groundworks, roads and hydrological engineering works, and 14% to renovation and repair. Large infrastructure works (e.g. the Betuwelijn Railway and the High-Speed Railway Line (HSL)) and land reclamation projects (e.g. IJburg, a new residential neighbourhood in Amsterdam, and Maasvlakte-2, which is an extension to the Port of Rotterdam), are bulk users of fill sand and other land-raising material.

In total, the Netherlands consumes an annual 150 million tonnes of building materials.

These materials are not only used for expanding the built environment, but also for renovating existing buildings and replacing demolished buildings. In the Netherlands, between 1997 and 2011, over 1 million houses were built while 200.000 houses were demolished. During the same period, more than 16 million square metres in new office space were added to the building stock, while almost 2 million were demolished or converted to other uses.

8.2 / MATERIALS SOURCED FROM DUTCH SOIL AND SEA

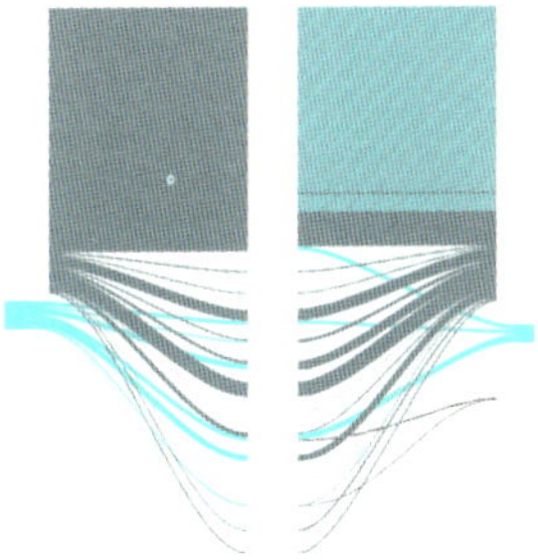

The Netherlands has major onshore and offshore sources of building materials; particularly sand, gravel and clay. About 60 million tonnes of sand are extracted from the North Sea each year, not counting sand extracted for the construction of the Maasvlakte-2. Of these 60 million tonnes, about 35 million are used as fill sand for land raising; the remainder is used for coastal maintenance.

Other primary building materials, such as timber and steel (including raw materials for steel production), have to be imported. Two thirds of all tropical hardwood imported into the Netherlands (close to 300,000 tonnes in 2010) is used in construction. This timber mainly comes from Malaysia, Brazil, Indonesia and Cameroon. Iron ore is mostly imported from Brazil, Canada, Sweden, Australia and South Africa. Of the 34 million tonnes of iron ore imported each year, close to 75% is re-exported.

The construction of the Maasvlakte-2 extension to the Port of Rotterdam (2008 – 2013) has taken a massive amount of building materials – over 435 million tonnes. The bulk of this amount (430 million tonnes) consisted of sand, 90% of which was extracted offshore. In addition, the project used 0.2 million tonnes of clay and about 5 million tonnes of stone rubble from Norway.

The use of secondary materials, such as recycled steel and recycled concrete aggregate, has significantly increased in

USE OF BUILDING MATERIALS FOR DIFFERENT HOUSING TYPES, IN TONNES (THE NETHERLANDS, 2013)

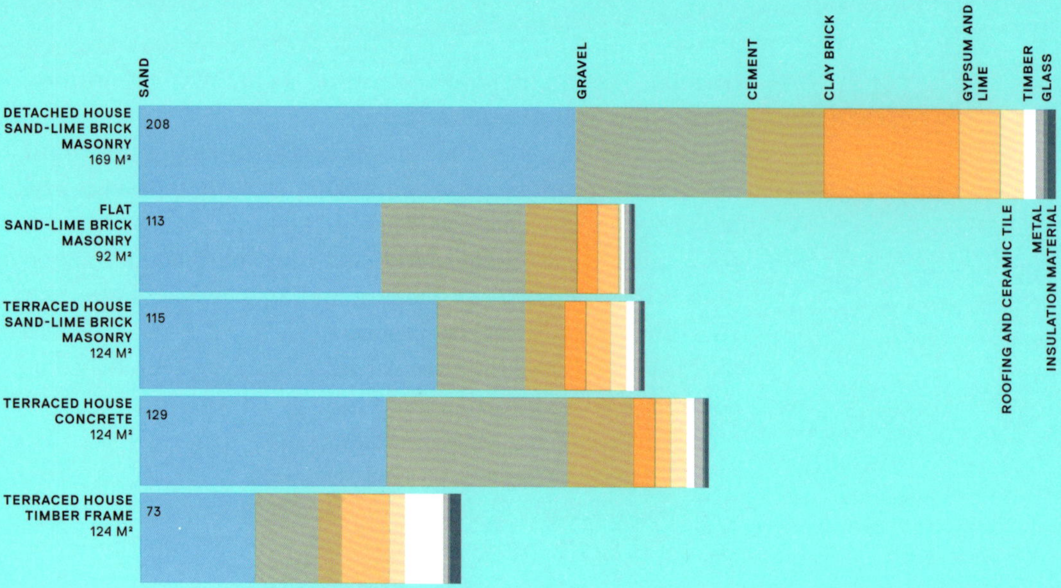

HOUSING IN THE NETHERLANDS: CONSTRUCTION AND DEMOLITION, IN THOUSANDS OF DWELLINGS PER YEAR

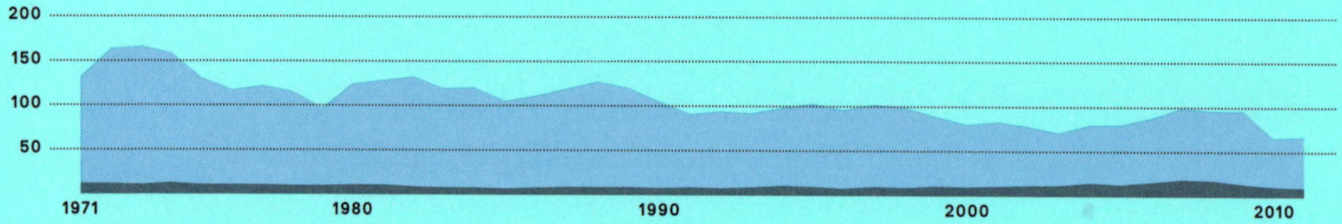

OFFICE SPACE IN THE NETHERLANDS: STOCK CHANGES, IN MILLION M² OF RENTABLE FLOOR SPACE

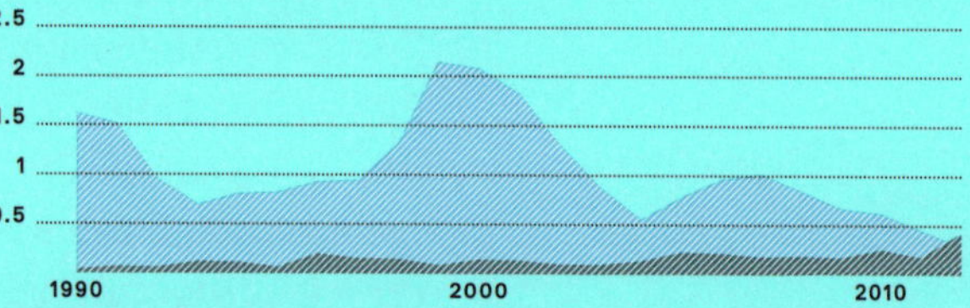

MUTATION

- NEW CONSTRUCTION
- DEMOLITION
- NEW CONSTRUCTION OR REFITTED
- DEMOLITION OR OTHER FUNCTION

8.1 / A HOUSE IS MADE OF MORE THAN BRICKS

It takes 130 tonnes of building materials to build an average Dutch house, as well as 450 tonnes of sand for the foundation. A huge amount of building materials is needed for housing construction, plus twice as much for non-residential construction, groundworks, roads and hydrological engineering works. Demolition waste is mostly reused or recycled.

Sources: Agentschap NL, Bak RL, CBS, CE, DGMR, MRPI, Nationale Milieudatabase – all adapted by PBL

EXTRACTION, IMPORT, CONSUMPTION AND EXPORT OF BUILDING MATERIALS, IN MILLION TONNES (THE NETHERLANDS, 2010)

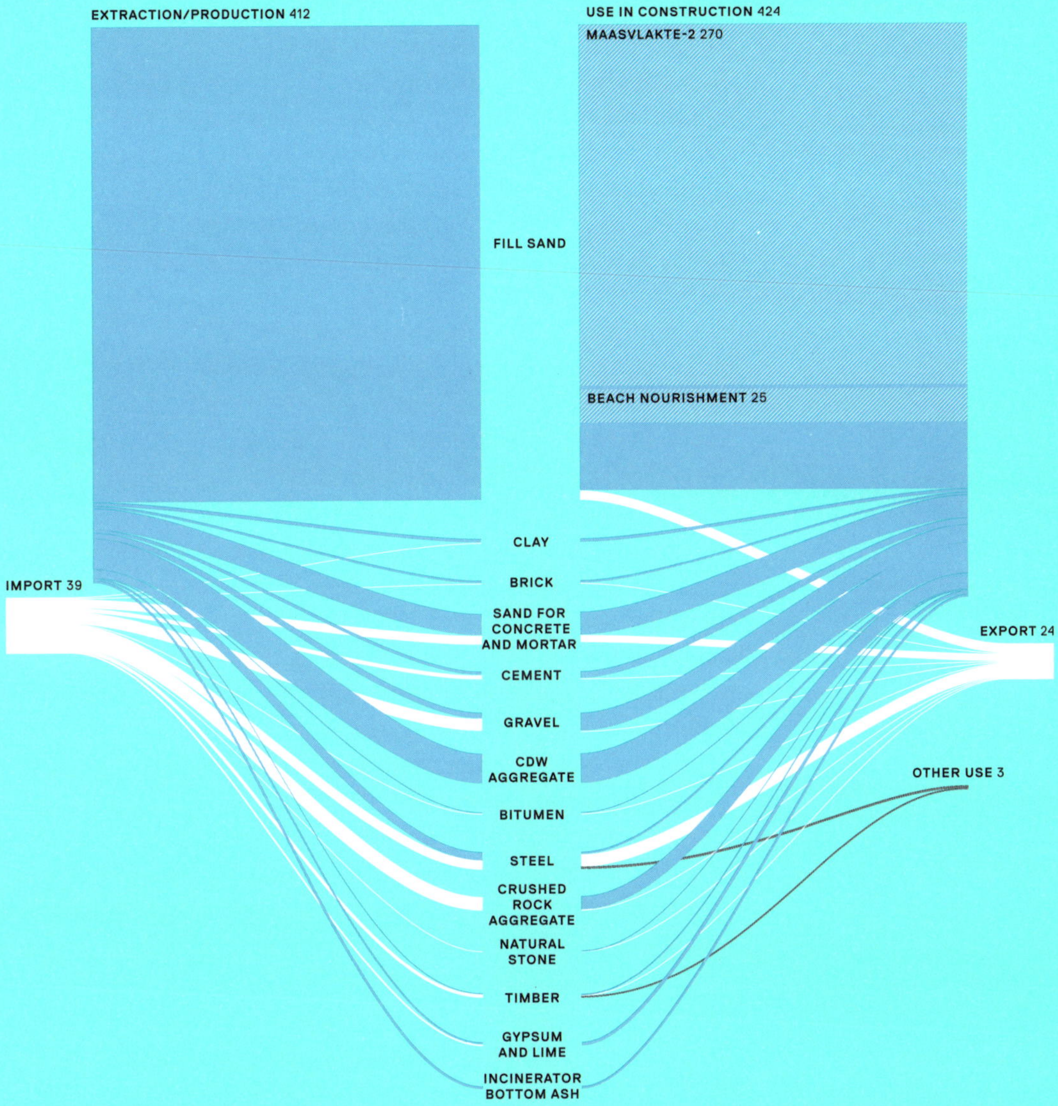

8.2 / MATERIALS SOURCED FROM DUTCH SOIL AND SEA

Sand, clay and CDW aggregate (recycled construction and demolition waste) are mostly sourced within the Netherlands or from the North Sea. Sand is required for construction in low-lying areas, coastal maintenance and land reclamations, such as Maasvlakte-2. Gravel, crushed rock, timber and natural stone are mostly imported.

Sources: CBS, CBS/PBL/WUR, CE, KNB, Probos, Stichting Bouwen met Staal, VBW-asfalt, World Steel Association – all adapted by PBL recent years. Furthermore, primary building materials are increasingly being substituted by industrial residues, such as fly ash and furnace slag (in cement production) and bottom ash from coal-fired power plants (in road construction). The Dutch *Grondbank* ('soil bank') facilitates the exchange, cleaning and reuse of excavated soil between construction sites.

8.3 / NO CONSTRUCTION WITHOUT PITS

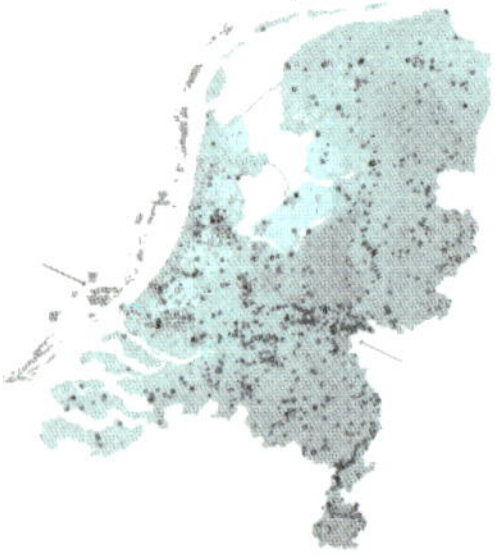

The most important building materials are sourced within the Netherlands itself. Sand, gravel and clay are resources typical of delta areas, and are also abundantly present in the Dutch river delta. However, extraction possibilities are limited.

Over the course of thousands of years, about 225 billion cubic metres of sand, clay and gravel were deposited on the Netherlands; 20% by the rivers and 80% by the sea. This is enough to cover the entire country with a layer that is 6 metres high. About a thousand years ago, natural sediment supply was cut off when the Dutch started to build sea and river dykes. Dykes protect the land against flooding, but also prevent sediment from being deposited on to the land. As a result, over the past centuries, the Netherlands has missed out on an estimated 13 billion cubic metres of sediment. This is equivalent to twice the volume of the IJsselmeer lake.

However, the Netherlands needs sediment input to preserve its lowlands, now more than ever before. The land is subsiding due to drainage, peat oxidation and clay shrinkage, while the sea level is rising. To compensate for land subsidence and sea level rise, the Netherlands would need to be raised by 140 million cubic metres of soil, each year. As this is not feasible or realistic, the country is increasingly dependent on artificial flood protection structures, such as dykes.

Even though the supply of new sediment has been negligible over the past thousand years, the Netherlands has been extracting huge amounts of sand, clay and gravel in recent centuries. Extraction of these surface minerals has left distinct traces in the landscape; there are numerous former pits and quarries all over the country. Traditionally, extraction sites were located mostly along the rivers. However, when urbanisation accelerated and (rail)road construction increased – in the second half of the 19th century and again after World War II – deep sand pits were dug close to new city and town expansions and road construction sites. Between 1960 and 2010, the built-up area of the Netherlands, including infrastructure, doubled to about 15% of the country's total area. As a result of this massive construction activity, the Netherlands is strewn with hundreds of former sand pits, which have filled with water and may be up to 40 metres deep.

Some of these sand pits were designed, from the time of excavation, to become recreational lakes; others developed as such, later on. Examples of post-war sand pit lakes are the Sloterplas and Gaasperplas near Amsterdam, the Valkenburgse Meer near Leiden, the Maarsseveense Plassen near Utrecht, the Hoornse Plas near Groningen and the Albaplas near Apeldoorn. An older sand pit lake is the IJzeren Man lake near Vught, which was excavated during the second half of the 19th century.

Compared to onshore sand extraction, the effects of offshore extraction – in the North Sea and the IJsselmeer – are less visible, but no less profound. Apart from the ecological impacts, offshore sand extraction may conflict with offshore wind parks, cables and pipelines, as well as shipping.

Sand extraction pits are like counter-moulds of growing cities and towns; what is added to the latter, has to be removed from the former. By using extraction pits as recreational lakes for urbanites, their counter-moulds become part of the city itself.

8.4 / THE WORLD KEEPS ON BUILDING

The demand for building materials is enormous – not only in the Netherlands, but also worldwide. Global demand is expected to increase strongly in the coming decades, as a result of population growth, rising prosperity, and increasing dwelling sizes per capita and household. Massive construction activity will be needed to house the projected 2.7 billion new urban inhabitants by 2050. By that time, more than two thirds

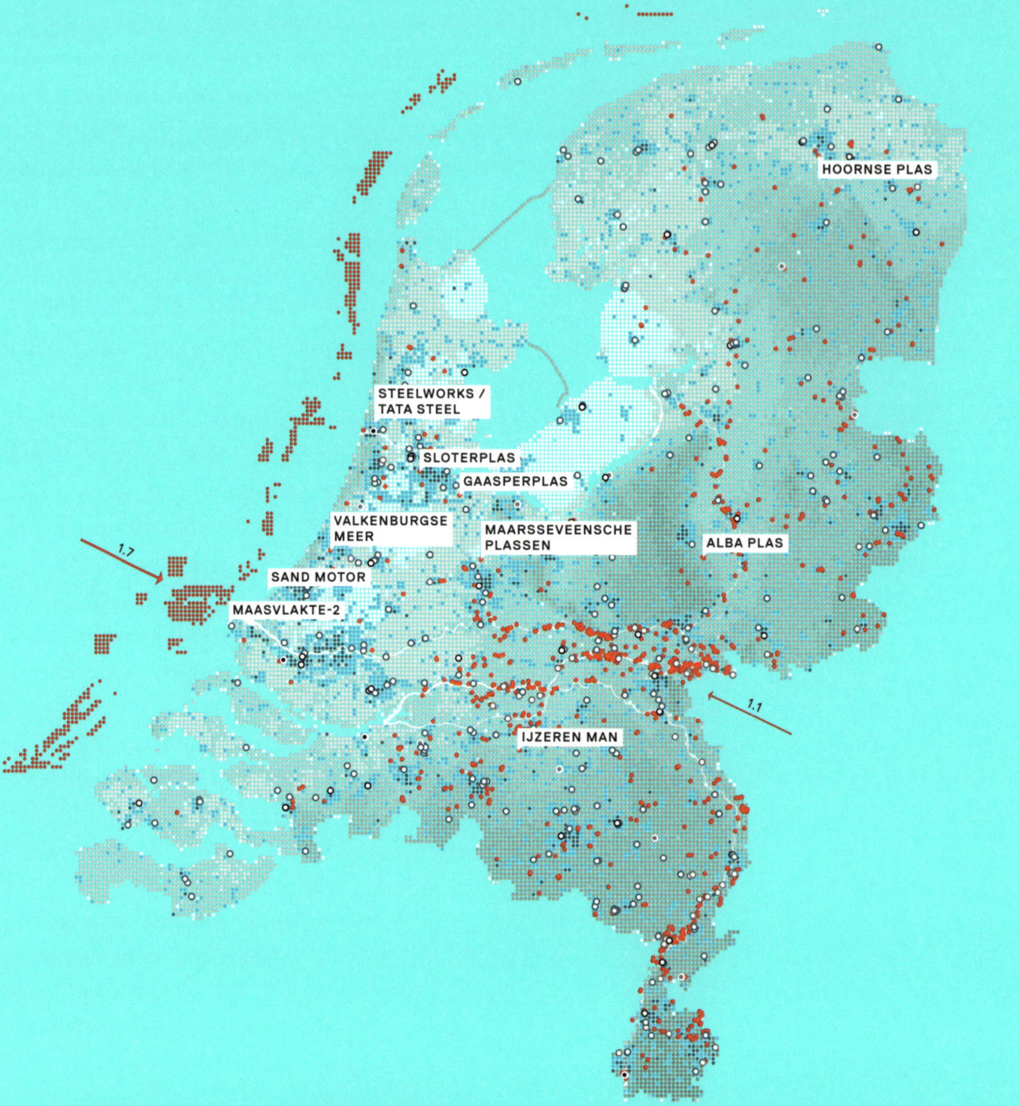

FACTORY (2012)

- ASPHALT
- CEMENT
- CLAY BRICKS
- CONCRETE
- SAND-LIME BRICKS

NATURAL DEPOSITS OF SAND IN ESTUARIES OF THE RHINE AND MEUSE, IN MILLION TONNES PER YEAR

1.1

BUILT-UP AREA AND INFRASTRUCTURE

1960 2010

SAND EXTRACTION SITE

EXTRACTION SITE OR QUARRY

HEIGHT IN METRES

<-5 -5–-2.5 -2.5–0 0–5 5–10 10–20 20–50 50–100 100–200 >200

8.3 / NO CONSTRUCTION WITHOUT PITS

The Netherlands has been extracting clay, sand and gravel for centuries. This has left traces in the landscape; there are hundreds of former extraction pits, some of which now serve as recreational lakes. Natural sediment supply (sand, clay, gravel) has practically ceased due to the construction of dykes, separating the land from rivers and the sea.

Sources: Alterra, CBS, LISA, RWS – all adapted by PBL

DOMESTIC CONSUMPTION OF CONSTRUCTION MINERALS, IN TONNES PER CAPITA, PER YEAR (2000)

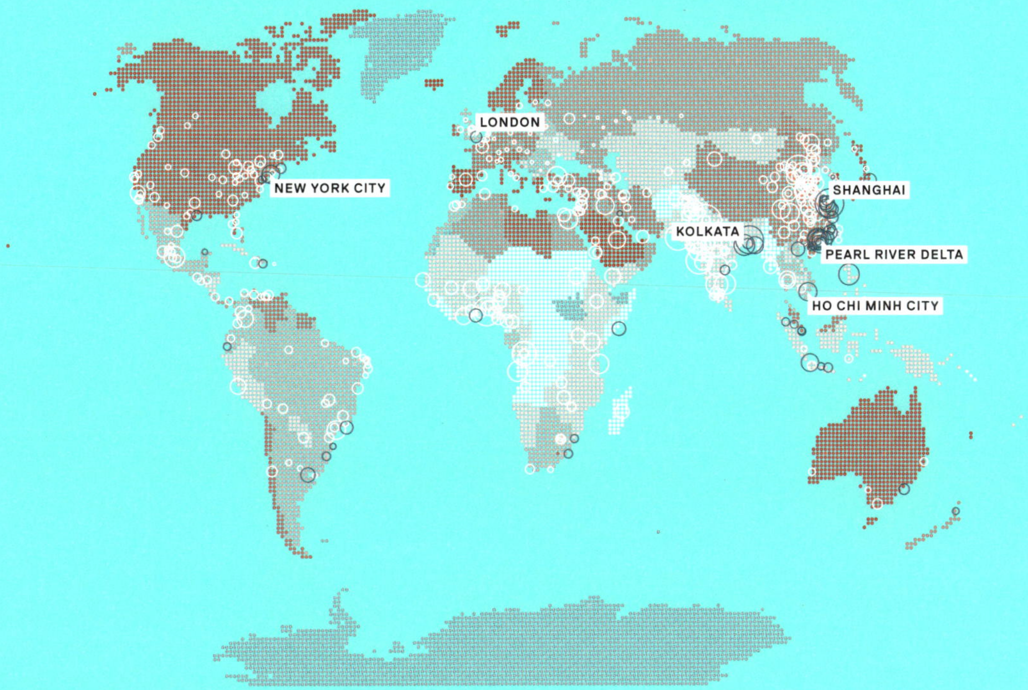

DOMESTIC CONSUMPTION OF CONSTRUCTION MINERALS (INDEX 1970=100)

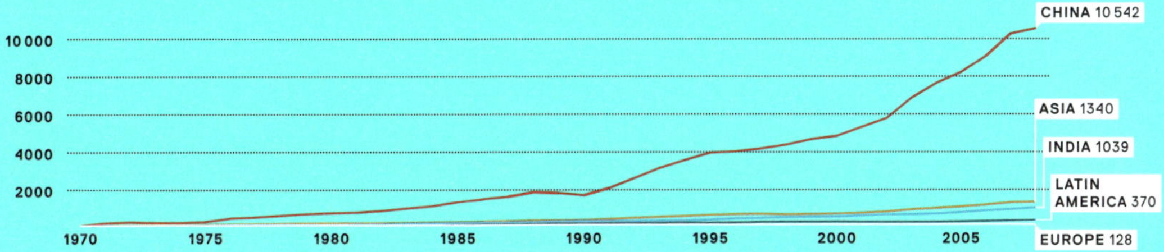

URBAN AGGLOMERATIONS
(>1 MILLION INHABITANTS IN 2010)

POPULATION INCREASE
(2010–2025)

- 50 000
- 500 000
- 1 000 000
- 10 000 000

FLOOD-PRONE COASTAL CITIES

DOMESTIC CONSUMPTION OF CONSTRUCTION MINERALS, IN TONNES PER CAPITA, PER YEAR (2000)

<0.5 | -1.5 | -2.5 | -3.5 | -4.5 | -7.5 | >7.5

NO DATA

8.4 / THE WORLD KEEPS ON BUILDING

The coming decades will see massive construction activity, worldwide, particularly in Asia, due to economic and population growth and shorter construction–demolition cycles. This will increase the pressure on the economically attractive, already densely populated delta areas, which are vulnerable to flooding, land subsidence and decreased sediment supply.

Sources: CSIRO/UNEP, Eurostat, Institute of Social Ecology Vienna, Steinberger et al., UN – all adapted by PBL of the world population will live in urban areas; in 2010, this was slightly more than half. Furthermore, buildings are being replaced sooner than before, resulting in shorter construction-demolition cycles.

In Asia, in particular, the demand for building materials is high. Urbanisation rates are much higher there than in the Western world. Due to growing prosperity and a decreasing household size, per-capita consumption of building materials is also increasing. Thus, the consumption of construction minerals in China since 1970 saw more than a hundredfold increase.

Reduced sediment supply and land subsidence are not only a problem in the Netherlands, but also in other densely populated, intensively used delta areas and coastal zones around the world. If climate change continues, sea levels keep rising and extreme storms become more frequent, these areas are at increased risk of flooding. Flood-prone areas include megacities and key economic regions around the world, such as New York, London, Kolkata, Ho Chi Minh City, Shanghai and the Pearl River Delta. In many cases, reduced sediment supply downstream is caused by hydropower dams upstream, which limit river flow and sediment load.

8.5 / THE CITY AS AN EXTRACTION SITE

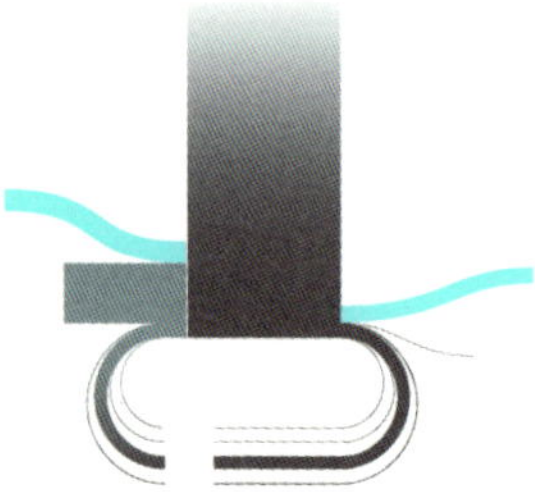

Until 2050, global population growth and urbanisation will continue. This growth will require new input of construction materials; demand cannot be met by reusing existing stocks. However, in many European countries, populations are expected to stabilise or even decline in the next decades; here, the need for city expansions and infrastructure additions – and hence the need for additional building materials – will likely be reduced. The current high office vacancy rates could be a foretaste of Europe's future. Building activities will likely shift from new construction to management, preservation, maintenance, restoration, renovation, transformation and reuse for other purposes.

REUSE OF MATERIALS FROM THE BUILDING STOCK, IN MILLION TONNES (THE NETHERLANDS, 2010)

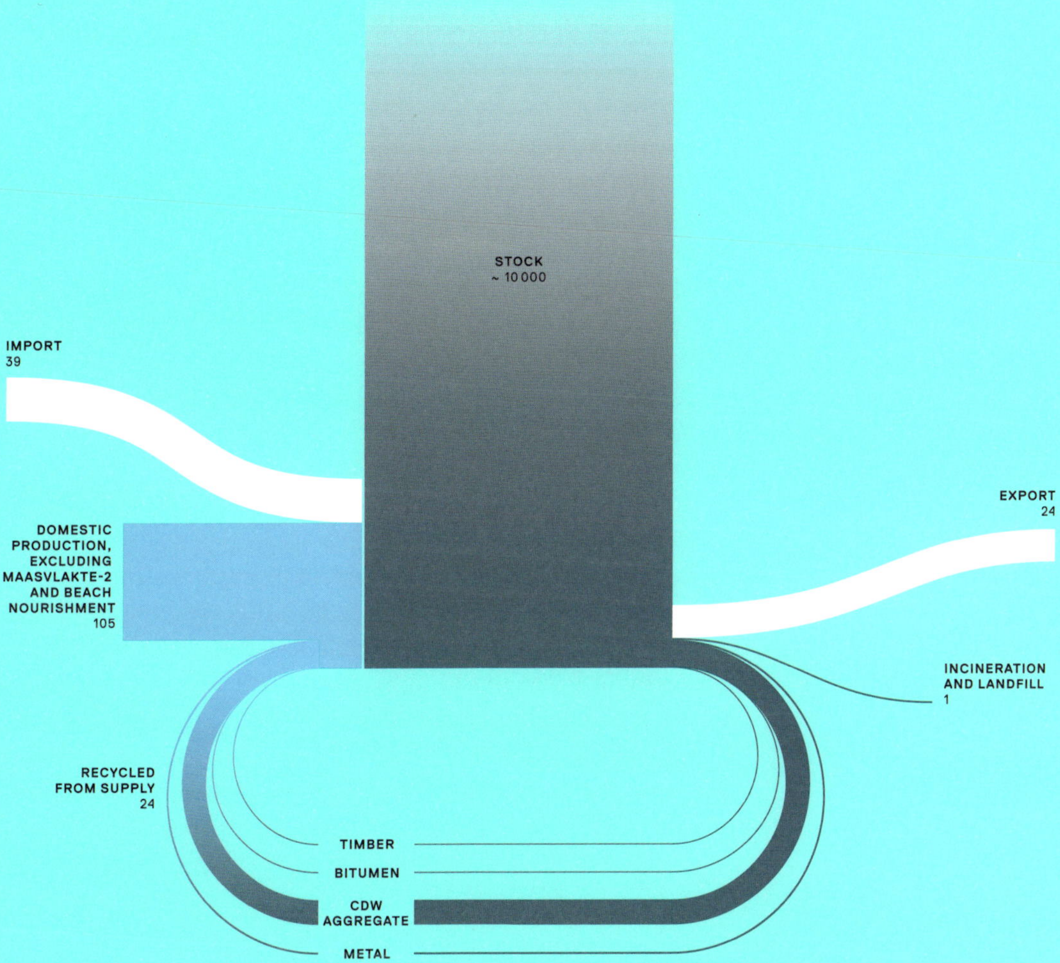

8.5 / THE CITY AS AN EXTRACTION SITE

As the European population is expected to stabilise or even decline, the focus of building activities may shift from growth and new construction to upkeep and reuse. Large-scale reuse of demolition waste, such as steel, is becoming increasingly attractive. The urban building stock is an inexhaustible source of valuable, reusable raw materials.

Sources: CE, CBS, CBS/PBL/WUR KNB, Probos, VBW-asfalt, Stichting Bouwen met Staal, World Steel Association – all adapted by PBL

Use and reuse will become more important than new construction. If buildings have to be replaced, their materials can be recycled and reused in new construction projects. In the Netherlands, over 95% of steel and stony materials from demolition waste are already being reused or recycled. The stony material is reused as fill material and in foundations, and increasingly as a substitute for primary minerals in concrete production. Steel is either being reused directly or melted down and recast. Cities are 'urban mines' of valuable, reusable construction materials, and could become largely self-sufficient.

Already, the total amount of steel in the built environment of, for example, the United States has more or less stabilised. At about 11 tonnes of steel per capita, the country has reached its saturation point; the demand for steel can now be met by reusing existing stocks.

Reuse and recycling are also attractive in terms of energy use and CO_2 emission reduction. Building activity accounts for about 30% of global CO_2 emissions. Recycling and reuse of energy-intensive building materials, such as steel and aluminium, can make a real difference. Making steel from scrap metal requires around 45% less energy than making it from iron ore. The longer these materials are used and reused, the more of their original energy cost can be recovered.

In an ideal world of recycling, waste does not exist. What we would call waste or rubbish simply serves as raw material for the next cycle. The question is whether this perfect world of 100% recycling has ever existed, or can ever exist. Animals, plants and, particularly, human civilisations leave traces that are not erased in subsequent cycles but that remain long after they were left – from dinosaur bones, to ashes and potsherds.

9.1 / SEVEN TIMES THE BODY WEIGHT

Humans have always produced waste. However, the volume and nature of waste flows have changed over time; worldwide, there is more waste today than ever before, and the amount keeps growing. The average Dutch citizen currently discards 530 kilograms of waste per year. This is seven times the average adult body weight, and four times as much as in 1950. In recent years, however, waste production has slightly decreased in the Netherlands.

Forty-nine per cent of household waste is being collected separately, leaving 51% of unsorted household waste. The main components of household waste are organic (vegetables, fruit and garden waste), paper and cardboard. Sixty per cent of all discarded paper and glass is collected separately; for plastic this is only 13%.

Contemporary households own more things than ever before, and throw more things away. In other words, the turnover rate is higher. Goods such as clothing and furniture are much less often mended, repaired or reused than in the past. Many products now come as disposables, such as diapers and plastic packaging material. However, some waste flows have decreased or completely disappeared; the production of coal ash, for example, ceased when the Netherlands switched from burning coal over to natural gas in the 1960s.

Waste production appears to be correlated with economic prosperity. Waste growth tends to stagnate during economic downturns. This was particularly the case during the oil crisis of the 1970s and the economic recession of the 1980s, and has also been observed in recent years as a result of the present economic crisis.

Household waste is only the tip of the iceberg. The majority of waste (85%) is produced by businesses. This share amounts to an additional 3000 kilograms of waste per Dutch citizen per year.

WASTE, IN KG PER CAPITA, PER YEAR (THE NETHERLANDS, 2010)

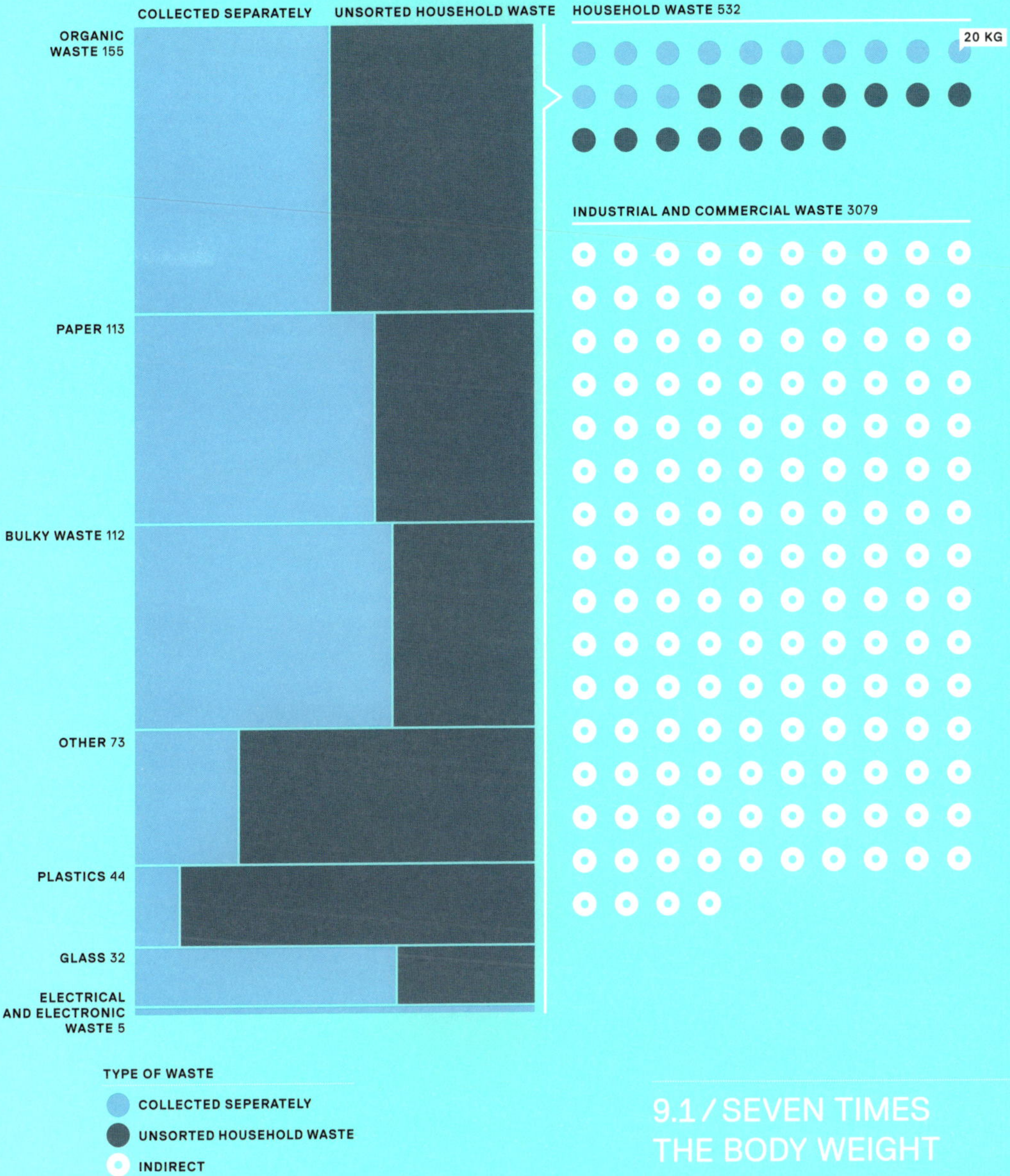

9.1 / SEVEN TIMES THE BODY WEIGHT

The average Dutch citizen discards 530 kilograms of waste per year, four times as much as in 1950. Part of this waste–particularly paper, glass and bulky waste–is collected separately. The contribution of households to total waste production is relatively small; 85% of all waste is produced by businesses.

Sources: CBS/PBL/WUR, RWS, RWS – adaptation by PBL

WASTE SOURCES AND TREATMENT, IN KILOTONNES (THE NETHERLANDS, 2010)

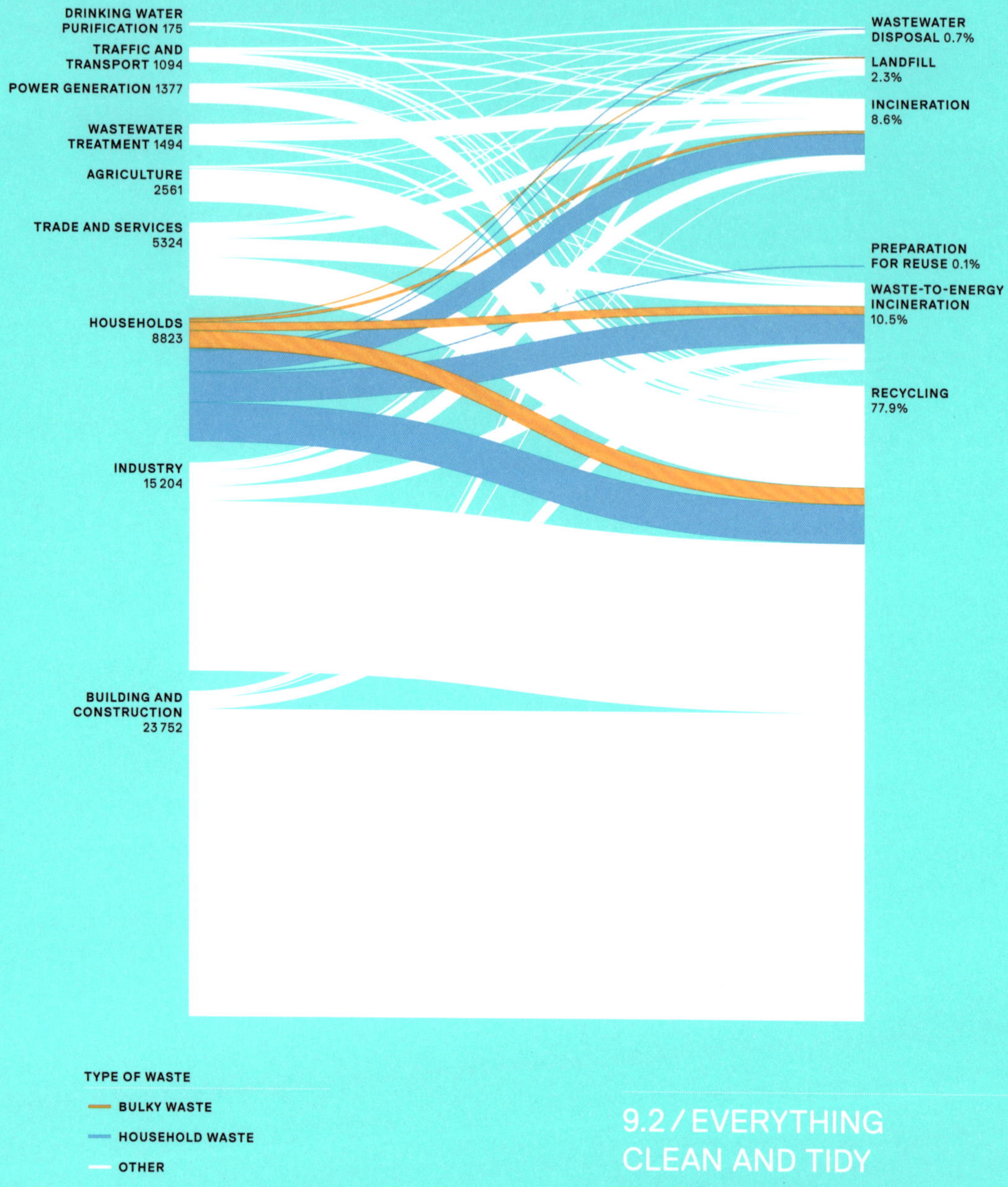

9.2 / EVERYTHING CLEAN AND TIDY

In the Netherlands, waste management appears to be a problem solved. Seventy-five per cent of all waste is recycled. Residual waste is mostly incinerated, where it contributes to electricity generation. Landfill and wastewater disposal, common practice 30 years ago, are hardly used anymore. Dutch incineration plants are now processing waste from London and southern Italy.

Sources: CBS/PBL/WUR, RWS – adaptation by PBL

9.2 / EVERYTHING CLEAN AND TIDY

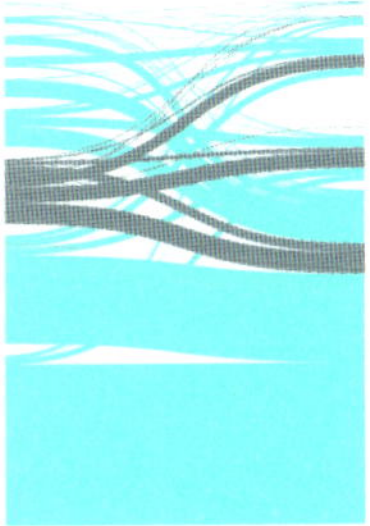

Waste management in the Netherlands appears to be a problem solved; partly thanks to sophisticated logistics. Back in 1980 most household waste ended up in landfills, but now it is efficiently recycled or incinerated. Large-scale industrial waste scandals are also a thing of the past. For only a few dimes per person per day, we dispose of our waste in a clean and proper manner.

Better still, our waste is put to good use, as more than 75% is recycled, and a part of the 20% that is incinerated thus contributes to heat and electricity generation. No more than 2% of Dutch waste ends up as landfill.

Waste management in the Netherlands has become so efficient that the current capacity of Dutch incinerator plants is larger than the domestic supply of waste for incineration. This overcapacity allows these plants to import waste from other countries. Waste from London and southern Italy, for example, is being incinerated at the Port of Rotterdam. From a European perspective, incineration of imported waste in the Netherlands is good for the environment, because it generates energy and the waste does not end up as landfill in other countries. Furthermore, in addition to generating energy, waste incineration also benefits the Dutch economy. This is particularly the case if the incinerators can operate non-stop. However, all this waste could also be recycled. This appears to be a case of 'lock-in': the incinerator plants want to keep on burning waste and generate electricity, but this stands in the way of more recycling.

9.3 / CITIES ARE WASTING WASTE

The increase in waste flows is primarily an urban issue – not only because urban populations are growing so rapidly, but also because urbanites on average produce two to four times more waste per person than do rural inhabitants. The latter generally are poorer; therefore, they consume less and reuse and recycle more. In 1900, the global urban population produced 300,000 tonnes of waste per day. A hundred years

UNSORTED HOUSEHOLD WASTE, PER MUNICIPALITY (2011)

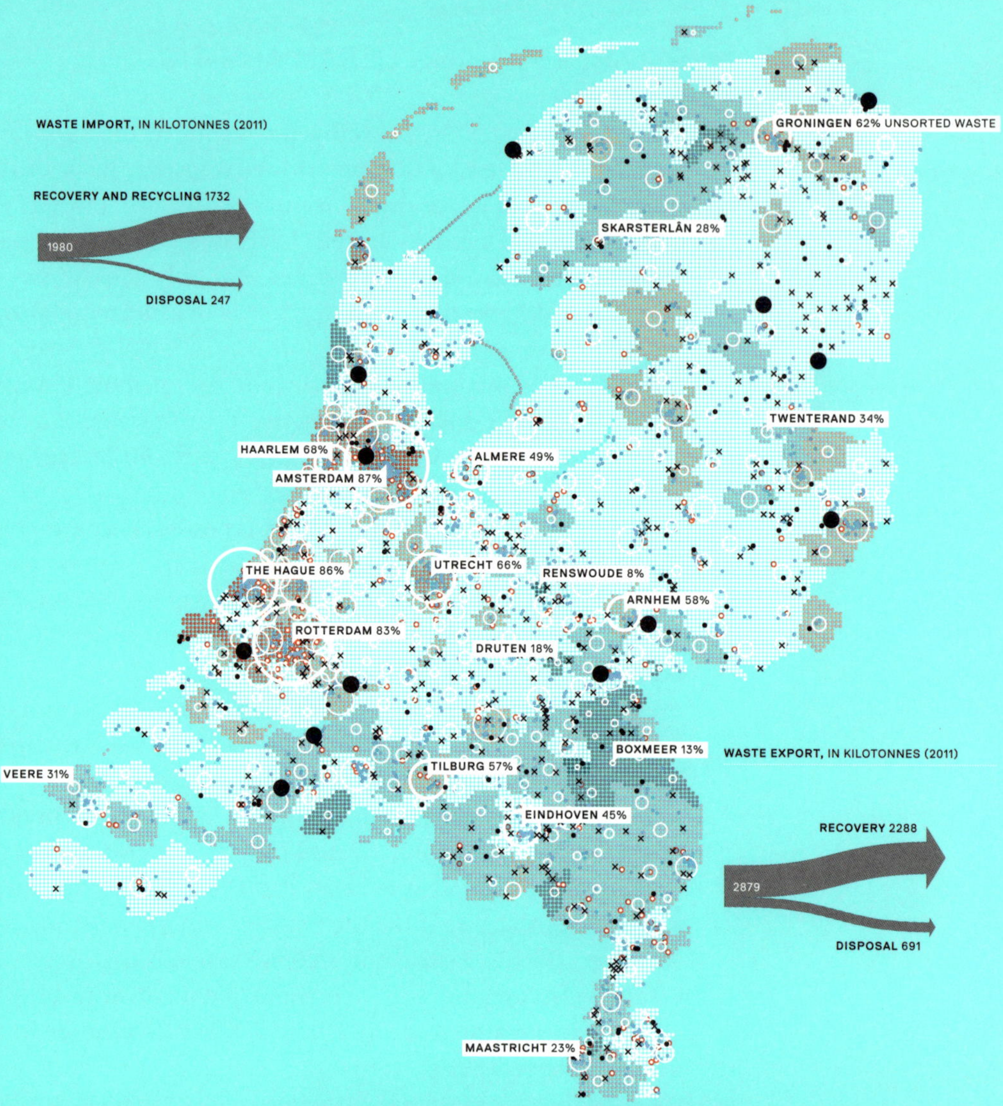

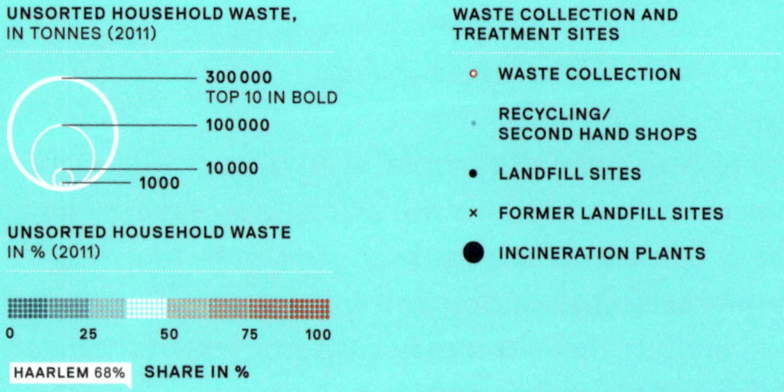

9.3 / CITIES ARE WASTING WASTE

Reuse, waste separation and recycling are effective ways to reduce the amount of household waste. Reuse has become easier thanks to online platforms, such as eBay, for buying and selling used goods. So far, sorted waste collection has been more successful in smaller municipalities than in large cities. Thus, in terms of recycling, the greatest gains can be achieved in cities.

Sources: CBS, LISA – all adapted by PBL

later they produced ten times this amount: 3 million tonnes per day. By 2025, this figure is expected to have doubled to 6 million tonnes per day.

These quantities are an enormous burden on urban environments; particularly in less developed countries where waste management is not well-organised. In countries with many people living below the poverty line, the enormous waste flows are leading to deplorable conditions. In some cities, the slums are overflowing with rubbish. Numerous people live and work on the vast rubbish dumps of big cities.

In Dutch cities, however, the treatment of waste is well-organised. Waste separation and recycling are effective ways to reduce the amount of residual waste. Many Dutch municipalities collect sorted waste door-to-door and have household waste recycling centres. Reuse has also gained popularity, mainly thanks to the rise of online platforms such as eBay for buying and selling used goods. These platforms also facilitate sharing and leasing.

However, more waste is recycled and reused in rural areas and small towns than in cities, where a larger share of plastic and organic waste ends up in incinerators. Thus, in terms of recycling there is still plenty of room for improvement in cities.

9.4 / FROM LANDFILLS AND INCINERATION TO RECYCLING

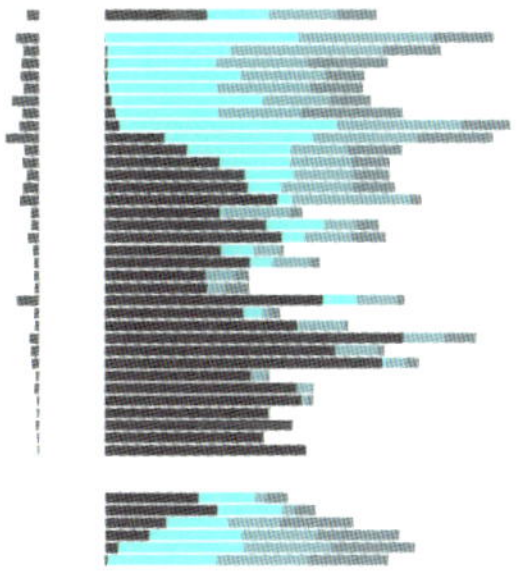

European countries differ considerably in their waste production and waste management. Rich countries such as the Netherlands produce more household waste per head of population than less prosperous countries. However, waste management also significantly improves with increasing prosperity; progressing from waste dumping to well-managed landfills, from simply burning waste to waste-to-energy incineration, and finally to more and more recycling. The richer European countries aim to further reduce the amount of waste going into landfills and incinerators; the Netherlands aims for a 50% reduction in incinerated waste, over the following decade.

GDP, IN EUROS PER CAPITA (2011) / MUNICIPAL WASTE, IN KG PER CAPITA, PER YEAR (2011)

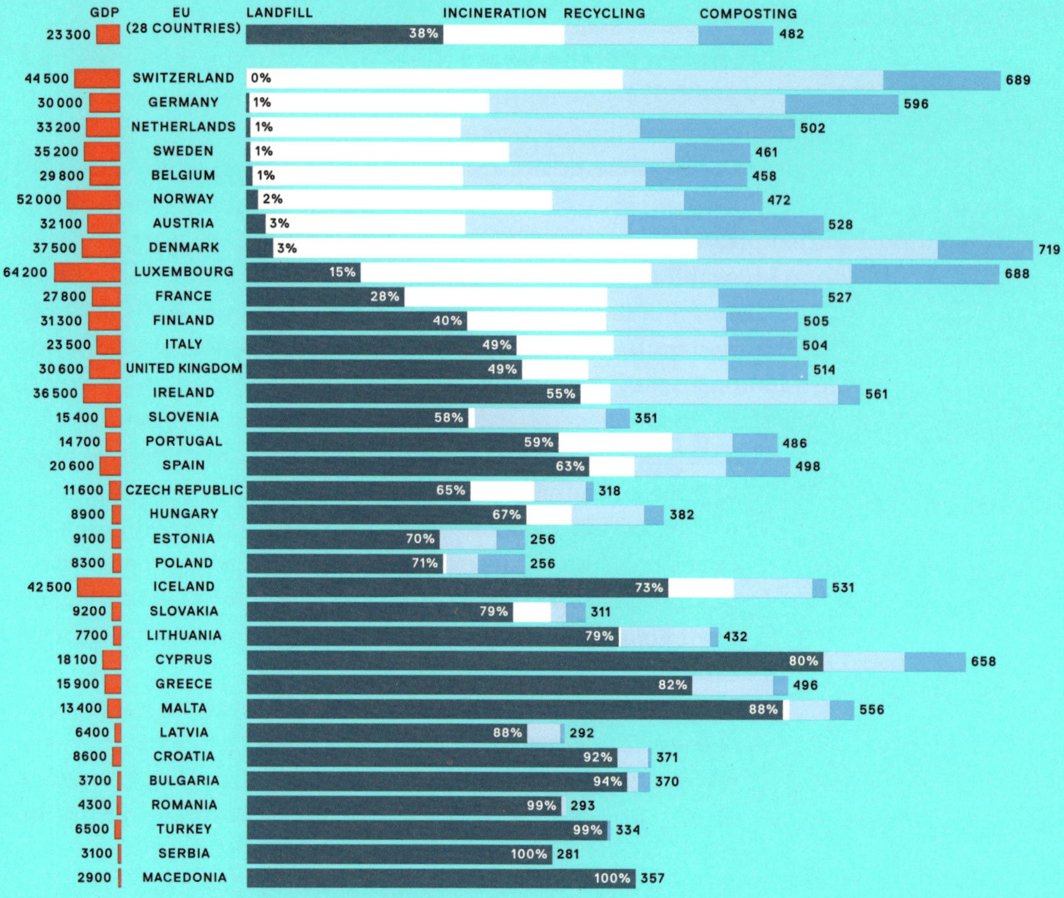

MUNICIPAL WASTE IN THE NETHERLANDS, IN KG PER CAPITA, PER YEAR

9.4 / FROM LANDFILLS AND INCINERATION TO RECYCLING

In Europe rich countries produce more household waste per capita than less prosperous countries. As prosperity increases, waste management practices are becoming more advanced. For Europe, recycling is increasingly attractive from an economic and geopolitical point of view. Recycling forms the basis of a more circular economy.

Sources: CBS/PBL/WUR, Eurostat

For Europe, recycling is becoming increasingly more attractive, also from an economic and geopolitical point of view. Europe depends on other countries for many raw materials, and these materials are likely to become scarcer and more expensive in the future, due to global economic and population growth. Therefore, Europe should carefully manage its current resources, including the materials present in products and waste.

A growing number of companies and regions aim for a circular economy, in which production cycles are closed as much as possible. This means that products are increasingly being designed in such a way that materials can easily be recovered at the end of the product life cycle. Waste prevention and reuse are the guiding principles of this approach. A circular economy would also allow a shift from buying and selling products to buying and selling services, which would facilitate product sharing, reuse and recycling.

A circular economy goes beyond waste-to-energy incineration and recycling. In this system, waste is no longer viewed as waste, but as a resource for new products.

9.5 / WASTE TRAVELS THE WORLD

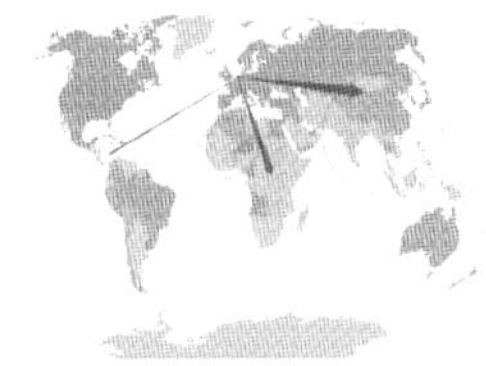

Across the globe, population growth and increasing prosperity lead to growing waste flows. The continuing spread of waste increasingly endangers the environment for both humans and animals. For example, large quantities of plastics end up in nature areas and oceans.

Waste, however, also offers opportunities. If waste is more recycled and reused, we make better use of the valuable materials it contains. As was common practice in the Netherlands decades ago, many poor countries have a lively tradition of recycling and reuse. Over the years, people developed their own informal collection systems, which support a broad sub-economy based on recycling. These days, they process not only local waste, but also scrap metal, paper, plastics, and discarded electronic parts and equipment, known as e-waste, from the Netherlands and other Western countries. Processing e-waste is profitable because electronic devices often contain valuable

DUTCH EXPORT OF SCRAP METAL, PAPER AND PLASTIC WASTE TO NON-EUROPEAN COUNTRIES, IN MILLION EUROS (2012) / **PLASTIC SOUP AND REGIONS WITH ILLEGAL WASTE DUMPS**

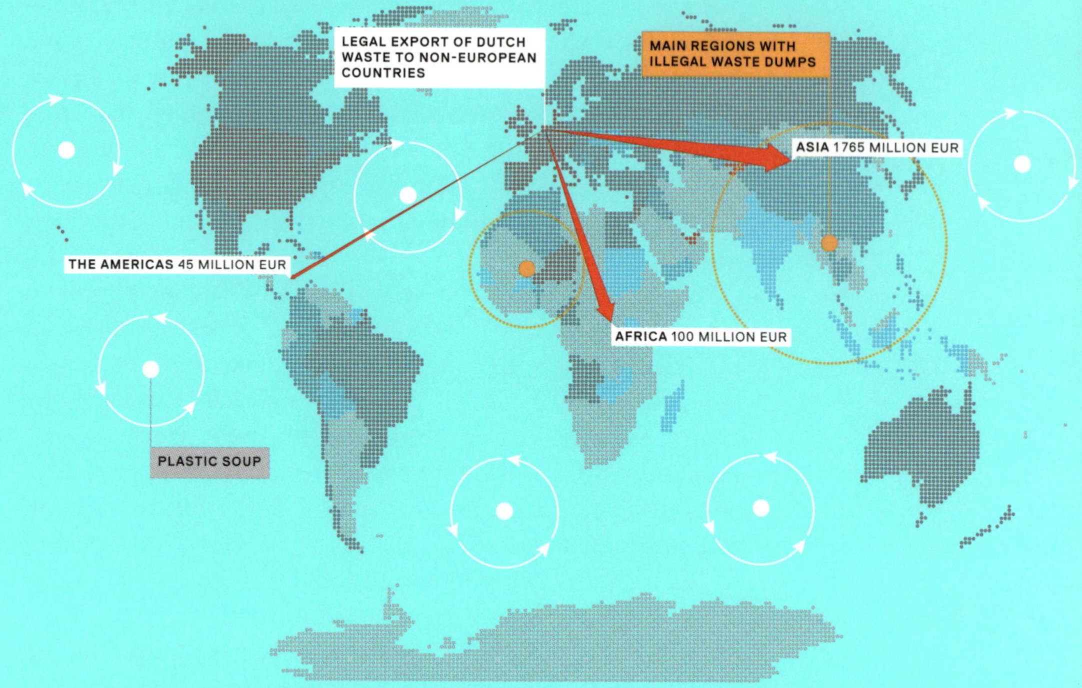

DUTCH EXPORT OF SCRAP METAL, PAPER AND PLASTIC WASTE, IN MILLION EUROS

9.5 / WASTE TRAVELS THE WORLD

The global urban population produces 3 million tonnes of waste per day, and this amount keeps increasing. Less-developed countries, in particular, have difficulties managing their waste streams. These problems are exacerbated by imported waste, such as e-waste, from Western countries. The last often contains toxic substances that may cause health problems.

Sources: CBS, INECE, UNEP, UNSD – all adapted by PBL

metals such as copper, nickel, iron and even gold. However, great care must be taken to avoid unsafe exposure, because e-waste may contain hazardous substances. According to the UNEP (United Nations Environment Programme), the available data on e-waste is limited, and in poorer countries, particularly in Africa and Asia, waste dumps are known where e-waste is not being processed safely.

Insight into stocks and waste flows is still limited. This forms an important barrier to the sustainable use of various materials and scarce resources. Leading institutions, such as the World Bank, call for improved registration of the transportation and use of materials and resources, and they clearly consider this to be an initiative for cities to pursue.

‘If the supply of energy failed, modern civilisation would come to an end as abruptly as does the music of an organ deprived of wind.’ The English radiochemist and Nobel Prize winner Frederick Soddy wrote this a hundred years ago, but his words are still relevant today; human civilisation, particularly the modern way of life, requires a constant and uninterrupted supply of energy. The majority of our daily activities are only possible thanks to the use of energy.

10.1 / A FULL TANK PER DAY

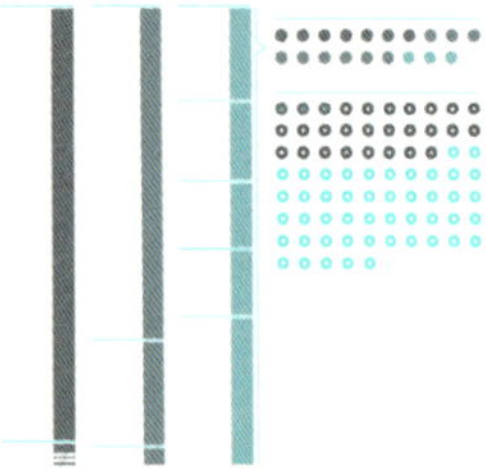

The average Dutch household uses an annual 57 gigajoules of energy within the home. Natural gas accounts for 75% of this amount (1500 m^3) and electricity for 25% (3400 kWh). Natural gas is mostly used for heating and hot water supply, while the bulk of electricity is used for washing and drying. The average annual household bill for natural gas and electricity is 1750 euros, which is about 6% of the average disposable income and close to 9% of below average incomes.

Households also consume a considerable amount of energy outside the home; particularly in the form of fuel for cars, motorcycles, mopeds and leisure vessels. On average, this comes to an annual 37 gigajoules per household, corresponding to over 1100 litres of petrol or diesel, or nearly 2000 euros. Thus, households spend more money on energy for transport than on that used at home.

Household consumption of natural gas has been decreasing for years, mostly thanks to better heat insulation – double glazing and cavity wall insulation, in particular. Electricity consumption, however, keeps on rising; even though electrical appliances have become more energy-efficient, they have also become bigger, and people use more and more of them. The same applies to private cars; engines have become more fuel-efficient, but car ownership has also grown and cars have become bigger and heavier (although recently this trend has halted). Furthermore, people are using their cars more often and for greater distances. As a result, total energy consumption from private car use increased, considerably, between 1990 and 2008, and since has stabilised.

In addition to direct energy consumption, households also account for a considerable amount of indirect energy consumption. This is the energy consumed during the production of goods and services that households buy or use; it is 'hidden' in everything that people buy, from a jar of peanut butter, to a tablet, to a home-delivered online purchase. Indirect energy consumption amounts to an annual 372 gigajoules per household, 138 gigajoules of which are domestically generated within the Netherlands and 244 gigajoules in other countries.

ANNUAL DOMESTIC ENERGY CONSUMPTION, IN GIGAJOULES (2009) (1 GIGAJOULE = 1 000 000 000 JOULES)

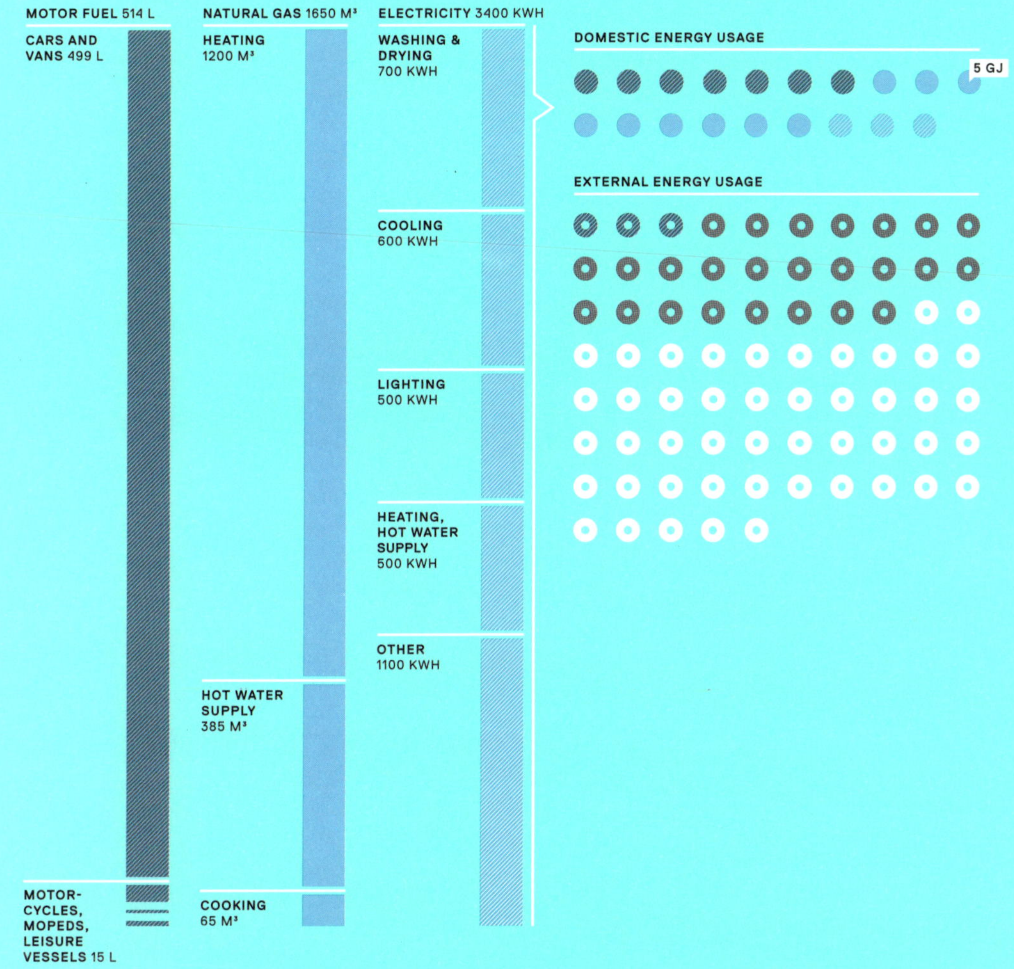

DOMESTIC ENERGY CONSUMPTION

- MOTOR FUEL
- NATURAL GAS
- ELECTRICITY

INDIRECT ENERGY CONSUMPTION

- PUBLIC TRANSPORT (INCLUDING FERRIES, TAXIS AND AEROPLANES)
- PUBLIC AND PRIVATE CONSUMPTION IN THE NETHERLANDS
- PRODUCTION OF GOODS, TRANSPORT AND SERVICES IN OTHER COUNTRIES (IMPORT)

10.1 / A FULL TANK PER DAY

The average Dutch household uses 466 gigajoules of energy per year. This is equivalent to 40 litres of petrol per day. One fifth of this amount is used directly, at home or for own transport. A much larger share is due to 'hidden' energy consumption: the energy required to produce the food and goods that households buy.

Sources: CBS/PBL/WUR, WIOD

ENERGY BALANCE OF THE NETHERLANDS, IN PETAJOULES (2011) (1 PETAJOULE = 1 000 000 000 000 000 JOULES)

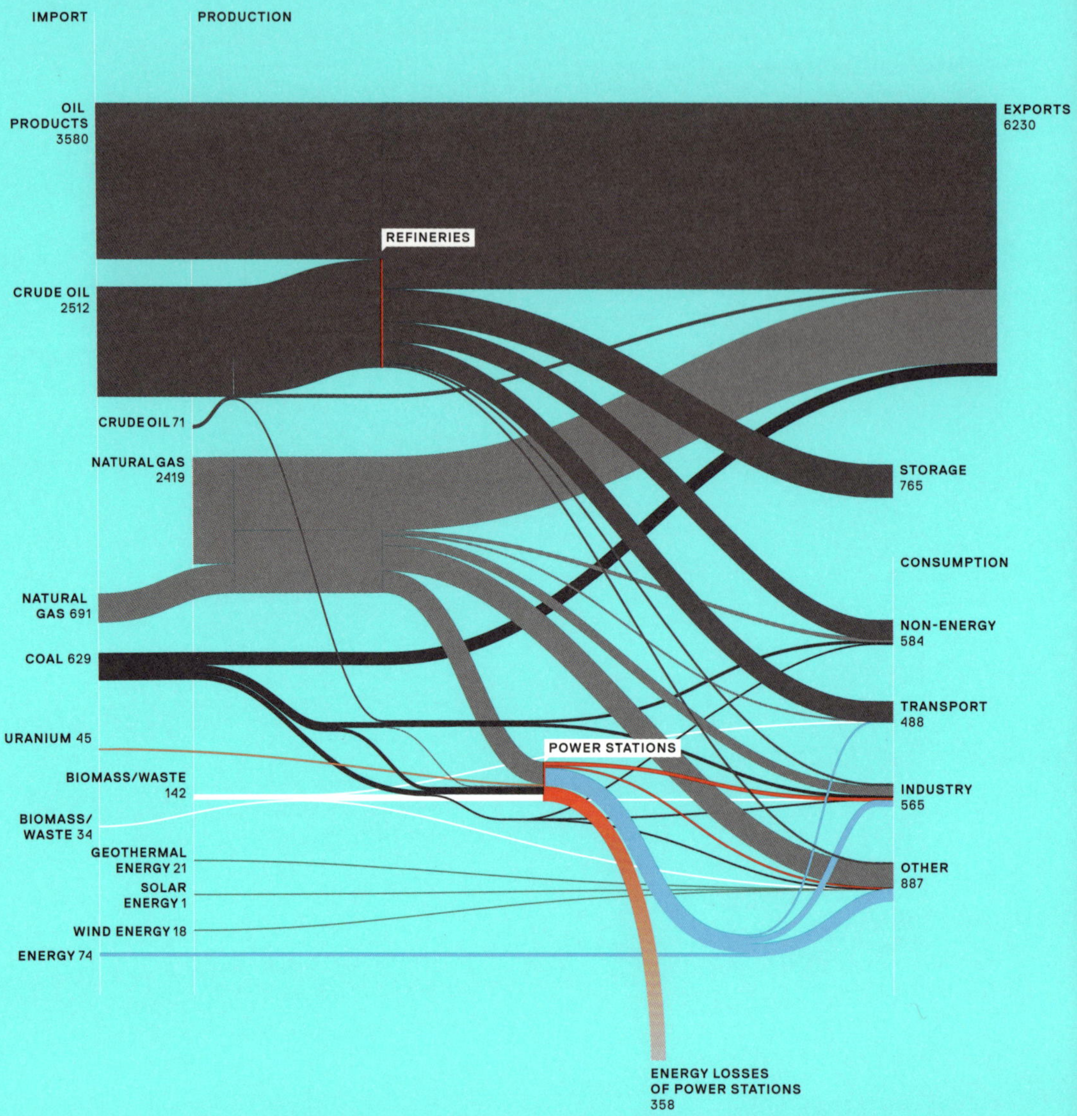

10.2 / THE NETHERLANDS RUNS ON OIL AND NATURAL GAS

The main flows in the Dutch energy system are oil and natural gas. These fuels are both imported and exported, and in the Netherlands converted into electricity, heat, mobility and non-energy products, such as plastics. Biomass (e.g. imported wood pellets or agricultural residues), wind and solar energy meet over 4% of the energy demand.

Source: IEA

Adding direct and indirect energy consumption together, the average Dutch household has a total annual energy use of 466 gigajoules. This is equivalent to 40 litres of petrol per day.

10.2 / THE NETHERLANDS RUNS ON OIL AND NATURAL GAS

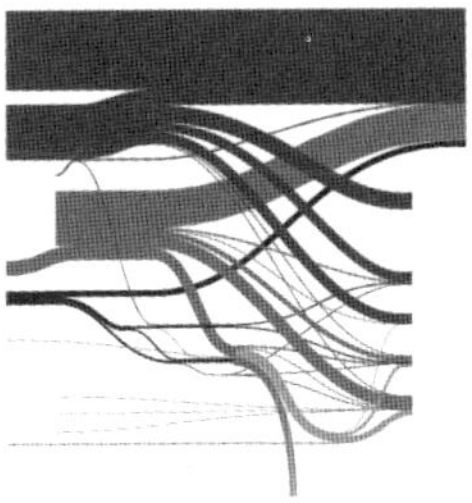

The Dutch energy system is largely dependent on oil and natural gas. Furthermore, the Netherlands plays an important role in the international trade and distribution of oil, natural gas and coal. Fossil-fuel import is three times higher and export two times higher than domestic fuel consumption.

The Netherlands has to import almost all of its oil. About 75% of imported oil is re-exported, often after processing. The remainder is used within the Netherlands; mostly as raw material and motor fuel. As for natural gas, the Netherlands' own reserves provide for 75% of demand; the remainder is covered by import. The Netherlands also exports natural gas from its own gas fields and re-exports imported gas. The total export volume is equal to two thirds of the annual yield from Dutch gas fields. Thus, the Netherlands is both importer and exporter of natural gas.

Dutch electricity import and export levels are much lower, at least in terms of petajoules. However, relative to total domestic electricity consumption, cross-border electricity trade is still substantial. These amounts vary considerably between years.

Within the Netherlands, oil and natural gas are converted to electricity, heat, mobility and various non-energy products, such as plastics. These energy conversions not only take place in large-scale power stations and factories, but also on smaller scales; for example, in car engines and household heating systems.

In addition to fossil fuels, biomass and other renewable sources also contribute to the Dutch energy supply, but to a much smaller extent. Biomass, wind and solar energy together meet over 4% of the current energy demand in the Netherlands.

Energy efficiency is never 100%; heat is lost in each conversion or processing step. Heat loss not only occurs from car engines but also in power stations, which produce electricity as well as heat. Power stations usually discharge this heat into the environment via cooling water, resulting in a heat loss of 40%. Heat loss from car engines is even higher, at 75%.

In general, yield losses cannot be avoided, but they can often be reduced. For example, energy yields can be significantly improved if residual heat from power stations is recovered and reused, rather than discharged into the environment.

10.3 A / EUROPE'S GAS HUB

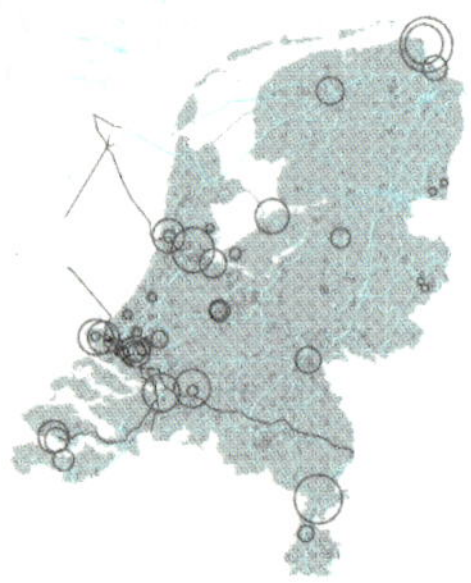

The Netherlands is an important node in the global energy network, and also has an excellent nation-wide energy infrastructure. The energy consumed within the Netherlands comes from both domestic and various global sources; coal from Australia, natural gas from Russia, oil from Saudi Arabia, biofuel from Brazil and electricity from Germany, imported by ship, pipeline or electricity cable. The natural gas network extends from deep into the North Sea to far beyond Europe's borders, into Iran, Russia and Algeria.

Within the Netherlands, energy is delivered to users via petrol stations as well as natural gas pipelines, heat networks and electricity cables reaching into every Dutch home. The Dutch natural gas network measures 135,000 kilometres of pipeline; the electricity network cables stretch over 300,000 kilometres.

The Dutch energy infrastructure is not only extensive, but also highly advanced. This high-tech infrastructure allows the Netherlands to serve as a hub for natural gas distribution across north-western Europe, even once the Dutch gas fields will be exhausted. Via this hub natural gas and biomethane can be distributed to other European countries or temporarily stored in underground fields.

MAIN INFRASTRUCTURE FOR NATURAL GAS AND PETROLEUM / POWER STATIONS (>60 MW) (2012)

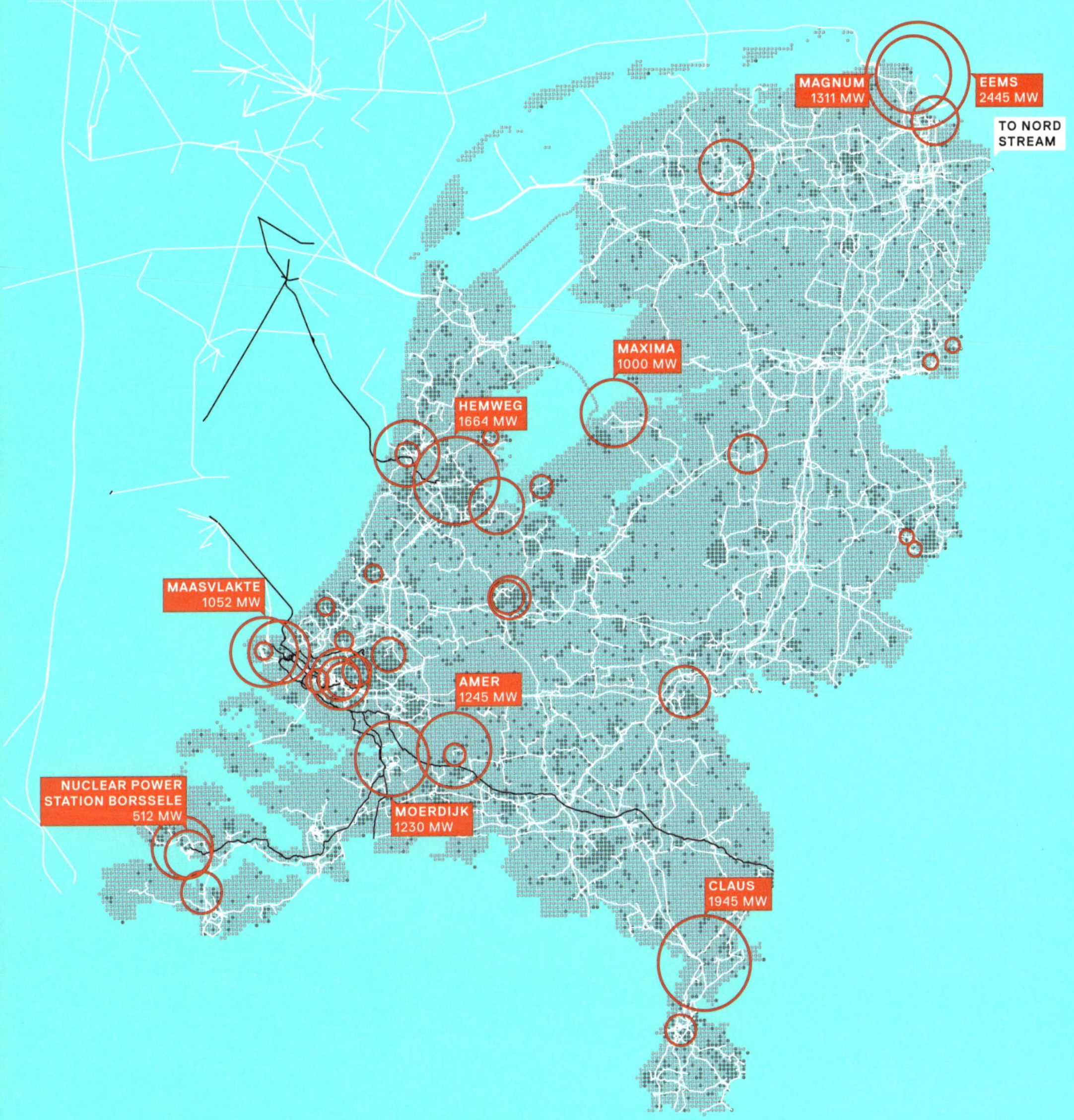

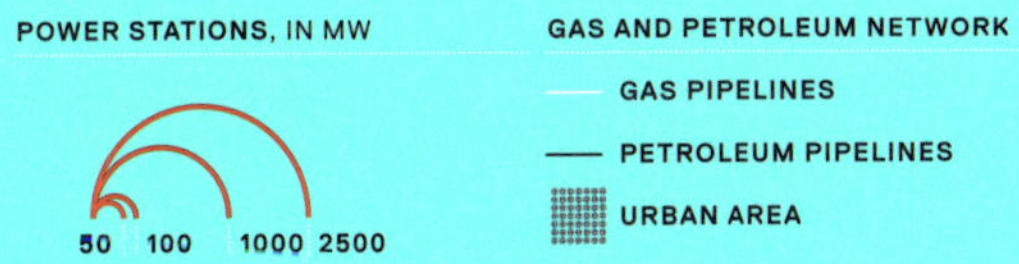

10.3 A / EUROPE'S GAS HUB

The Netherlands has an excellent gas infrastructure, with extensive pipeline networks on land and in the North Sea. The Netherlands aims to use this infrastructure to provide gas services across Europe; the country is to become a 'gas roundabout' (gas hub) for international distribution and storage of natural gas and CO_2.

Sources: ECN, LISA, Risicoregister/RIVM – adaptation by PBL

MAIN INFRASTRUCTURE FOR ELECTRICITY / POWER STATIONS (>60 MW), WIND TURBINES AND WASTE-TO-ENERGY (WTE) INCINERATORS (2012)

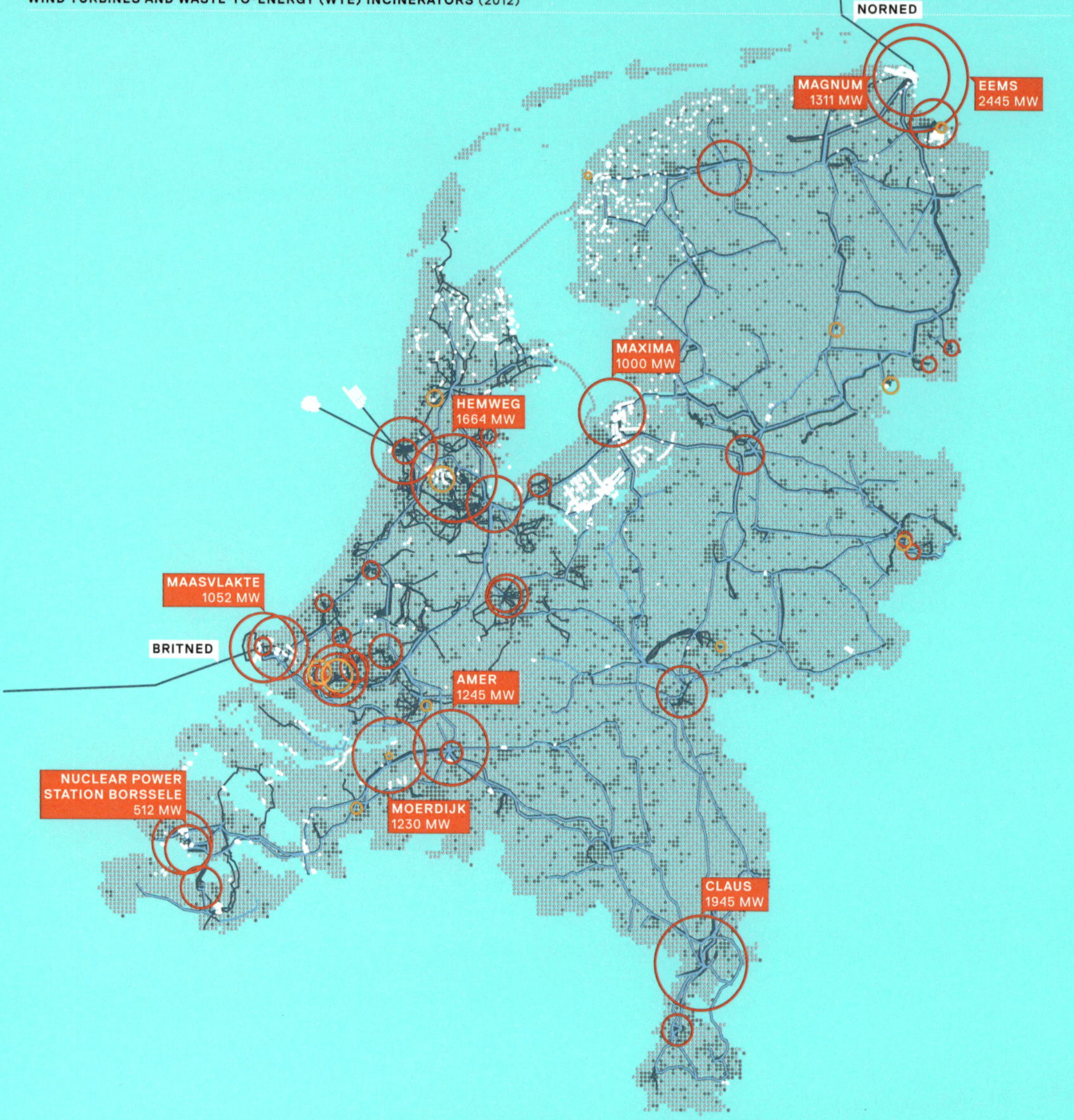

POWER GENERATION IN MW

50 100 1000 2500

- POWER STATIONS
- WASTE-TO-ENERGY (WTE) INCINERATORS
- WIND TURBINES

ELECTRICITY NETWORK

- HIGH-VOLTAGE OVERHEAD POWER LINES
- HIGH-VOLTAGE UNDERGROUND POWER LINES
- URBAN AREA

10.3 B / ELECTRICITY INCREASINGLY MORE OFTEN CROSSES NATIONAL BORDERS

The Dutch electricity network connects power stations to end users, ranging from industry to individual households. New wind parks require the network to be extended, both onshore and offshore. The electricity infrastructure is also becoming more international; for instance, through increasing trade with Germany and new connections to the United Kingdom.

Sources: IDON, LISA, RWS, TenneT, Windenergie-nieuws – all adapted by PBL

10.3 B / ELECTRICITY INCREASINGLY MORE OFTEN CROSSES NATIONAL BORDERS

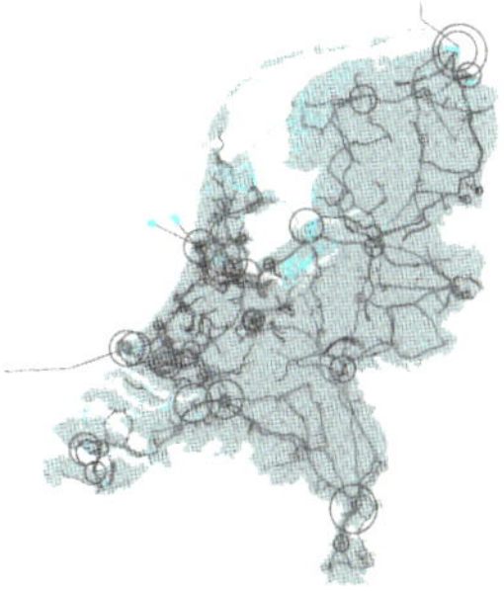

The electricity infrastructure is also becoming ever more international. The Netherlands is trading electricity with neighbouring countries; in the long run, the entire European market is to be served through a single, interconnected transmission network. Partly for this reason, cable links between the Netherlands and the United Kingdom and Norway have recently been constructed. International electricity grids also provide flexibility to respond to natural variability in wind and solar power supply.

10.4 / CO_2 AS A BY-PRODUCT OF PROSPERITY AND POVERTY

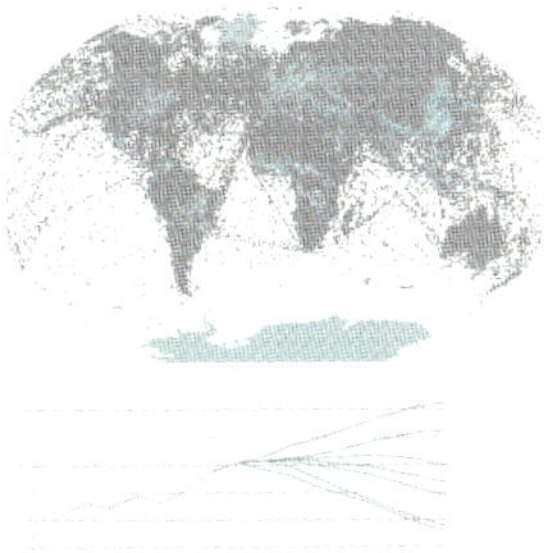

Across the world, energy supply mostly depends on fossil fuels; particularly coal, oil and natural gas. In addition, wood is a common fuel in many poor areas of the world. Burning wood and fossil fuels results in the emission of carbon dioxide (CO_2). The scientific consensus is that anthropogenic emissions of CO_2 and other greenhouse gases very likely lead to warming of the earth and its atmosphere. Global warming has irreparable consequences for ecosystems, agriculture and urban populations.

The threats of global warming call for a radical change in our energy system. This will not be easy, because CO_2 production is interwoven with many human activities.

The measures that are needed to reduce carbon emissions differ between countries and regions. North America, Europe and Australia have high emission levels due to their energy-intensive standard of living, including the massive use of cars, electrical appliances and machines. The emerging economies of China and India have high emission levels because of their recent rapid development as a 'factory of the world', resulting in proportionally high energy use. In contrast, the high emission levels of Central Africa are due to poverty combined with a rapid population growth. Here, energy consumption is relatively low but carbon emission levels are still high, because

CO_2 EMISSIONS (2005)

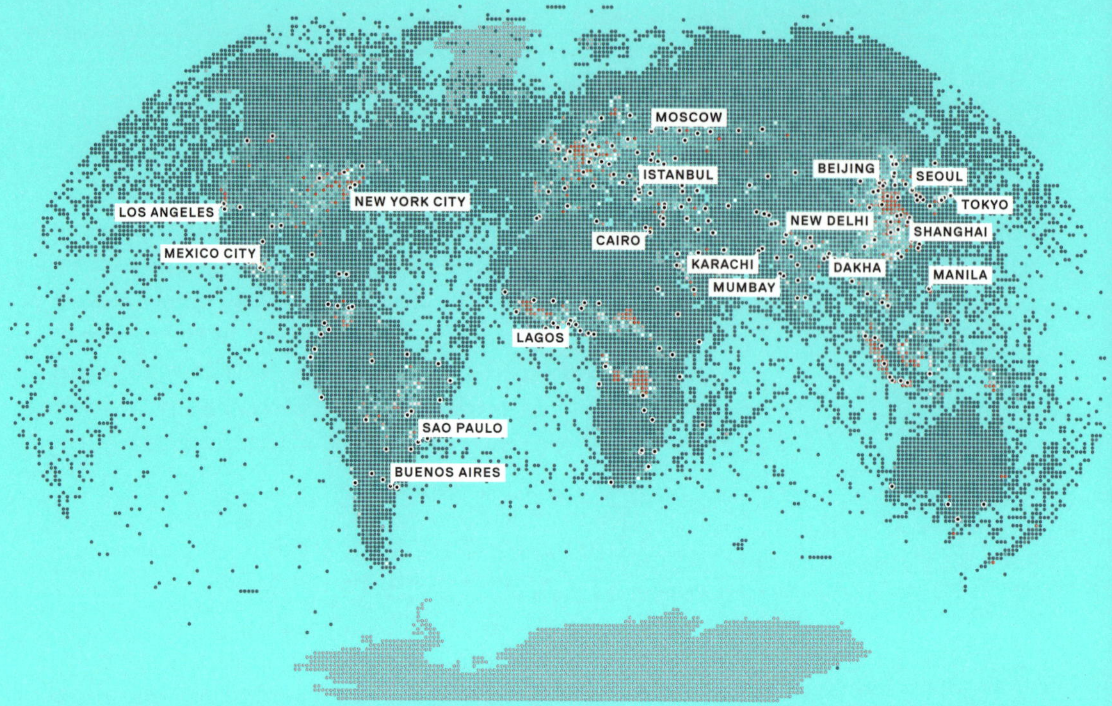

IMPACT OF EMISSION REDUCTION OPTIONS ON GLOBAL GREENHOUSE GAS EMISSIONS, IN GIGATONNES CO_2 eq PER YEAR

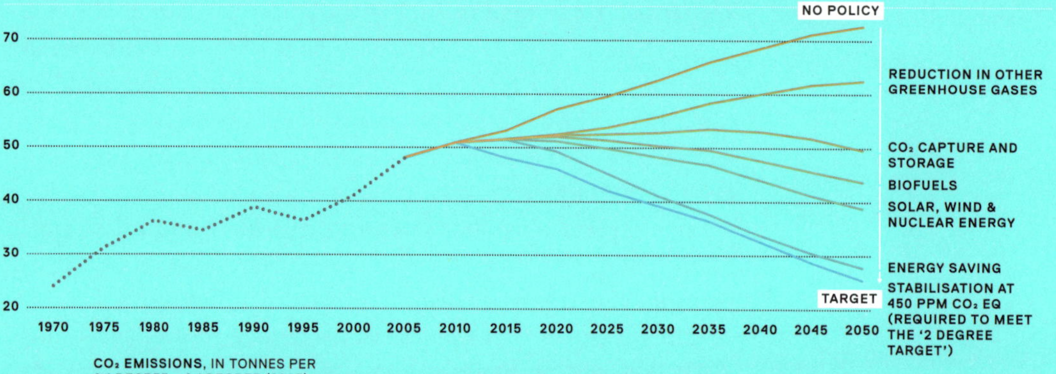

CO_2 EMISSIONS, IN TONNES PER 0.1 DEGREE × 0.1 DEGREE (2005)

POPULATION IN MAJOR CITIES (2010)

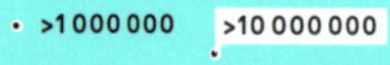

10.4 / CO_2 AS A BY-PRODUCT OF PROSPERITY AND POVERTY

Carbon dioxide (CO_2) is released when we burn fossil fuels, such as coal, oil and natural gas. Rich countries and emerging economies have high CO_2 emission levels. Emission levels in Africa are also high, but this is due to deforestation and the use of wood for fuel. To stop global warming, CO_2 emissions must be drastically reduced.

Sources: JRC, PBL

of the extensive use of coal and wood for fuel and the widespread clearing of forests to create farmland. Because of these international differences in carbon emission patterns, countries may require different mitigation strategies.

The measures needed to reduce carbon emissions are collectively known as 'the energy transition'. Although there is no standard recipe for energy transition, there are three essential ingredients, which vary in importance between countries and regions. First, we have to reduce harmful emissions from fuel combustion; for example, by substituting coal with natural gas or sustainably produced biomass, and by capturing and storing CO_2 instead of releasing it into the atmosphere. Second, we have to generate more low-carbon energy; the options for Europe are wind and solar energy, nuclear energy, hydropower and geothermal energy. And third, we need to save energy wherever possible; the less energy we use, the less CO_2 is released into the atmosphere.

10.5 / AN ENERGETIC FUTURE

To limit global warming, international agreements have been reached to reduce carbon emissions. According to these agreements, global CO_2 emissions must be halved by 2050, relative to 1990 levels. Of the more than 200 countries of the world, 138 countries have adopted climate policies, some more far-reaching than others. The European Union aims for an 80% to 95% emission reduction by 2050.

Achieving these reduction targets will be difficult; particularly, because energy consumption keeps rising. Global energy consumption is projected to increase by 80% between now and 2050. Energy consumption in the Netherlands will rise less steeply, but still by 20% to 50% if no energy saving measures are taken. To meet the growing energy demand while achieving an 80% to 95% emission reduction will require a radical change in Europe's energy system.

One step in the right direction is to further improve energy efficiency. With current technologies the Netherlands could achieve energy savings of up to 30% compared to autonomous growth – a 10% to 20% reduction in present consumption

ENERGY MIX OF THE NETHERLANDS (2012) AND TWO POSSIBLE SCENARIOS IN WHICH CO_2 EMISSIONS ARE REDUCED BY 80%, BY 2050

TOTAL DOMESTIC ENERGY DEMAND, INCLUDING ELECTRICITY AND HEAT, NATURAL GAS FOR HEATING, AND TRANSPORT FUELS; EXCLUDING INDUSTRIAL FEEDSTOCK (2012)

OPTION 1: A LOW-CARBON ENERGY SYSTEM BY 2050, DUE TO THE LARGE-SCALE APPLICATION OF RENEWABLE ENERGY SOURCES

OPTION 2: TOTAL DOMESTIC ENERGY DEMAND BY 2050, ASSUMING MASSIVE ENERGY SAVING AND MASSIVE DEPLOYMENT OF CCS

ENERGY SOURCE

- FOSSIL FUEL
- FOSSIL FUEL WITH CARBON CAPTURE AND STORAGE
- BIOMASS WITH CARBON CAPTURE AND STORAGE
- BIOMASS
- WIND ENERGY
- SOLAR POWER
- AMBIENT HEAT

10.5 / AN ENERGETIC FUTURE

Meeting the CO_2 reduction targets in the Netherlands requires a radical energy transition. The future energy mix is still uncertain, but it will undoubtedly require energy saving and efficiency improvements, a switch to non-fossil energy sources, and further deployment of carbon capture and storage.

Source: PBL

levels. For example, energy can be saved by using more fuel-efficient cars and by better insulating buildings to reduce heat consumption.

This, however, will not be enough. It will also be necessary to change the energy system; particularly, the ways in which energy is supplied. We need to generate more solar, wind and hydropower, and possibly also nuclear and/or biomass energy. Or, when using fossil fuels, we have to capture the CO_2 and reuse or store it.

To make the energy transition a success, we will have to deploy all known, tried and tested technologies and energy sources. However, all of these have their own limitations. For example, some are still too expensive, such as offshore wind energy. Others, such as nuclear energy, onshore wind energy and carbon capture and storage (CCS), are less popular because of their effects on the environment; whether these will ever have sufficient public support remains to be seen.

It is still uncertain what our energy system in 2050 will look like, but the building blocks described above will undoubtedly be part of it. If, in the Netherlands, we achieve only moderate energy savings and want to use mainly renewable energy, we will have to pull out all the stops; we will need much more biomass, much more wind energy, much more solar power and ambient heat. However, if we succeed in achieving massive energy savings, we should be able to meet emission reduction targets with an energy mix based on fossil fuels and biomass. However, this would require massive deployment of carbon capture and storage (CCS) systems in power plants. In the case of biomass-based electricity generation, CCS may even result in a net reduction in atmospheric CO_2.

REFERENCES

ON BEING SMART ABOUT CITIES

- **Airoldi M, Biscarini L and Saracina V. (2010)**
  The Global Infrastructure Challenge: Top Priorities for the Public and Private Sectors. Boston Consulting Group, Milan.
- **Angel S. (2012)**
  Planet of cities, the Lincoln Institute of Land Policy, Cambridge (US).
- **The Arts Council of Great Britain (1987)**
  Le Corbusier: Architect of the Century, Catalog of the exhibition, 5 March – 7 June 1987, Hayward Gallery, London.
- **Ausubel JH and Herman R. (eds.) (1988)**
  Cities and Their Vital Systems: Infrastructure, Past, Present, and Future, National Academy, Washington DC.
- **Barber BR. (1984)**
  Strong Democracy: Participatory Politics for a New Age, University of California Press, Oakland.
- **Berman M. (1983)**
  All that is solid melts into air. The experience of modernity, Verso Books, London.
- **Biswas AK and Brabeck Letmathe P. (2014)**
  The Third World's Drinking Problem, Project Syndicate, 23 February 2014. www.project-syndicate.org.
- **Chakrabarti V. (2013)**
  A Country of Cities: A Manifesto for an Urban America, Metropolis Books.
- **CPCB (Central Pollution Control Board), Ministry of Environment and Forests, Government of India (2013)**
  Performance evaluation of sewage treatment plants under control of NRCD, Delhi.
- **Crutzen PJ. (2002)**
  Geology of mankind, Nature 415, 23 (3 January 2002).
- **Doshi V, Schulman G and Gabaldon D. (2007)**
  Light! Water! Motion! Strategy and Business, 47:39–53.
- **FAO (2013)**
  The State of Food Insecurity in the World: The multiple dimensions of food security. Food and Agriculture Organization (FAO), Rome.
- **Farrao P and Fernandez JE. (2013)**
  Sustainable Urban Metabolism. MIT Press, Cambridge (US).
- **Flint A. (2009)**
  Wrestling with Moses. How Jane Jacobs took on the New York's master builder and transformed the American city, Random House, New York.
- **Graedel TE, Alwood J, Birat J-P, Reck BK, Sibley SF, Sommermann G, Buchert M and Hagelüken C. (2011)**
  Recyling rates of metals – a status report. A report by the working group on the global metal flows to the International Resource Panel, United Nations Environment Programme (UNEP).
- **Graham S and Marvin S. (2001)**
  Splintering Urbanism: Networked Infrastructures, Technological Mobilities, Routledge London and New York.
- **Greenfield A and Kim N. (2013)**
  Against the smart city (The city is here for you to use), Kindle eBook.
- **The Guardian (2014)**
  China's toxic air pollution resembles nuclear winter, say scientists, http://www.theguardian.com/world/2014/feb/25/china-toxic-air-pollution-nuclear-winter-scientists, 27 February 2014, accessed on 28 March 2014.
- **Hajer MA. (1995)**
  The Politics of Environmental Discourse, Ecological Modernization and the Policy Process, Oxford University Press, Oxford.
- **Hajer MA. (2009)**
  Policy Making in the Age of Mediatization, Oxford University Press, Oxford.
- **Hajer MA. (2011)**
  The Energetic Society, PBL Netherlands Environmental Assessment Agency, The Hague.
- **Hajer MA and Wagenaar H. (2003)**
  Deliberative Policy Analysis: Understanding Governance in the Network Society, Cambridge University Press.
- **Hall P. (1986)**
  Governing the Economy, Oxford University Press, New York.
- **Hall P. (1988)**
  Cities of Tomorrow: An Intellectual History of Urban Planning and Design in the Twentieth Century, (1988, 1996, 2002), Blackwell Publishing, Oxford.
- **Hatzelhoffer L, Humboldt K, Lobeck M and Wiegandt CC. (2012)**
  Smart City in Practice - Converting Innovative Ideas into Reality, Jovis Verlag GmbH, Berlin.
- **Hoornweg D and Freire M. (2013)**
  Building sustainability in an urbanizing world, A Partnership Report, Urban Development Series Knowledge Papers, no. 17.
- **Kemp-Benedict E, Heaps C and Raskin P. (2002)**
  Global Scenario Group Futures: Technical Notes. PoleStar Series Report 9. Stockholm Environment Institute, Stockholm.
- **Kuecker GD. (2013)**
  Building the Bridge to the Future: New Songdo City from a Critical Urbanism Perspective. Essay Prepared for SOAS, University of London Centre of Korean Studies Workshop New Songdo City and South Korea's Green Economy: An Uncertain Future, 5 June 2013.
- **Lipsky M. (1980)**
  Street-level bureaucracy – Dilemmas of the individual in public service, Russell Sage Foundation, New York.
- **OECD (2012)**
  OECD Environmental Outlook to 2050, OECD Publishing, Paris.
- **OECD (2013)**
  Urbanisation and Green Growth in China, OECD Regional Development Working Papers, 2013/07, OECD Publishing, Paris.
- **Olivier JGJ, Janssens-Maenhout G, Muntean M and Peters JAHW. (2013)**
  Trends in global CO_2 emissions, 2013 report, PBL Netherlands Environmental Assessment Agency, The Hague, and the Joint Research Centre (JRC), Ispra.
- **PBL (2012)**
  Roads from Rio+20 Pathways to achieve global sustainability goals by 2050, PBL Netherlands Environmental Assessment Agency, The Hague.
- **Pizzi A. (2014)**
  Apostles of cleanliness - The 19th-century Sanitary Movement denied the germ theory of disease, yet created our public health infrastructure, http://pubs.acs.org/subscribe/journals/mdd/v05/i05/html/05ttl.html, accessed on 3 March 2014.
- **Premalatha S, Tauseef M, Abbasi T and Abbasi SA. (2013)**
  The promise and the performance of the world's first two zero carbon eco-cities, Renewable and Sustainable Energy Reviews 25; 660–669.
- **Pressman JL and Wildavsky A. (1984)**
  Implementation, third edition expanded, 1 January 1984, University of California Press.
- **Raworth K. (2012)**
  A safe and just space for humanity. Can we live within the doughnut? Oxfam Discussion Papers.
- **Richter M. (2013)**
  Business model innovation for sustainable energy: German utilities and renewable energy. Energy Policy, Volume 62 (2013) 1226–1237.
- **Rockström J, Steffen W, Noone K, Persson Å, Chapin III FS, Lambin EF, Lenton TM, Scheffer M, Folke C, Schellnhuber HJ, Nykvist B, De Wit CA, Hughes T, Van der Leeuw S, Rodhe H, Sörlin S, Snyder PK, Costanza R, Svedin U, Falkenmark M, Karlberg L, Corell RW, Fabry VJ, Hansen J, Walker B, Liverman D, Richardson K, Crutzen P and Foley JA. (2009)**
  A safe operating space for humanity, Nature, 461: 472–475.

- **Schattschneider E. (1960)**
The Semisovereign People: a realist's view of democracy in America, Holt, Rhinehart and Winston, New York.
- **Scott JC. (1998)**
Seeing Like a State: How Certain Schemes to Improve the Human Condition Have Failed. Yale University Press.
- **Steffen W, Sanderson A, Tyson PD, Jäger J, Matson PA, Moore III B, Oldfield F, Richardson K, Schellnhuber HJ, Turner BL and Wasson RJ. (2004)**
Global Change and the Earth System: A Planet Under Pressure. Published by Springer-Verlag, Berlin Heidelberg New York.
- **Swilling M. (2012)**
Economic crisis, long waves and the sustainability transition: An African perspective, Environmental Innovation and Societal Transitions 6 (2013) 96–115.
- **Swilling M. (2014a)**
Towards Sustainable Urban Infrastructures for the Urban Anthropocene, Contribution to Allen A, Lampis A and Swilling M. (Eds.), Untamed Urbanism. New York: Routledge, Forthcoming.
- **Swilling, M. (2014b)**
Ecocultural Assemblages in the Urbanizing Global South. Draft submitted for publication in Pretty, J., Boehme, S. and Bharucha, Z. Ecocultures: Blueprints for Sustainable Communities. (in press)
- **Swilling M and Annecke E. (2012)**
Just Transitions: Explorations of Sustainability in an Unfair World. Cape Town: UCT Press and Tokyo: United Nations University Press.
- **Swilling M, Robinson B, Marvin S and Hodgson M. (2012)**
Reshaping Urban Infrastructure: Material Flow Analysis and Transitions Analysis in an Urban Context. Journal of Industrial Ecology, 16(6):789–800.
- **Throgmorton J. (1996)**
Planning as Persuasive Storytelling: The Rhetorical Construction of Chicago's Electric Future, University of Chicago Press.
- **Townsend AM. (2013)**
Smart Cities: Big Data, Civic Hackers, and the Quest for a New Utopia, W. W. Norton and Company, 7 October 2013.
- **UN (United Nations) (2012)**
World Population Prospects: The 2012 Revision, New York, http://esa.un.org/unpd/wpp/index.htm, visited 6 March 2014.
- **UNEP (2013a)**
City-Level Decoupling: Urban resource flows and the governance of infrastructure transitions. Full report by the Working Group on Cities of the International Resource Panel. Swilling M, Robinson B, Marvin S and Hodson M., United Nations Environment Programme (UNEP).
- **UNEP (2013b)**
City-Level Decoupling: Urban resource flows and the governance of infrastructure transitions. Summary by the Working Group on Cities of the International Resource Panel. Swilling M, Robinson B, Marvin S and Hodson M., United Nations Environment Programme (UNEP).
- **WHO and Unicef (2013)**
Progress on sanitation and drinking water. 2013 Update, World Health Organization and Unicef.
- **Worldbank (2014)**
http:/data.worldbank.org/indicator/CM.MKT.LCAP.CD/countries?display=graph, accessed on 24 April 2014.

01 DEMOGRAPHY

- **CBS (2005)**
Binnenlandse migratie: verhuismotieven en verhuisafstand, Bevolkingstrends, 2e kwartaal 2005 [Domestic migration, motives for moving and moving distance, Population trends, 2nd quarter 2005 (in Dutch)], Statistics Netherlands, The Hague/Heerlen.
- **McEvedy C and Jones R. (1978)**
Atlas of World Population History (1978), Penguin Books, London.
- **PBL (2013)**
Welvaart en Leefomgeving – Horizonscan [Welfare, Prosperity and Quality of the Living Environment (in Dutch)], PBL Netherlands Environmental Assessment Agency, The Hague.
- **UN (2011)**
World Urbanization Prospects, the 2011 Revision, Data on Urban and Rural Populations, United Nations, accessed on 14 April 2014.

02 AIR

- **MNP (2005)**
Fijn stof nader bekeken [A closer look at particulate matter (in Dutch)]. MNP Report number 500037008, Netherlands Environmental Assessment Agency, Bilthoven.
- **OECD (2012)**
OECD Environmental Outlook to 2050: The Consequences of Inaction, OECD Publishing, doi: 10.1787/9789264122246-en, Organisation for Economic Co-operation and Development, Paris.
- **PBL (2010)**
Assessment of the Human Environment 2010. PBL Report number 500206001, PBL Netherlands Environmental Assessment Agency, The Hague.
- **Sigman R, Hilderink H, Delrue N, Braathen N-A, Leflaive X. (2012)**
'Health and Environment', in OECD Environmental Outlook to 2050: The Consequences of Inaction, OECD Publishing. Doi, 10.1787/env_outlook-2012-9-en, Organisation for Economic Co-operation and Development, Paris.
- **US EPA (2008)**
Reducing Urban Heat Islands: Compendium of Strategies, http://www.epa.gov/heatisland/resources/pdf/BasicsCompendium.pdf, United States Environmental Protection Agency, Washington.
- **WHO (2006)**
WHO Air quality guidelines for particulate matter, ozone, nitrogen dioxide and sulfur dioxide, Global update 2005, Summary of risk assessment. <http://whqlibdoc.who.int/hq/2006/WHO_SDE_PHE_OEH_06.02_eng.pdf>, World Health Organization, Geneva.

03 WATER

- **Mekonnen MM and Hoekstra AY. (2011)**
National water footprint accounts: the green, blue and grey water footprint of production and consumption, Value of Water Research Report Series No.50, UNESCO-IHE, Delft.
- **Nibud (2014)**
http://www.nibud.nl/uitgaven/huishouden/gas-elektriciteit-en-water.html, National Institute for Family Finance Information (Nibud), accessed on 7 January 2014

04 FOOD

- **Backer KD and Miroudot A. (2013)**
Mapping Global Value, Chains, OECD Trade Policy Papers, No. 159, OECD Publishing Organisation for Economic Co-operation and Development, Paris.
- **Backus G, Meeusen M, Dagevos H, Van 't Riet J, Bartels J, Onwezen MC and Grievink JW. (2011)**
Voedselbalans 2011. Deel I [Food balance 2011. Part 1 (in Dutch)], LEI, Agricultural Economics Research Institute (part of Wageningen University and Research Centre), The Hague/Wageningen.
- **Beusen AHW, Van Beek LPH, Bouwman AF and Middelburg JJ. (2014)**
Exploring changes in nitrogen and phosphorus biogeochemistry in global rivers in the twentieth century, Global Biogeochemical Cycles, February 2014. (paper submitted)
- **Felperlaan A, Ariesen M and De Boer A. (2010)**
Sustainable Cocoa for the Dutch Market, Analysis of the Dutch cocoa sector, Amsterdam/Utrecht, CREM/Dutch sustainable trade.

- **Van Gelder JW and Herder A. (2012)**
Soja Barometer 2012, Een onderzoeksrapport voor de Nederlandse sojacoalitie [Soya Barometer 2012, A study conducted for the Dutch soya coalition (in Dutch)], Profundo, Amsterdam.
- **Knijff A, Bolhuis J, Van Galen MA and Beukers R. (2011)**
Verduurzaming voedselproductie: inzicht in productie, import, export en consumptie van voedsel [Sustainable food production; insight into the production, import, export and consumption of food (in Dutch)]. LEI Agricultural Economics Research Institute (part of Wageningen University and Research Centre) (2011): pp. 15–29.
- **Lesschen JP, Van den Berg M, Westhoek HJ, Witzke HP and Oenema O. (2011)**
Greenhouse gas emission profiles of European livestock sectors. In: Animal Feed Science and Technology (2011) 166–167: pp. 1–796.
- **Mekonnen MM and Hoekstra AY. (2011)**
National water footprint accounts: the green, blue and grey water footprint of production and consumption, Value of Water Research Report Series No. 50, UNESCO-IHE, Delft.
- **PBL (2012a)**
The Netherlands in 21 infographics, PBL Netherlands Environmental Assessment Agency, The Hague.
- **PBL (2012b)**
Roads from Rio+ 20: Pathways to achieve global sustainability goals by 2050. PBL Netherlands Environmental Assessment Agency, The Hague.
- **PBL (2012c)**
Assessment of the Human Environment 2012, PBL Netherlands Environmental Assessment Agency, The Hague.
- **PBL (2013a)**
Leren van het energieke platteland [Learning from the energetic countryside (in Dutch)], PBL Netherlands Environmental Assessment Agency, The Hague.
- **PBL (2013b)**
De macht van het menu [The power of the menu (in Dutch)]. PBL Netherlands Environmental Assessment Agency, The Hague.
- **Pereira HM, Leadley PW, Proença V, Alkemade R, Scharlemann JP, Fernandez-Manjarrés JF, Araújo MB, Balvanera P, Biggs R, Cheung WW, Chini L, Cooper HD, Gilman EL, Guénette S, Hurtt GC, Huntington HP, Mace GM, Oberdorff T, Revenga C, Rodrigues P, Scholes RJ, Sumaila UR and Walpole M. (2010)**
Scenarios for global biodiversity in the 21st century. Science, 330(6010).
- **Šebek LBJ and Temme EHM. (2009)**
De humane eiwitbehoefte en eiwitconsumptie en de omzetting van plantaardig eiwit naar dierlijk eiwit. [Human protein requirements and protein intake and the conversion of vegetable protein into animal protein (in Dutch)]. Livestock Research Lelystad (Animal Sciences Group) (Animal Sciences Group), part of Wageningen University and Research Centre.
- **Wascher DM, Roos-Klein Lankhorst J, Agricola HJ and De Jong A. (2010)**
SUSMETRO : Impact Assessment Tools for Food Planning in Metropolitan Regions: IA tools and serious gaming in support of sustainability targets for food planning, nature conservation and recreation. Alterra, Wageningen University and Research Centre, Wageningen, p. 66.
- **Weiss F and Leip A. (2012)**
Greenhouse gas emissions from the EU livestock sector: a life cycle assessment carried out with the CAPRI model. In: Agriculture, Ecosystems & Environment (2012) 149: pp. 124 – 134.

05 BIOTA

- **Buis, J. (1985)**
Historia Forestis: Nederlandse Bosgeschiedenis [Forest History of The Netherlands], Volumes I and II, HES Studia Historica, parts I and II, published as a doctoral thesis, Agricultural University Wageningen and HES Publishers, Utrecht (in Dutch).
- **Municipality of Amsterdam: Bureau Onderzoek en Statistiek, (2013), Het Grote Groenonderzoek 2013 [Comprehensive Green Research (in Dutch)**
Project number: 13124, Amsterdam.
- **PBL (2012a)**
Nature Outlook 2010–2040. PBL publication number: 500414010, PBL Netherlands Environmental Assessments Agency, The Hague.
- **PBL (2012b)**
Voorbij de EHS. Koers voor het nieuwe natuurbeleid, verslag van debat & ontwerpatelier tijdens de Manifestatie De Groene Golflengte van 5 t/m 8 september 2011 op Radio Kootwijk [Beyond the Dutch National Ecological Network (EHS), report on debate and design during a radio event]. PBL Netherlands Environmental Assessments Agency, The Hague.

06 MOBILITY

- **CBS (2004)**
Sociaal-economische trends, 4e kwartaal 2004, Woon-werkverkeer [Socio-economic trends, 4th quarter 2004, on commuter traffic (in Dutch)] Statistics Netherlands, The Hague/Heerlen.
- **KiM (2010)**
Verklaring mobiliteit en bereikbaarheid, 1985–2008 [Explanation mobility and accessibility, 1985–2008 (in Dutch)], KiM Netherlands Institute for Transport Policy Analysis, The Hague.
- **PBL (2009)**
Openbaar vervoer, ruimtelijke structuur en flankerend beleid: de effecten van beleidsstrategieën [Public stransport, spatial structure and flanking policy; the impact of policy strategies (in Dutch)], PBL Netherlands Environmental Assessment Agency, The Hague.
- **PBL (2010)**
De staat van de ruimte 2010: de herschikking van stedelijk Nederland [Spatial development 2010. Rearrangement of Dutch urban areas (in Dutch)]. PBL Netherlands Environmental Assessment Agency, The Hague.
- **PBL (2011)**
The energetic society. PBL Netherlands Environmental Assessment Agency, The Hague.
- **RPB (2005)**
Verkenning van regionale luchthavens [Exploration of regional airports (in Dutch)]. NAi Uitgevers, Netherlands Institute for Spatial Research, The Hague.
- **RPB (2007)**
De staat van de ruimte 2007, Nederland zien veranderen [Spatial development 2007 (in Dutch)]. NAi Uitgevers, Netherlands Institute for Spatial Research, The Hague.

07 CARGO

- **CBS (2012)**
Monitor Logistiek en Supply Chain Management rapportage 2010 [Monitor Logistics and Supply Chain Management, 2010 (in Dutch)]. Statistics Netherlands, The Hague/Heerlen.
- **CBS (2014)**
StatLine: Bbp, productie en bestedingen; productie en inkomens naar bedrijfstak [GDP, production and spending, production and income per business sector (in Dutch)], accessed on 10 February 2014. Statistics Netherlands, The Hague/Heerlen.
- **CPB/MNP/RPB (2006)**
Welfare, Prosperity and Quality of the Living Environment, a scenario study on the Netherlands in 2040. CPB Netherlands Bureau for Economic Policy Analysis, The Hague, Netherlands Environmental Assessment Agency (MNP), Bilthoven, Netherlands Institute for Spatial Research (RPB), The Hague.
- **EEA (2009)**
Towards a resource-efficient transport

system - TERM 2009: indicators tracking transport and environment in the European Union, EEA Report No. 2, European Environment Agency, Copenhagen.
- **IEA (2012)**
  CO_2 emissions from fuel combustion. International Energy Agency, Paris.
- **KiM (2011)**
  Mobiliteitsbalans 2010 [Mobility assessment 2010 (in Dutch)]. KiM Netherlands Institute for Transport Policy Analysis, The Hague.
- **PBL (2012)**
  Elektrisch rijden in 2050: Gevolgen voor de leefomgeving [Electric driving in 2050; consequences for the human environment (in Dutch)]. PBL Netherlands Environmental Assessment Agency, The Hague.

08 BUILDING MATERIALS

- **Bijleveld MM, Bergsma GC and Van Lieshout M. (2013)**
  Milieu-impact van betongebruik in de Nederlandse bouw; Status quo en toetsing van verbeteropties [Environmental impact of the use of concrete in Dutch construction; status quo and review of improvement options (in Dutch)]. CE Delft, Delft.
- **Cement&BetonCentrum (2014)**
  (http://www.cementenbeton.nl/betonmarkt, cementmarkt), accessed on 10 February 2014.
- **Deltares (2008)**
  Staat en Toekomst van de Delta; Achtergronddocument Thema Veiligheid [State and Future of the Delta; background (ocument on Safety (in Dutch)]. Deltares, Delft.
- **Deltares (2011)**
  Sedimentperspectief op de Zuidwestelijke Delta [Sedirr ent perspective on the south-western delta (in Dutch)]. Deltaris, Delft.
- **Hendriks ChF and Janssen GMT. (2004)**
  A New vision on the Building Cycle. Æneas Technical Publishers, Boxtel.
- **Krausmann F, Fischer-Kowalski M, Schandl H and Eisenmenger N. (2008)**
  The global socio-metabolic transition: past and present metabolic profiles and their future trajectories. In: Journal of Industrial Ecology 12(5–6), 637–657.
- **Müller DB, Wang T and Duval B. (2011)**
  Patterns of Iron Use in Societal Evolution. In: Environmental Science and Technology, Volume 45, no. 1.
- **Müller DB. (2006)**
  Stock dynamics for forecasting material flows – Case study for housing in The Netherlands. In: Ecological Economics, Volume 59, issue 1.
- **MWH (2012)**
  Productie en verbruik van beton- en metselzand en (gebroken) grind in 2010; Stand van het Zand XVI; Lint aan het Grind XIV [Production and use of sand for concrete production and bricklaying and (crushed) gravel (in Dutch)]. Montgomery Watson Harza, Arnhem.
- **Oldenburger J, De Groot C and Winterink A. (2012)**
  Nederlandse houtstromen in beeld [Dutch timber flows (in Dutch)]. Stichting Probos, Wageningen.
- **Project organisation Maasvlakte 2 (2014)**
  (http://www.maasvlakte2.com/en/index/show/id/691/Sand+and+rock%3A+a+status+report), accessed on 5 March 2014.
- **Rijkswaterstaat (2003)**
  Inventarisatie voor de Nota Ophoogzand (Intron) III [Inventory for the Policy Document on Elevation Sand (Intron) III (in Dutch)]. Intron, Sittard, VIBO (Verkeer en Waterstaat IPO Bouwgrondstoffen Onderzoek) Rijkswaterstaat, Dienst Weg- en Waterbouwkunde, Delft.
- **Rijkswaterstaat (2006)**
  Scenariostudie BSA-granulaten; aanbod en afzet van 2005 tot 2025 [Scenario study BSA granulates; supply and demand, 2005–2025 (in Dutch)]. Intron, Sittard, Rijkswaterstaat, Dienst Weg- en Waterbouwkunde, Delft.
- **Rijkswaterstaat (2014)**
  Noordzeeloket [North Sea office] (http://www.noordzeeatlas.nl/Kaart/zand_en_schelpwinning.htm), accessed on 5 March 2014.
- **Steinberger JK, Krausmann F and Eisenmenger N. (2010)**
  Global patterns of materials use: a socioeconomic and geophysical analysis. In: Ecological Economics, Volume 69, issue 5.
- **UN (2012)**
  World Urbanization Prospects, The 2011 Revision. United Nations Department of Economic and Social Affairs, Population Division, New York.
- **UNEP (2013)**
  Recent trends in material flows and resource productivity in Asia and the Pacific. United Nations Environment Programme (UNEP) Regional Office for Asia and the Pacific, Bangkok, Thailand.
- **UNEP SBCI (United Nations Environment Programme, Sustainable Buildings/Climate Initiative) (2009)**
  Buildings and Climate Change; Summary for Decision-Makers. UNEP Sustainable Buildings and Climate Initiative, Paris.

09 WASTE

- **Carabain C, Spitz G and Keulemans S. (2012)**
  Nederlanders & afval: Jonge en oudere Nederlanders over afval [The Dutch & waste; young and elderly Dutch people talk about waste (in Dutch)]. NCDO Dutch expertise and advisory centre for citizenship and international cooperation, Amsterdam.
- **PBL (2013)**
  Green Gains; in search of opportunities for the Dutch economy. PBL Netherlands Environmental Assessment Agency, The Hague.
- **Rijkswaterstaat (2013)**
  Nederlands afval in cijfers, gegevens 2006–2010 [Data on Dutch waste, 2006–2010 (in Dutch)]. Utrecht.
- **UNEP (2012)**
  Global Environment Outlook 5: Environment for the Future We Want. United Nations Environment Programme, Nairobi.
- **World Bank (2013)**
  What a waste: A Global Review of Solid Waste Management. Washington.

10 ENERGY

- **Dutch Government (2014)**
  http://www.rijksoverheid.nl/onderwerpen/gaswinning-en-infrastructuur/gaspositie-van-nederland/gasrotonde, accessed on 30 January 2014
- **ECN (2012)**
  Energietrends 2012 (Energy trends 2012 (in Dutch)], Energy research Centre of the Netherlands, Petten/The Hague.
- **European Parliament (2014)**
  http://www.europarl.europa.eu/aboutparliament/nl/displayFtu.html?ftuId=FTU_5.7.2.html, accessed on 15 January 2014.
- **PBL (2011)**
  Exploration of pathways towards a clean economy by 2050: How to realise a climate-neutral Netherlands, PBL Netherlands Environmental Assessment Agency, The Hague.
- **PBL (2012a)**
  Roads from Rio 20+; Pathways to achieve global sustainability goals by 2050, PBL Netherlands Environmental Assessment Agency, The Hague.
- **PBL (2012b)**
  The Netherlands in 21 infographics, PBL Netherlands Environmental Assessment Agency, The Hague.
- **PBL (2013a)**
  De ruimtelijke impact van hernieuwbare energie: een verkenning [Outlook on the spatial impact of renewable energy (in Dutch)], PBL Netherlands Environmental Assessment Agency, The Hague.

- **PBL (2013b)**
  Trends in Global CO_2 Emissions: 2013 Report, PBL Netherlands Environmental Assessment Agency, The Hague.
- **PBL (2014)**
  Infographics on global CO_2 emissions. http://infographics.pbl.nl/website/globalco2/, PBL Netherlands Environmental Assessment Agency, The Hague
- **Sijmons D, Hugtenburg J, van Hoorn A, Feddes F (eds.) (2014)**
  Ontwerpen voor het postfossiele landschap [Designs for post fossil landscapes (in Dutch)], Nai Netherlands Architecture Institute, Rotterdam.

DATA SOURCES INFOGRAPHICS

01 DEMOGRAPHY

INFOGRAPHIC 1.1

- **CBS (2014)**
  Statline database: Life expectancy (from 1950 onwards (per year)), accessed on 11 April 2014, Statistics Netherlands, The Hague/Heerlen.
- **NIDI (2003)**
  Population Atlas of the Netherlands (demographic developments from 1850 to the present day), Netherlands Interdisciplinary Demographic Institute The Hague.

INFOGRAPHIC 1.2A

- **CBS (2013)**
  Statline database on population, generation, gender and origins, 1 January, accessed on 27 March 2014, Statistics Netherlands, The Hague/Heerlen.

INFOGRAPHIC 1.2B

- **CBS (2013)**
  Statline database on population, generation, gender and origins, 1 January, accessed on 27 March 2014, Statistics Netherlands, The Hague/Heerlen.

INFOGRAPHIC 1.3A

- **CBS (2014)**
  StatLine database: Population dynamics; birth, death and migration per region, 24 September 2013, accessed on 27 March 2014, Statistics Netherlands, The Hague/Heerlen.

INFOGRAPHIC 1.3B

- **CBS (2014)**
  StatLine database: Population dynamics; birth, death and migration per region, 24 September 2013, accessed on 27 March 2014, Statistics Netherlands, The Hague/Heerlen.

INFOGRAPHIC 1.4

- **PBL/CBS (2013)**
  Regionale bevolkings- en huishoudensprognose 2013–2040 [Regional Population and Household Prognoses, 2013–2040 (in Dutch)], PBL Netherlands Environmental Assessment Agency, The Hague/Bilthoven; Statistics Netherlands, The Hague/Heerlen.

INFOGRAPHIC 1.5

- **ESRI (2014)**
  DeLorme Publishing Company, Inc
- **PBL (2012)**
  Roads from Rio+20: Pathways to achieve global sustainability goals by 2050, PBL Netherlands Environmental Assessment Agency, The Hague.
- **PBL (2014)**
  GISMO model, OECD baseline scenario, PBL Netherlands Environmental Assessment Agency, The Hague.
- **UNEP (2014)**
  UNEP Environmental Data Explorer – The Environmental Database, accessed on 2 March 2014, United Nations Environment Programme.

02 AIR

INFOGRAPHIC 2.1

- **MNP (2005)**
  Fijn stof nader bekeken [A closer look at particulate matter (in Dutch)], MNP report number 500037008, Netherlands Environmental Assessment Agency (MNP), Bilthoven.

INFOGRAPHIC 2.2

- **PBL (2009)**
  Report 2009. Concentratiekaarten voor grootschalige luchtverontreiniging in Nederland [Concentration maps of large-scale air pollution in the Netherlands (in Dutch)]. PBL Netherlands Environmental Assessment Agency, The Hague.
- **RIVM (2009)**
  <http://www.rivm.nl/Documenten_en_publicaties/Wetenschappelijk/Kaarten/Milieu_Leefomgeving/GCN_concentratiekaartbestanden>, National Institute for Public Health and the Environment (RIVM), Bilthoven.

INFOGRAPHIC 2.3

- **RIVM (2011)**
  Emissieregistratie, Kaart Fijnstof (PM_{10}) [Pollutant Release and Transfer Register, map on particulate matter], 2011, http://www.emissieregistratie.nl/ERPUBLIEK/bumper.en.aspx, National Institute for Public Health and the Environment (RIVM), Bilthoven.

INFOGRAPHIC 2.4

- **JRC and PBL (2005)**
  EDGAR – Emissions Database for Global Atmospheric Research, <http://edgar.jrc.ec.europa.eu/>, Joint Research Centre, Ispra
- **PBL (2009)**
  Growing within limits. A Report to the Global Assembly 2009 of the Club of Rome, PBL Netherlands Environmental Assessment Agency, The Hague.

INFOGRAPHIC 2.5

- **OECD (2012)**
  OECD Environmental Outlook to 2050: The Consequences of Inaction, http://dx.doi.org/10.1787/888932571532 and http:/dx.doi.org/10.1787/888932571589, OECD Publishing, doi: 10.1787/9789264122246-en, Organisation for Economic Co-operation and Development, Paris.

03 WATER

INFOGRAPHIC 3.1

- **CBS/PBL/Wageningen UR (2011)**
  Huishoudelijk waterverbruik per inwoner, 1995–2010 [household water use per inhabitant, 1995–2010 (indicator 0037, version 06, 15 July 2011) (in Dutch)]. www.compendiumvoordeleefomgeving.nl. Statistics Netherlands (CBS), The Hague/Heerlen, PBL Netherlands Environmental Assessment Agency, The Hague and Wageningen University and Research Centre, Wageningen.
- **Mekonnen MM and Hoekstra AY. (2011)**
  National water footprint accounts: the green, blue and grey water footprint of production and consumption, Value of Water Research Report Series No.50, UNESCO-IHE, Delft.

INFOGRAPHIC 3.2

- **CBS (2014)**
  Statline database: Bodemgebruik, uitgebreide gebruiksvorm [Statline database on land use], accessed on 11 April 2014, Statistics Netherlands (CBS), The Hague/Heerlen.
- **CBS/PBL/Wageningen UR (2013)**
  Watergebruik landbouw, 2001–2011 [water use in agriculture, 2001–2011 (indicator 0014, version 10, 9 July 2013) (in Dutch)].

www.compendiumvoordeleefomgeving.nl. Statistics Netherlands (CBS), The Hague/Heerlen, PBL Netherlands Environmental Assessment Agency, The Hague and Wageningen University and Research Centre, Wageningen.

- **CBS/PBL/Wageningen UR (2014)**
  Waterwinning en waterverbruik in Nederland, 1976–2011 [water extraction and water use in the Netherlands, 1976–2011 (indicator 0057, version 10, 28 January 2014) (in Dutch)]. www.compendiumvoordeleefomgeving.nl. Statistics Netherlands (CBS), The Hague/Heerlen, PBL Netherlands Environmental Assessment Agency, The Hague and Wageningen University and Research Centre, Wageningen.
- **Droogers F. (2009)**
  Verbetering bepaling actuele verdamping voor het strategisch waterbeheer [Improvement determination of current evaporation for strategic water management (in Dutch)], STOWA (Dutch foundation of applied research on water management), Utrecht.
- **Geudens P. (2012)**
  Drinkwaterstatistieken 2012 [Drinking water statistics 2012 (in Dutch)], VEWIN (Association of Dutch Water Companies), Rijswijk.
- **Klijn F. (2012)**
  Zoetwatervoorziening in Nederland – aangescherpte landelijke knelpuntenanalyse 21e eeuw [Freshwater supply in the Netherlands – thorough analysis of bottlenecks (in Dutch)], Deltares, Delft.

INFOGRAPHIC 3.3

- **Deltaprogramma (2013)**
  Deltascenario's voor 2050 en 2100, Nadere uitwerking 2012–2013 [Delta scenarios for 2050 and 2100; further elaboration 2012–2013 (in Dutch)], The Hague.
- **Eurostat/GISCO database (2010)**
  Data on watersheds, accessed in 2010.
- **H+N+S Landscape Architects (2012)**
  Werkboek Deelprogramma Nieuwbouw en Herstructurering [work book sub-programme on newbuilds and restructuring (in Dutch)], H+N+S Landscape Architects Amersfoort.
- **Ministry of Infrastructure and the Environment (2012)**
  Structuurvisie Infrastructuur en Ruimte [Planning Vision for Infrastructure and Landscape (in Dutch)], The Hague.
- **Noordhoff Atlasproducties (2010)**
  De Bosatlas van Nederland Waterland [Atlas of the Netherlands water country (in Dutch)], Noordhoff plublishers, Groningen.
- **PBL (2010)**
  Basiskaart Aquatisch: de Watertypenkaart. Het oppervlaktewater in de TOP10NL geclassificeerd naar watertype [Basic acquatic map of water types. Surface water in the top 10 of the Netherlands, classified according to water type (in Dutch)], PBL Netherlands Environmental Assessment Agency, The Hague.
- **PBL (2011)**
  Climate adaptation in the Dutch Delta, PBL Netherlands Environmental Assessment Agency, The Hague.

INFOGRAPHIC 3.4

- **Gleeson T, Wada Y, Van Beek LPH and Bierkens MFP. (2012)**
  Water balance of global aquifers revealed by groundwater footprint, In: Nature 488, 197–200.
- **Natural Earth data (2014)**
  Area of dense human habitation. Urban Areas, http://www.naturalearthdata.com/downloads/50m-cultural-vectors/50m-urban-areas/, accessed on 11 April 2014.
- **PBL (2012)**
  Water Footprint: Useful for sustainability policies? PBL Netherlands Environmental Assessment Agency, The Hague.
- **Wada Y. (2013)**
  Human and climate impacts on global water resources, Utrecht University, Faculty of Geosciences, Utrecht.

INFOGRAPHIC 3.5

- **OECD (2012)**
  OECD Environmental Outlook to 2050: The Consequences of Inaction; baseline scenario, Organisation for Economic Co-operation and Development, Paris.
- **Wada Y, van Beek LPH, Sperna Weiland FC, Chao BF, Wu Y-H and Bierkens MFP. (2012)**
  Past and future contribution of global groundwater depletion to sea-level rise, In: Geophysical Research Letters, Vol. 39, L09402, New Jersey.

04 FOOD

INFOGRAPHIC 4.1

- **GfK (2013), RIVM (2011) and Milieucentraal (2014)**
  Voedselverspilling 062 [Food waste 062], adaptation by PBL Netherlands Environmental Assessment Agency, The Hague.
- **PBL (2012)**
  The Netherlands in 21 Infographics, PBL Netherlands Environmental Assessment Agency, The Hague.
- **UNESCO-IHE (2011)**
  National water footprint accounts: the green, blue and grey water footprint of production and consumption, Value of Water Research Report Series No.50, UNESCO-IHE, Delft, adaptation by PBL Netherlands Environmental Assessment Agency.

INFOGRAPHIC 4.2

- **CBS (2010)**
  Dierlijke mest en mineralen 2009 [Animal manure and nutrients 2009 (in Dutch)], Statistics Netherlands, The Hague/Heerlen, adaptation by PBL Netherlands Environmental Assessment Agency.
- **LEI (2011)**
  Verduurzaming voedselproductie: inzicht in productie, import, export en consumptie van voedsel [Sustainable food production; insight into production, import, export and consumption of food (in Dutch)] pp. 15–29, Agricultural Economics Research Institute (LEI, part of Wageningen University and Research Centre), Wageningen.
- **PDV (2009)**
  Productschap dierenvoerder [Animal feed commodity board], adaptation by PBL Netherlands Environmental Assessment Agency.
- **PZ (2010)**
  Statistisch jaaroverzicht 2009 [Statistical annual report 2009, Dutch Dairy Board (in Dutch)], adaptation by PBL Netherlands Environmental Assessment Agency.

INFOGRAPHIC 4.3

- **Alterra (2010)**
  Impact Assessment Tools for Food Planning in Metropolitan Regions : IA tools and serious gaming in support of sustainability targets for food planning, nature conservation and recreation. Alterra, Wageningen University and Research Centre, Wageningen, p. 66, adaptation by PBL Netherlands Environmental Assessment Agency.
- **CBS**
  Landbouwtelling [Agricultural census (in Dutch)], adaptation by LEI, adaptation by PBL Netherlands Environmental Assessment Agency.
- **LEI (Wageningen University and Research Centre) (2012)**
  Ruimtelijke verdeling in SO, www.agrimatie.nl, Agricultural Economics Research Institute (LEI, part of Wageningen University and Research Centre), adaptation by PBL Netherlands Environmental Assessment Agency.
- **LISA (2012)**
  Dutch National Database of Employment and Firms, adaptation by PBL Netherlands Environmental Assessment Agency.

INFOGRAPHIC 4.4

- **FAO (2010)**
  Global Forest Resources Assessment 2010, countries data en forest cover (215m raster), Food and Agriculture Organization of the United Nations, Rome
- **PBL (2010)**
  GLOBIO GBO4 BL, PBL Netherlands Environmental Assessment Agency, The Hague.
- **PBL (2012)**
  IMAGE RIO+20 baseline scenario, PBL Netherlands Environmental Assessment Agency, The Hague.

INFOGRAPHIC 4.5

- **PBL (2012)**
  The Netherlands in 21 Infographics, PBL Netherlands Environmental Assessment Agency, The Hague.

05 BIOTA

INFOGRAPHIC 5.1

- **PBL and Wageningen UR (in prep.)**
  Leefomgevingsbalans 2014 [Assessment of the Human Environment 2014 (in Dutch)]. PBL Netherlands Environmental Assessments Agency, The Hague, Wageningen University and Research Centre, Wageningen.

INFOGRAPHIC 5.2

- **Alterra (2009)**
  HGN: Historisch Grondgebruik Nederland [History of land use in the Netherlands (in Dutch)], Alterra, Wageningen University and Research Centre, Wageningen.
- **Buis J. (1985)**
  Historia Forestis: Nederlandse bosgeschiedenis [History of Dutch forests (in Dutch)], Utrecht HES, Vol.2.
- **TNO (2006)**
  Paleogeografische reconstructies van NL [Paleogeographical reconstructions (in Dutch)], Netherlands Organisation for Applied Scientific Research, Utrecht

INFOGRAPHIC 5.3

- **AHN (2012)**
  Topografische Dienst Nederland (2012) [Dutch topographical service], AHN-2, Algemeen Hoogtebestand Nederland [Database of local land levels in the Netherlands], http://www.ahn.nl/.
- **Alterra (2008)**
  Natura 2000 gebieden 2011 [Natura 2000 areas, 2011 (in Dutch)]; version 4 January 2011, Alterra, Wageningen University and Research Centre, Wageningen.
- **Alterra (2009)**
  LGN6, Landelijk Grondgebruiksbestand 6 [LGN6, National land use, data set 6 (in Dutch)], Alterra, Wageningen University and Research Centre, Wageningen.
- **Ministry of Agriculture, Nature and Food Quality (former Dutch Ministry of LNV) (2007)**
  EHS 2007; Netto Ecologische Hoofdstructuur [National Ecological Network 2007 (in Dutch)], The Hague.
- **PBL (2008)**
  GWB-gebieden 2008; ook waterwingebieden en boringsvrije zones [GWB areas 2008; also water extraction areas and drilling-free zones (in Dutch)], PBL Netherlands Environmental Assessment Agency, The Hague.
- **Rijkswaterstaat (2009)**
  Primaire Waterkeringen 2009; Dijkringlijnen [Primary dykes 2009 (in Dutch)], The Hague.
- **RUG/PBL/Alterra (2010)**
  HSM: Hotspotmonitor [Hot spot monitor (in Dutch)], University of Groningen (RUG), Groningen; PBL Netherlands Environmental Assessment Agency, The Hague; Alterra, Wageningen University and Research Centre, Wageningen.

INFOGRAPHIC 5.4

- **FAO (2013)**
  Roundwood – Production 1961–2012, Environmental Data Explorer, Food and Agricultural Organization of the United Nations Environment Programme (UNEP).
- **PBL (2013)**
  IMAGE model, PBL Netherlands Environmental Assessment Agency, The Hague.
- **PBL and UBC (2011)**
  Change in biomass of fish groups, 2004–2050, Baseline Scenario. From: PBL Netherlands Environmental Assessment Agency (2011). EU Resource Efficiency Perspectives in a Global Context, PBL Netherlands Environmental Assessment Agency, The Hague; University of British Columbia, Vancouver.

INFOGRAPHIC 5.5

- **Alterra (2008)**
  Natura 2000 gebieden 2011 [Natura 2000 areas, 2011 (in Dutch)], version 4 January 2011, Alterra, Wageningen University and Research Centre, Wageningen.
- **Dutch National Cycling Platform (2012a)**
  Landelijke Fietsknooppunten, 2012 [National bicycle bottlenecks 2012 (in Dutch)], Dutch National Cycling Platform, Amersfoort.
  Dutch National Cycling Platform (2012b)
  Landelijke Fietsroutes, 2012 [National bicycle routes, 2012 (in Dutch)], Dutch National Cycling Platform, Amersfoort.
- **Ministry of Agriculture, Nature and Food Quality (former Dutch Ministry of LNV) (2007)**
  EHS 2007; Netto Ecologische Hoofdstructuur [EHS 2007; Dutch National Ecological Network (in Dutch)], The Hague.
- **Municipality of Amsterdam (1992)**
  Beschermde Flora en Fauna [Protected Flora and Fauna (in Dutch)], www.maps.amsterdam.nl, accessed on 2 December 2013.
- **Municipality of Amsterdam: Bureau Onderzoek en Statistiek, (2013)**
  Het Grote Groenonderzoek 2013 [Department of research and statistics; The large green research 2013 (in Dutch)], Project number: 13124, Amsterdam.
- **Municipality of Amsterdam (2011)**
  Groenstructuur Amsterdam [Green structure Amsterdam (in Dutch), www.maps.amsterdam.nl, geoportal accessed on 2 December 2013.
- **Municipality of Amsterdam (2013a)**
  Bijzondere Kades [Special quays (in Dutch)], www.maps.amsterdam.nl, accessed on 2 December 2013.
- **Municipality of Amsterdam (2013b)**
  Monumentale bomen [Monumental trees (in Dutch)], geoportal accessed on 2 December 2013.
- **PBL (2009)**
  Waterwegen A1 [Waterways A1 (in Dutch)], PBL Netherlands Environmental Assessment Agency, The Hague.
- **RUG/PBL/Alterra (2010)**
  HSM: Hotspotmonitor [HSM; hot spot monitor (in Dutch)], University of Groningen (RUG), Groningen; PBL Netherlands Environmental Assessment Agency, The Hague; Alterra, Wageningen University and Research Centre, Wageningen.

06 MOBILITY

INFOGRAPHIC 6.1

- **Amsterdam Airport Schiphol (2013)**
  Traffic Review 2012, Amsterdam Airport Schiphol.
- **CBS (2010/2011)**
  Onderzoek Verplaatsingsgedrag [Research on mobility behaviour (in Dutch)], Statistics Netherlands (CBS), The Hague.
- **CBS (2010/2011)**
  Onderzoek Verplaatsingen in Nederland [Research on mobility in the Netherlands (in Dutch)], Statistics Netherlands (CBS), The Hague/Heerlen.
- **CBS (2014)**
  Statline database: Mobiliteit in Nederland; vervoerwijzen en motieven, regio's [Mobility in the Netherlands;

transport modes and motives, regions (in Dutch)], accessed on 11 April 2014, Statistics Netherlands (CBS), The Hague/Heerlen.
- **KiM (2013)**
Data Mobiliteitsbalans [Mobility assessment data (in Dutch)], KiM Netherlands Institute for Transport Policy Analysis, The Hague.
- **KiM (2013)**
Schiphol Enquête [Schiphol survey (in Dutch)], adaptation by KiM Netherlands Institute for Transport Policy Analysis, The Hague
- **Rijkswaterstaat**
Mobiliteitsonderzoek Nederland [Mobility research on the Netherlands (in Dutch)], The Hague.

INFOGRAPHIC 6.2

- **CBS (2013)**
Forenzen naar woongemeente (2011) – maatwerktabel [Commuters per municipality of residence (2011) – custom-made table (in Dutch)], Statistics Netherlands (CBS), The Hague/Heerlen.
- **Deltarail and Prorail**
ASWIN database, adaptation by PBL Netherlands Environmental Assessment Agency.
- **Goudappel Coffeng and Rijkswaterstaat**
INWEVA database, adaptation by PBL Netherlands Environmental Assessment Agency.

INFOGRAPHIC 6.3

- **Alterra**
Historische spoorwegen, Historisch Grondgebruik Nederland [historical rail road, historical landuse the Netherlands (in Dutch)] – Alterra, Wageningen University and Research Centre, Wageningen – adaptation by PBL Netherlands Environmental Assessment Agency.
- **CBS**
Bodemgebruik (land use (in Dutch)], Statistics Netherlands (CBS), The Hague/Heerlen.
- **LISA (2012)**
Dutch National Database of Employment and Firms.
- **PBL**
Historische wegen en stations [Historical roads and railways stations (in Dutch)], PBL Netherlands Environmental Assessment Agency.
- **Rijkwaterstaat**
Nationaal WegenBestand [National database of roads (in Dutch)], Rijkwaterstaat The Hague.

INFOGRAPHIC 6.4

- **OECD (2012)**
OECD Environmental Outlook to 2050: The Consequences of Inaction – baseline scenario, Organisation for Economic Co-operation and Development, Paris.

INFOGRAPHIC 6.5

- **PBL (2012)**
Monitor Structuurvisie Infrastructuur en Ruimte [Planning Vision for Infrastructure and Landscape (in Dutch)], PBL Netherlands Environmental Assessment Agency, The Hague.

07 CARGO

INFOGRAPHIC 7.1

- **CBS (2013)**
StatLine database: Goederenvervoer; vervoerwijzen, vervoerstromen van en naar Nederland [Goods transport; modes of transport, transport flows to and from the Netherlands (in Dutch)]. Statistics Netherlands (CBS), The Hague/Heerlen, data extracted on 18 December 2013, adaptation by PBL Netherlands Environmental Assessment Agency.
- **CBS/PBL/Wageningen UR (2013)**
Vervoersprestaties in het goederenvervoer, 1985–2010 [Results goods transport, 1985–2010 (in Dutch)] (indicator i-nl-0025, version 06). www.compendiumvoordeleefomgeving.nl. Statistics Netherlands (CBS), The Hague/Heerlen; PBL Netherlands Environmental Assessment Agency, The Hague; Wageningen University and Research Centre, Wageningen, data extracted on 7 November 2013.

INFOGRAPHIC 7.2

- **CBS (2013)**
StatLine database: Internationale handel en doorvoer; waarde en gewicht, goederenhoofdstukken [International trade and transit; value and weights, chapters on goods (in Dutch)]. Statistics Netherlands (CBS), The Hague/Heerlen, data extracted on 23 September 2013, adaptation by PBL Netherlands Environmental Assessment Agency.

INFOGRAPHIC 7.3

- **CBS (2013)**
StatLine database: Goederenvervoer; vervoerwijzen, vervoerstromen van en naar Nederland [Goods transport; modes of transport, transport flows to and from the Netherlands (in Dutch)]. Statistics Netherlands (CBS), The Hague/Heerlen, data extracted on 18 December 2013, adaptation by PBL Netherlands Environmental Assessment Agency.
- **Deltarail and Prorail (2013)**
ASWIN database, adaptation by PBL Netherlands Environmental Assessment Agency.
- **Eurostat Geographic Information System of the European Commission (GISCO) (2010)**
European road network, adaptation by PBL Netherlands Environmental Assessment Agency.
- **Rijkswaterstaat (2013)**
INWEVA database, adaptation by PBL Netherlands Environmental Assessment Agency.

INFOGRAPHIC 7.4

- **CBS (2013a)**
StatLine database: Internationale handel; in- en uitvoer volgens SITC-indeling 2012 [International trade; import and export according to SITC division 2012 (in Dutch)]. Statistics Netherlands (CBS), The Hague/Heerlen, data extracted on 25 October 2013, adaptation by PBL Netherlands Environmental Assessment Agency.
- **CBS (2013b)**
StatLine database: Invoer en uitvoer van vaste minerale brandstoffen 2012 [Import and export of solid mineral fuels (in Dutch)]. Statistics Netherlands (CBS), The Hague/Heerlen, extracted 25 October 2013), adaptation by PBL Netherlands Environmental Assessment Agency.
- **CBS (2013c)**
StatLine database: Invoer en uitvoer van bloemen en bollen 2012 [Import and export of flowers and bulbs, 2012 (in Dutch)]. Statistics Netherlands (CBS), The Hague/Heerlen, data extracted on 24 October 2013, adaptation by PBL Netherlands Environmental Assessment Agency.

INFOGRAPHIC 7.5

- **Port of Rotterdam (2012)**
Haven in cijfers 2010–2011–2012 [Data on the port, 2010–2011–2012 (in Dutch)]. Port of Rotterdam, Rotterdam.
- **UNCTAD (2012)**
United Nations Conference on Trade and Development, adaptation by PBL Netherlands Environmental Assessment Agency.

08 BUILDING MATERIALS

INFOGRAPHIC 8.1

- **Agentschap NL (2013)**
Referentiewoningen nieuwbouw 2013 [New-build reference housing 2013

(in Dutch)]. Agentschap NL, Dutch Ministry of the Interior and Kingdom Relations, The Hague, adaptation by PBL Netherlands Environmental Assessment Agency.

- **Bak RL, office space data (2013)**
  Adaptation by PBL Netherlands Environmental Assessment Agency.
- **Bijleveld MM, Bergsma GC and Van Lieshout M. (2013)**
  Milieu-impact van betongebruik in de Nederlandse bouw; Status quo en toetsing van verbeteropties [Environmental impact of the use of concrete in Dutch construction; Status quo and review of improvement options (in Dutch)]. CE Delft, Delft, adaptation by PBL Netherlands Environmental Assessment Agency.
- **CBS (2013)**
  StatLine database: Historie Woningbouw [History of housing construction (in Dutch)], Statistics Netherlands, The Hague/Heerlen, adaptation by PBL Netherlands Environmental Assessment Agency.
- **DGMR ingenieursbureau**
  Materialisatie referentiewoningen [Materialisation of reference buildings (in Dutch)], adaptation by PBL Netherlands Environmental Assessment Agency.
- **Nationale Milieudatabase**
  Milieuprestaties bouwmaterialen [Environmental performance of building materials (in Dutch)], (http://www.milieudatabase.nl/), adaptation by PBL Netherlands Environmental Assessment Agency.
- **Stichting Milieu Relevante Product Informatie (MRPI)**
  Materialisatie referentiewoningen [Materialisation of reference buildings (in Dutch)], (http://www.mrpi.nl/), adaptation by PBL Netherlands Environmental Assessment Agency.

INFOGRAPHIC 8.2

- **Bijleveld MM, Bergsma GC and Van Lieshout M. (2013)**
  Milieu-impact van betongebruik in de Nederlandse bouw; Status quo en toetsing van verbeteropties [Environmental impact of the use of concrete in Dutch construction; Status quo and review of improvement options (in Dutch)]. CE Delft, Delft, adaptation by PBL Netherlands Environmental Assessment Agency.
- **Branchevereniging VBW-asfalt (Vakgroep Bitumineuze Werken)**
  Adaptation by PBL Netherlands Environmental Assessment Agency.
- **CBS (2013a)**
  StatLine database: Goederensoorten naar EU, niet-EU; minerale brandstoffen en chemie [Goods categories, EU and non-EU; fossil fuels and chemistry (in Dutch)], accessed on 18 December 2013, Statistics Netherlands, The Hague/Heerlen, adaptation by PBL Netherlands Environmental Assessment Agency.
- **CBS (2013b)**
  StatLine database: Milieurekeningen; winning, invoer en uitvoer van materialen naar soort, Fysieke materiaalstromen 2010 [environmental accounts; sourcing, import and export of materials per type, Physical material flows 2010 (in Dutch)], accessed on 18 December 2013, Statistics Netherlands, The Hague/Heerlen, adaptation by PBL Netherlands Environmental Assessment Agency.
- **CBS/PBL/Wageningen UR (2013)**
  Winning en verbruik van oppervlaktedelfstoffen, 1980–2011 [Extraction and use of surface minerals, 1980–2011 (indicator 0067, version 13, 12 March 2013) (in Dutch)]. www.compendiumvoordeleefomgeving.nl, Statistics Netherlands (CBS), The Hague/Heerlen; PBL Netherlands Environmental Assessment Agency, The Hague, and Wageningen University and Research Centre, Wageningen, adaptation by PBL Netherlands Environmental Assessment Agency.
- **KNB (2013)**
  Jaarverslag KNB 2012 [Annual Report KNB 2012 (in Dutch)], KNB Dutch Association for Building Ceramics, Velp, adaptation by PBL Netherlands Environmental Assessment Agency.
- **Oldenburger J, De Groot C and Winterink A. (2012)**
  Nederlandse houtstromen in beeld [Dutch timber flows (in Dutch)]. Stichting Probos, Wageningen, adaptation by PBL Netherlands Environmental Assessment Agency.
- **Stichting Bouwen met Staal**
  Gegevens over gebruik en hergebruik van staal in de bouwsector [Data on use and reuse of steel in the Dutch building sector (in Dutch)], (http://www.bouwenmetstaal.nl/), adaptation by PBL Netherlands Environmental Assessment Agency.
- **World Steel Association (2013)**
  Steel Statistical Yearbook 2013, adaptation by PBL Netherlands Environmental Assessment Agency.

INFOGRAPHIC 8.3

- **Alterra (2010)**
  Historisch Grondgebruik Nederland 1960 [Historical land use in the Netherlands 1960 (in Dutch)]. Alterra, Wageningen University and Research Centre, Wageningen, adaptation by PBL Netherlands Environmental Assessment Agency.
- **CBS (2013)**
  Bestand bodemgebruik 2010 [Land-use data 2010 (in Dutch)]. Statistics Netherlands, The Hague/Heerlen, adaptation by PBL Netherlands Environmental Assessment Agency.
- **LISA**
  Dutch National Database of Employment and Firms, adaptation by PBL Netherlands Environmental Assessment Agency.
- **Rijkswaterstaat (2005)**
  Sediment in (be)weging; Sedimentbalans Rijn-Maasmonding periode 1990–2000 [Sediment balance Rhine-Meuse estuary, 1990–2000 (in Dutch)]. RWS-RIZA, The Hague, adaptation by PBL Netherlands Environmental Assessment Agency.
- **Rijkswaterstaat (2006)**
  Actueel Hoogtebestand Nederland [Up-to-date Height Model of The Netherlands]; AHN1, http://www.ahn.nl) Rijkswaterstaat, The Hague, adaptation by PBL Netherlands Environmental Assessment Agency.

INFOGRAPHIC 8.4

- **CSIRO and UNEP (2013)**
  Asia-Pacific and Latin American Material Flows online database (http://www.cse.csiro.au/forms/form-material-flows.aspx), Commonwealth Scientific and Industrial Research Organisation and United Nations Environment Programme, accessed on 16 December 2013, adaptation by PBL Netherlands Environmental Assessment Agency.
- **Eurostat Database (2013)**
  Material Flow Accounts (http://appsso.eurostat.ec.europa.eu/nui/show.do?dataset=env_ac_mfa), accessed on 26 March 2013, adaptation by PBL Netherlands Environmental Assessment Agency.
- **Institute of Social Ecology Vienna, Alpen Adria Universität Klagenfurt-Graz-Wien (2014)**
  (http://www.uni-klu.ac.at/socec/downloads/Online_data_version_2_0_public.xls), accessed on 30 January 2014, adaptation by PBL Netherlands Environmental Assessment Agency.
- **Steinberger J, Krausmann F and Eisenmenger N. (2010)**
  The global patterns of materials use: a socioeconomic and geophysical analysis. In: Ecological Economics 69(5), 1148–1158, adaptation by PBL Netherlands Environmental Assessment Agency.
- **UN (2011)**
  World Urbanization Prospects, the 2011 Revision (http://esa.un.org/unup/GIS-Files/gis_1.htm), United Nations, accessed on 5 March 2014, adaptation by PBL Netherlands Environmental Assessment Agency.

INFOGRAPHIC 8.5

- **Bijleveld MM, Bergsma GC and Van Lieshout M. (2013)** Milieu-impact van betongebruik in de Nederlandse bouw; Status quo en toetsing van verbeteropties [Environmental impact of the use of concrete in Dutch construction; Status quo and review of improvement options (in Dutch)], CE Delft, Delft, adaptation by PBL Netherlands Environmental Assessment Agency.
- **Branchevereniging VBW-asfalt (Vakgroep Bitumineuze Werken)** Adaptation by PBL Netherlands Environmental Assessment Agency.
- **CBS (2013)** StatLine database: Milieurekeningen; winning, invoer en uitvoer van materialen naar soort, Fysieke materiaalstromen 2010 [Environmental accounts; sourcing, import and export of materials per type, Physical material flows 2010 (in Dutch)], Statistics Netherlands, The Hague/ Heerlen, adaptation by PBL Netherlands Environmental Assessment Agency.
- **CBS/PBL/Wageningen UR (2013)** Winning en verbruik van oppervlaktedelfstoffen, 1980–2011 [Extraction and use of surface minerals, 1980–2011 (indicator 0067, version 13, 12 March 2013) (in Dutch). www.compendiumvoordeleefomgeving.nl. Statistics Netherlands (CBS), The Hague/Heerlen; PBL Netherlands Environmental Assessment Agency, The Hague and Wageningen University and Research Centre, Wageningen, adaptation by PBL Netherlands Environmental Assessment Agency.
- **KNB (2013)** Jaarverslag KNB 2012 [Annual Report KNB 2012 (in Dutch)], KNB Dutch Association for Building Ceramics, Velp, adaptation by PBL Netherlands Environmental Assessment Agency. **Oldenburger J, De Groot C and Winterink A. (2012)** Nederlandse houtstromen in beeld [Dutch timber flows (in Dutch)]. Stichting Probos, Wageningen, adaptation by PBL Netherlands Environmental Assessment Agency.
- **Stichting Bouwen met Staal** Gegevens over gebruik en hergebruik van staal in de bouwsector [Data on use and reuse of steel in the Dutch building sector (in Dutch)], (http://www.bouwenmetstaal.nl/), adaptation by PBL Netherlands Environmental Assessment Agency.
- **World Steel Association (2013)** Steel Statistical Yearbook 2013, adaptation by PBL Netherlands Environmental Assessment Agency.

09 WASTE

INFOGRAPHIC 9.1

- **CBS/PBL/Wageningen UR (2013)** Samenstelling van huishoudelijk restafval, 1940–2011 [Compositions of household waste, 1940–2011 (in Dutch)] (indicator 0141, version 13 Juny 2013). www.compendiumvoordeleefomgeving.nl. Statistics Netherlands (CBS), The Hague/Heerlen; PBL Netherlands Environmental Assessment Agency, The Hague; Wageningen University and Research Centre, Wageningen, data extracted on 14 October 2013.
- **Rijkswaterstaat (2013)** Nederlands afval in cijfers, gegevens 2006–2010 [Data on Dutch waste, 2006–2010 (in Dutch)], Rijkswaterstaat, Utrecht.
- **Rijkswaterstaat (2014)** Afvalmonitor: Gescheiden ingezameld huishoudelijk afval 2010 [Waste monitor; separated collected household waste, 2010 (in Dutch)], Rijkswaterstaat, Utrecht, data extracted on 25 November 2013, adaptation by PBL Netherlands Environmental Assessment Agency.

INFOGRAPHIC 9.2

- **CBS/PBL/Wageningen UR (2013)** Verwerking van afval van huishoudens, 1985–2010 [Processing of household waste, 1985–2010 (in Dutch)] (indicator 0392, September 2012). www.compendiumvoordeleefomgeving.nl. Statistics Netherlands (CBS), The Hague/Heerlen; PBL Netherlands Environmental Assessment Agency, The Hague; Wageningen University and Research Centre, Wageningen, data extracted on 10 October 2013.
- **Rijkswaterstaat (2013)** Nederlands afval in cijfers, gegevens 2006–2010 [Data on Dutch waste, 2006–2010 (in Dutch)], Rijkswaterstaat, Utrecht, adaptation by PBL Netherlands Environmental Assessment Agency.

INFOGRAPHIC 9.3

- **CBS (2013)** StatLine database: Gemeentelijk afval; hoeveelheden 2011 [Municipal waste, 2011 (in Dutch)]. Statistics Netherlands (CBS), The Hague/Heerlen, data extracted on 25 November 2013), adaptation by PBL Netherlands Environmental Assessment Agency.
- **LISA (2012)** Dutch National Database of Employment and Firms, adaptation by PBL Netherlands Environmental Assessment Agency.

INFOGRAPHIC 9.4

- **CBS/PBL/Wageningen UR (2013)** Verwerking van afval van huishoudens, 1985–2010 [Treatment of household waste, 1985–2010 (in Dutch)] (indicator 0392, September 2012). www.compendiumvoordeleefomgeving.nl. Statistics Netherlands (CBS), The Hague/Heerlen; PBL Netherlands Environmental Assessment Agency, The Hague; Wageningen University and Research Centre, Wageningen, data extracted on 10 October 2013.
- **Eurostat (2013)** Municipal waste generation and treatment, by type of treatment method 2010 (indicator: tsdpc240). Eurostat, Luxembourg, data extracted on 14 October 2013.
- **Eurostat (2014)** Real GDP per capita, growth rate and totals 2010 (indicator: tsdec100). Eurostat, Luxembourg, data extracted on 27 January 2014.

INFOGRAPHIC 9.5

- **CBS (2013)** StatLine database: Internationale handel; in- en uitvoer volgens SITC-indeling 1997–2012 [International trade; import and export according to SITC division 1997–2012 (in Dutch)]. Statistics Netherlands (CBS), The Hague/ Heerlen, data extracted on 25 November 2013), adaptation by PBL Netherlands Environmental Assessment Agency.
- **INECE (2012)** Major destination areas for illicit waste shipments. International Network for Environmental Compliance and Enforcement (INECE). In: Vital Waste Graphics 3. Basel Convention, adaptation by PBL Netherlands Environmental Assessment Agency.
- **UNEP (2011)** UNEP Year Book 2011, United Nations Environment Programme, adaptation by PBL Netherlands Environmental Assessment Agency.
- **UNSD (2014)** Municipal waste collected per capita 2009 (version: March 2012). United Nations Statistics Division (UNSD), New York, data extracted on 21 November 2013, adaptation by PBL Netherlands Environmental Assessment Agency.

10 ENERGY

INFOGRAPHIC 10.1

- **CBS/PBL/Wageningen UR (2013)** Energieverbruik door huishoudens, 1990–2012 [Household energy use,

1990–2012 (in Dutch)] (indicator 0035, version 18, 3 December 2013). www.compendiumvoordeleefomgeving.nl. Statistics Netherlands (CBS), The Hague/Heerlen; PBL Netherlands Environmental Assessment Agency, The Hague; Wageningen University and Research Centre, Wageningen.
- **Timmer MP. (ed.) (2012)**
The World Input-Output Database (WIOD): Contents, Sources and Methods, WIOD Working Paper Number 10, downloadable from http://www.wiod.org/publications/papers/wiod10.pdf.

INFOGRAPHIC 10.2

- **IEA (2013)**
Energy Balances of OECD Countries, 2013 Edition, International Energy Agency, Paris.

INFOGRAPHIC 10.3A

- **ECN (2012)**
Energietrends 2012 [Energy trends 2012 (in Dutch)], Energy research Centre of the Netherlands, Petten/The Hague.
- **LISA (2012)**
Dutch National Database of Employment and Firms, adaptation by PBL Netherlands Environmental Assessment Agency.
- **Risicoregister/RIVM (2009)**
National Institute for Public Health and the Environment (RIVM), adaptation by PBL Netherlands Environmental Assessment Agency, adaptation by PBL Netherlands Environmental Assessment Agency.

INFOGRAPHIC 10.3B

- **Interdepartementale Directeuren Overleg Noordzee (2014)**
www.noordzeeloket.nl, accessed on 15 April 2014, adaptation by PBL Netherlands Environmental Assessment Agency.
- **LISA (2012)**
Dutch National Database of Employment and Firms, adaptation by PBL Netherlands Environmental Assessment Agency.
- **Rijkswaterstaat (2013)**
Afvalverwerking in Nederland, gegevens 2012 [Waste treatment in the Netherlands, data on 2012 (in Dutch)], adaptation by PBL Netherlands Environmental Assessment Agency.
- **TenneT (2014)**
www.hoogspanningsnet.com, accessed on 15 January 2014, adaptation by PBL Netherlands Environmental Assessment Agency.
- **Windenergie-nieuws (2013)**
Adaptation by PBL Netherlands Environmental Assessment Agency.

INFOGRAPHIC 10.4

- **JRC (2013)**
Edgar v4 Database, Joint Research Centre, data extracted from http://www.klimaatportaal.nl.
- **PBL (2009)**
Growing within limits. A Report to the Global Assembly 2009 of the Club of Rome, PBL Netherlands Environmental Assessment Agency, The Hague.

INFOGRAPHIC 10.5

- **PBL (2011)**
Model E-design, more info on http://www.pbl.nl/e-design/doel-en-opzet, PBL Netherlands Environmental Assessment Agency, The Hague.w

COLOPHON

AUTHORS

- **Maarten Hajer and Ton Dassen (eds.)**
- **Chapters Part 2:**
  Hans van Amsterdam, Maarten Baas, Arjan Harbers, Anton van Hoorn, Kersten Nabielek, Frank van Rijn, and Emma Westerduin (eds.)

EDITORS OF THE THEME CHAPTERS

- **Fred Feddes** (journalist and writer)
- **Nienke Noorman** (PBL)

TRANSLATION AND ENGLISH-LANGUAGE EDITING

- **Christien Ettema** (Shades of Green – De Groene Vertaler)
- **Annemieke Righart** (PBL)

DESIGN AND GRAPHICS

- **Catalogtree**

PRINTER

- **robstolk**

ACKNOWLEDGEMENT

Smart about Cities – Visualising the Challenge for 21st Century Urbanism has been publicised during the International Architecture Biennale Rotterdam (IABR) 2014 'Urban by Nature'.

We would like to thank the IABR people involved for the fruitful collaboration. Discussions held with George Brugmans, Marieke Francke, Jan Wilbers, Fanny Smelik and Dirk Sijmons were an important source of inspiration for us in the visualisation and work on the 10 metabolic flows of urban metabolism.

For their contribution to our work on these metabolic flows, we also would like to thank: Ruben Huele and Ester van der Voet of the Institute of Environmental Sciences (CML) of Leiden University; David Anink of W/E adviseurs, Utrecht; Mic Barendsz of Stichting Bouwen met Staal, Zoetermeer; Cees Maliepaard of Stichting Bouwkwaliteit (SBK), Rijswijk; Jeannette Levels-Vermeer of Milieu Relevante Product Informatie (MRPI), Nieuwegein; Marijn Bijleveld of CE Delft, Thomas Gleeson of McGill University, Montreal; Arjen Hoekstra of the University of Twente; Rens van Beek and Joost Gernaat, both of Utrecht University; Guus van den Berghe of Rijkswaterstaat; Jasper Hugtenburgh of H+N+S Landscape Architects; Sytske de Waart of Milieucentraal; Harold van der Meulen and Jos op de Weegh, both of LEI, part of Wageningen University and Research Centre; and Henk Hilderink of the National Institute for Public Health and the Environment.

Special thanks go to Zef Hemel of the Municipality of Amsterdam, David Laws of the University of Amsterdam and Mark Swilling of Stellenbosch University in South Africa for their review of the essay.

And, finally, we thank the many PBL colleagues without whose enthusiastic cooperation this book would not have seen the light of day.

DISTRIBUTION

- **nai010 publishers**
  Mauritsweg 23, 3012 JR Rotterdam
  info@nai010.com

nai010 publishers is an internationally orientated publisher specialized in developing, producing and distributing books in the fields of architecture, urbanism, art and design.
www.nai010.com

Available in North, South and Central America through Artbook | D.A.P., 155 Sixth Avenue 2nd Floor, New York, NY 10013-1507, tel +1 212 627 1999, fax +1 212 627 9484, dap@dapinc.com

Available in the United Kingdom and Ireland through Art Data, 12 Bell Industrial Estate, 50 Cunnington Street, London W4 5HB, tel +44 208 747 1061, fax +44 208 742 2319, orders@artdata.co.uk

Printed and bound in the Netherlands

- **PBL Netherlands Environmental Assessment Agency**
  is the national institute for strategic policy analyses in the fields of the environment, nature and spatial planning. We contribute to improving the quality of political and administrative decision-making, by conducting outlook studies, analyses and evaluations in which an integrated approach is considered paramount. Policy relevance is the prime concern in all our studies. We conduct solicited and unsolicited research that is both independent and always scientifically sound.
  www.pbl.nl/en

- **ISBN 978-94-6208-148-2**